SHOULD AULD ACQUAINTANCE
BE FORGOT

For Ilaria Poggiolini

SHOULD AULD ACQUAINTANCE BE FORGOT

THE GREAT MISTAKE OF SCOTTISH INDEPENDENCE

JOHN LLOYD

polity

First published in 2020 by Polity Press

Polity Press
65 Bridge Street
Cambridge CB2 1UR, UK

Polity Press
101 Station Landing
Suite 300
Medford, MA 02155, USA

ISBN-13: 978-1-5095-4266-6

A catalogue record for this book is available from the British Library.

Library of Congress Cataloging-in-Publication Data
Names: Lloyd, John, 1946- author.
Title: Should auld acquaintance be forgot : the great mistake of Scottish independence / John Lloyd.
Description: Cambridge ; Medford, MA : Polity, 2020. | Includes bibliographical references and index. | Summary: "An incisive critique of the quest for Scottish independence"-- Provided by publisher.
Identifiers: LCCN 2019038609 (print) | LCCN 2019038610 (ebook) | ISBN 9781509542666 (hardback) | ISBN 9781509542673 (paperback) | ISBN 9781509542680 (epub)
Subjects: LCSH: Self-determination, National--Scotland--History--21st century. | Nationalism--Scotland. | Scotland--History--Autonomy and independence movements. | Scotland--Politics and government--21st century.
Classification: LCC DA828 .L55 2020 (print) | LCC DA828 (ebook) | DDC 320.1/509411--dc23
LC record available at https://lccn.loc.gov/2019038609
LC ebook record available at https://lccn.loc.gov/2019038610

Typeset in 10.75 on 14 Adobe Janson by
Servis Filmsetting Ltd, Stockport, Cheshire
Printed and bound in Great Britain by CPI Group (UK) Ltd, Croydon

The publisher has used its best endeavours to ensure that the URLs for external websites referred to in this book are correct and active at the time of going to press. However, the publisher has no responsibility for the websites and can make no guarantee that a site will remain live or that the content is or will remain appropriate.

Every effort has been made to trace all copyright holders, but if any have been overlooked the publisher will be pleased to include any necessary credits in any subsequent reprint or edition.

For further information on Polity, visit our website: politybooks.com

CONTENTS

ACKNOWLEDGEMENTS

This book has benefited from advice and insights from many, some of whom have been consulted often, a few of whom don't want public thanks. Those who haven't said they don't include: Wendy Alexander, Ali Ansari, Brian Ashcroft, Arthur Aughey, Alex Bell, Miguel Beltran de Felipe, Paul Bew, Nigel Biggar, Lucy Hunter Blackburn, Keir Bloomer, Vernon Bogdanor, Nick Butler, Jim Campbell, Alan Cochrane, Maeve Connoly, Colin Copus, Gordon Craig, Alistair Darling, Chris Deerin, John Denham, Mure Dickie, Gerry Fisher, Jim Gallagher, Steven Gethins, Anthony Giddens, Brian Girvin, Rosemary Goring, Elga Graves, David Greig, Kevin Hague, Michael Ignatieff, Ian Jack, Alvin Jackson, Mark Jones, John Kay, Michael Keating, Christine Keay, Alex Kemp, Michael Kenny, George Kerevan, Colin Kidd, Calum MacDonald, John McClaren, Iain McClean, Greg McClymont, Gavin McCrone, Jim McColl, John Nicholson, Lindsay Paterson, Ray Perman, Jim Philips, Murray Pittock, David Purdie, Malcolm Rifkind, Graeme Roy, Christopher Rush, Michael Russell, Astrid Silins, Paul Silk, Jim Sillars, Lucas Stevenson, Adam Tomkins, Jim Tomlinson, David Torrance, David Ure, David Webster, Andrew Wilson, Janice Winter, Martin Wolf.

John Thompson and his colleagues at Polity Press – including Susan Beer, Julia Davis, Emma Longstaff and Evie Deavall – have been most helpful, efficient and attentive. My agent, Toby Mundy, was as always deeply and forensically engaged in the development of the book. My English–Jewish actor son, Jacob Fortune-Lloyd, played Macduff in the Globe Theatre's Macbeth in the summer and autumn of 2016, speaking in a strong Scots accent partly borrowed from me, but strengthened. It made me think about the pity of sundering a British state that had come to be largely accepting of human mixing – an element in my deciding to write this book.

INTRODUCTION:
BREAKING BRITAIN

The independence of Scotland would bring Great Britain to an end. That was the name given to the voluntary Union between Scotland and England in 1707 and, since it would finish Great Britain, it would destroy the United Kingdom as well, since the latter designation – the United Kingdom of Great Britain and Ireland – became the official title after the Union of Great Britain with Ireland in 1800. Without Scotland, Great Britain no longer exists: and without Great Britain, the United Kingdom no longer exists. The title survived the independence of the Republic of Ireland to become the United Kingdom of Great Britain and Northern Ireland, which has lasted for a century. In destroying that, the Scottish nationalists are playing for very high stakes indeed, whose outcome affects every part of the UK – though so far, only those living in Scotland have had a voice, and the understanding has been that the thinnest majority would be enough to declare independence.

This book argues the unionist case, believing, as most Scots showed they also did in the referendum on independence in 2014, that continued, and renewed Union will be better both for Scots and their fellow British citizens. But it must be better defended than it has been in the past. Some Scots politicians have done so: Gordon Brown, the former Prime Minister, in books, articles and speeches; Alistair Darling, in his leadership of the 2014 campaign against independence; Ruth Davidson, a popular, uplifting and moderate Conservative voice (she resigned from the leadership in August 2019).

But strong English voices are usually lacking. In the Scots referendum in particular, the position of the then Prime Minister, David Cameron, and of the other party leaders, was less one strongly protective of the rights of the citizens of the UK, and more a series of often sentimental pleas that Scotland remain in the Union. In the conclusion, I give the example of the sharp debates in Canada at the end of the 1990s over the secession of Quebec – debates won by the federalist politicians, who strongly argued for the rights of the federal state and pressed hard for recognition that the departure of a major province was a matter not only for its people, but for all the citizens of a Canada that would be diminished by secession. I believe it offers a model of vigorous support which should commend itself to unionists of every one of the four nations of the UK.

In some quarters, there is no defence. In August 2019, the shadow Chancellor, John McDonnell, indicated at an event in the Edinburgh Festival, that a Labour government would not try to block a second referendum on independence, saying 'We would let the Scottish people decide. That's democracy' – thus confirming the nationalists' view that the British as a whole had no interests, or rights, in the issue.

In the election of 12 December 2019, the Conservative Party led by Boris Johnson won a large majority of 80 in the House of Commons. The Scottish National Party were also winners, gaining 13 seats with 45 per cent of the vote, taking back several of the seats they had lost to Labour and the Conservatives in 2017. The Labour Party, with a far left manifesto, a fudged position on Brexit and a leader, Jeremy Corbyn, who had become unpopular, suffered most, losing 60 scats and 2.6m votes on 2017, most in constituencies in the Midlands and the North of England it had, in many cases, held for decades.

It meant that the new Prime Minister had large freedom of action, and no need for the support of the Northern Irish Democratic Unionists, a support whose cost and disagreements had added to the many woes of Theresa May, his predecessor. A scenario much discussed before the election, when a Tory victory seemed uncertain, in which Labour, Liberals and the SNP would combine to form a majority in the House, with a second referendum in Scotland the price of SNP support, simply disappeared. Nicola Sturgeon, the SNP leader, did, however, repeat her demand for a new referendum, and said it was inevitable that it would be conceded.

As she knew, it was far from inevitable – and, with polls showing that Scots were still doubtful about the adventure of independence in highly uncertain times, she is likely to have been glad of that. She also knew that with a trial in Edinburgh in March for her predecessor as leader, Alex Salmond, charged with several charges of sexual assault, coupled with growing scepticism about the SNP's record in providing efficient public services, 2020 was likely to be a tougher year than she had experienced in a six-year leadership marked by a succession of victories.

In the first two decades of the twenty-first century, the nationalists have come closer to the realization of their aim than at any other time. The moral and political case for Scots secession, the creation of an independent Scots state, has always relied on seeing England, or Englishness, or the English, as malign influences on the Scots; catching them in a political straitjacket which denies them the possibility of being fully themselves; possible only if the Scots nation secured a sovereign government. A nation should be governed by its own people, they believe: and the other British have not become, in over three centuries, their own people.

Early nationalists, like Hugh MacDiarmid, the Anglophobe poet who stands at the head of Scots twentieth-century cultural nationalism, believed that being Scots was to recognize, or find, an essence, which he sometimes described in racial terms, that was wholly opposed to that of the English, whom he hated.

Scottish nationalist leaders don't now promote a racial essence. Their nationalism is presented as civic: it has little to do with the anti-foreigner, anti-immigrant rhetoric that is often part of the various European nationalisms. It 'is built, not on ethnic homogeneity, but on a shared political identity'.[1] Scotland, with a naturally declining birth rate, needs immigrant labour and, unlike other states which are also ageing (most of those in Europe), its nationalist government actively seeks it. The suspicion that nationalism cannot be civic runs deep, especially among those who see the European Union as an alternative to it: but a civic, liberal nationalism is quite possible, if at times beset with un-civic temptations (see the Conclusion of this book).

It depends, however, on the essentialist argument of 'being ourselves' in government, since only ourselves can govern in the interests of the Scots people. In this, it must thus prove that the three-century-old Union of nations that is the United Kingdom has been, and certainly now is, illegitimate in the eyes of the people: unable to be successfully multinational, and at the same time successfully democratic. England dominates, and thus governs, Scotland against its wishes. Getting out is paramount for national political health.

There is something seductive about this, even if you aren't a nationalist. Many Scots, not previously inclined to nationalism, have turned during the past four decades towards the Scottish National Party, since 2007 the government in the Scots parliament and the country's most popular political party. Here's what a nationalist could argue: indeed, what nationalists *are* arguing.

As this is written, Westminster politics are turbulent and at times unseemly. Both the major parties, Conservative and Labour, committed themselves to delivering Brexit, citing the mandate given by a referendum in 2016, which brought in a 52-per-cent vote in favour of ending Britain's 45-year-old EU membership. Faced with this vote, a parliament largely composed of pro-EU members failed to find a majority for a plan acceptable to the EU and the UK parliament which would do so. The three-year inability to agree has made the UK an object of scorn and pity round the world.

Brexit, however delivered, would take Scotland out of the EU with the rest of Britain, though nearly two-thirds of Scots voted for remain. The nationalists argue that it would make Scots poorer, more isolated and would encourage the growth of chauvinism – an argument, scaled up to the rest of the UK, echoed by many millions. Scots, nationalists believe, would be cut off from those with whom they had forged close links, and from an EU which has brought Europeans together, helped the former communist states to make transitions to democracy and kept the peace in Europe for nearly seventy-five years.

Some of the richest states in the world, a nationalist would point out, are small: New Zealand (4.8m), Norway (5.26m), Finland (5.5m),

Denmark (5.75m): Scotland is in the middle of that pack, at 5.44m. They are able to get consensus on both social and economic issues, and to introduce needed reforms, more easily. Government depends on trust: and in small states, where the politicians are better known by and less distant from their electors, trust is easier to develop and keep.

Scots, most nationalists (and many non-nationalists) think, are a more moral people than the English, and are naturally social democratic in their politics. They need to break with the rest of the UK, where England tends to conservatism, in order to have a politics to which people can relate.

Scotland was a European nation state – one of the oldest. When the Union with England was agreed in 1707, its separate parliament was abolished, say nationalists, through a mixture of English bribery and opportunism, the English seizing the advantage when Scotland was weak. The lack of an independent political centre has weakened its culture and rendered it helpless when the elephant in the Union – England – goes on the rampage, as under Margaret Thatcher, UK Prime Minister from 1979 to 1990.

Besides, a nationalist might say, Scots are close to agreeing to leave the United Kingdom: the referendum in 2014 showed that 45 per cent of those living in Scotland voted for independence. Since the decision to leave the EU, the polls have at times shown a majority for independence as the consequences of Brexit become clearer, and as Boris Johnson, who attracted a popularity, or *un*popularity rating in Scotland of -37 in June 2019,[2] became Prime Minister (he entered 10 Downing Street on 24 July). Nearly all nationalists are certain that independence will come (and many Scots who wish to remain in the Union fear they're right). The nationalist vision is that this is the way Scotland's energy and talents will be released and Scots can make their own mark on the world. Voting for independence will bring Scots together.

The counter argument, the unionist argument, which informs this book, begins with an observation that has formed part of Scots life for most of the three centuries in which it became British as well as Scots. That is, that Scotland has remained distinctively Scottish, even where it was most, and most uncontroversially, unionist. Many – the larger part – of the events, movements and innovations that both Scots and non-Scots see as expressive of the nation appeared and were developed after the turn of the eighteenth century.

The Scots Enlightenment, that spurt of intellectual and practical exploration of the changing nature of the economy, society and morality, and the mapping of their future, took off in the mid eighteenth century, centred on Glasgow, Edinburgh and Aberdeen. Its American historian, Arthur Herman, subtitled his book on the enlightenment as 'The Scots' invention of the modern world', and wrote that 'the union with England and Wales in 1707 also created 'the conditions under which Scotland could emerge, not just as a modern nation but as the model for all nations which must pass through the fire of modernity, past, present and future.'[3] The two writers who still shine most brightly in the Scots, and international, firmaments – Robert Burns (1759–1796) and Walter Scott (1771–1832) – were enfolded in it, at times conflictually but never rebelliously: Burns was a British civil servant (customs officer) for part of his working life, while Scott in his writings and public life strove, with success, to integrate the stream of anti-regime Jacobinism into the dominant politics of increasingly settled unionist life.

The nineteenth century saw Scotland's emergence as one of the greatest manufacturing centres of the world, especially in engineering – spurred by technological breakthroughs, of which the most momentous for the future of industry and capitalism was the instrument maker James Watt's developments of the Devonshire preacher Thomas Newcomen's steam-driven pump into a steam engine that could drive machinery, from mills to locomotives. Britain's vast empire was the space within which Scots could and did become rulers, administrators, military leaders and scholars of other lands until deep into the twentieth century. Their contribution was both cruelly oppressive, as the eager supplying of opium to China's millions of addicts by the Scots William Jardine and James Matheson in the 1820s; and piously adventurous, as the carrying of Christianity to Africa by the missionary David Livingstone, son of Blantyre mill workers.

Assumption of the imperial right to create and develop as well as to command and suppress, were combined, as in the person of the 8th Earl of Elgin (1811–1863) (his father had purchased and repatriated the Elgin marbles, statuary from the Greek Acropolis, which remain in the British Museum), who virtually formed Canada as an autonomous state within the Empire. Later, having become High Commissioner in China, he achieved victory in the 2nd Opium War (1856–1860), ordered the destruction of the summer palace of Beijing as retaliation for the execution of twenty European and Indian captives; and then forced the Chinese authorities to cede Hong Kong to Britain in perpetuity. He had, however, Christian scruples about his part in winning a war waged for the right to sell opium to addicts, writing to his wife that 'I was never so ashamed of myself in my life.'

So deeply was Scotland invested in heavy industrial production and imperial governance that the decline of both hit it very hard in the twentieth century. Yet that century also saw the development of two movements of the left which, for much of the century, cemented the union for the working and lower middle classes, that is the majority: the spread of active trade unionism through the United Kingdom, most unions organized on an all-British basis; and the creation of a welfare state by a Labour government after the war, one whose main institutions in health, education and social care – roughly equal throughout the UK – remain.

Until the 1970s, unionism was, in Colin Kidd's words, 'banal ... a union so well established as to need no defence or justification'.[4] Indeed, after Scott, the Union and its effects had little presence in literature, either in Scotland or England (Ireland was a quite different matter: for the writers who had not left – as had George Bernard Shaw, Oscar Wilde, James Joyce and Samuel Beckett – Ireland's imperial subordination was *the* subject). To be sure, the Union, and English domination of it, was a matter for debate, criticism, and often biting wit in Scots conversations in a way it rarely was in England. But it was a fact of life, a background structure to quotidian reality.

The reason lay in the nature of the Union settlement itself, however chaotically and self-interestedly (on both sides) achieved. It lay 'precisely (in) the fact that Britishness sat lightly on top of the constituent national identities'.[5] The almost incredible lightness of being able to be Scots while also being British was and remains an extraordinary, if partly accidental, achievement. It is this which acts as the backstop to the unionist position and which, up to the present, has helped persuade Scots to remain within it.

The success of the nationalists poses, still, large questions. The economic issue tends to stand tallest in this: a view widely shared by economists is that the promises made by the SNP of a golden future come independence are largely spurious. The difficulties of launching a new nation state with a currency (the pound) of a state it has left and over which it has no control, and its application to join a European Union whose rules insist on its adoption of a currency (the Euro) the SNP leaders do not wish to join, are large.

The Scottish National Party government describes itself as 'social democratic', and emphasizes the benefits Scots enjoy, not available to the rest of the UK, such as free university education and free home care for the elderly. Yet these are available because of a large subsidy from the UK Treasury under a system known as the 'Barnett Formula' (after its creator, the former Labour Chief Secretary to the Treasury, Joel Barnett): in whatever ways that may be rationalized and accounted for, on independence something between £8bn and £10bn will disappear from Scotland's capacity for public-sector expenditure. At the same time, the best forecasts of the country's finances after secession, including the SNP's own, point to the need for sharply reduced public spending for some years. Further, according to analysis of the British Social Attitudes survey of 2010, 'it seems that Scotland is not so different after all. Scotland is somewhat more social democratic than England. However, for the most part the difference is one of degree rather than of kind and is no larger now than it was a decade ago. Moreover, Scotland appears to have experienced something of a drift away from a social democratic outlook during the course of the past decade, in tandem with public opinion in England.'[6]

A confident statement of long-term, deeply embedded difference between the English and the Scots in character, habits, and outlook is rarely possible, though the nationalists attempt to encourage it. SNP rhetoric on attitudes to immigration, for example, stress the openness of Scotland and the grudging, even hostile attitudes said to be those of the English. Yet England is far more multinational and diverse than Scotland: and Professor John Curtice, the pollster of reference at Strathclyde University, says that in aggregate, there is little difference between the way in which the two populations view immigrants. He also warns that these views can and do change quite rapidly and substantially, depending on circumstances.

Scotland's population – 5,062,000 in 2001, and 5,295,000 in 2011 (the census years) – remains overwhelmingly white: it is changing slowly, though change will tend to accelerate. On the census figures, Scots and other white British accounted for 95.47 per cent of the population in 2001, declining to 91.15 per cent in 2011. Other whites brought the 2001 total to 97.99, the 2011 total to 96.02 per cent. England had a population of 49,138,831 in 2001, rising to 53,012,456 in 2011. White British made up 88.3 per cent in 2001, 80.8 per cent in 2011. All whites were 91 per cent in 2001, 84.4 in 2011. England, too, has a large white majority: but it is both smaller than Scotland's and changing more rapidly than Scotland: some cities have, or are about to have, a minority white British population.

In Glasgow, Scotland's largest city – at 577,869 in 2001, 593,245 in 2011 – white Scots and other British made up 90.77 per cent in 2001, with all whites at 94.55 per cent; and 82.66 per cent in 2011, while all whites came out at 88.42 per cent. The Asian population – including Indian, Pakistani, Bangladeshi and Chinese – grew from 4.44 per cent of the population in 2001 to 8.05 per cent in 2011.

In Bradford, slightly smaller than Glasgow at 522,452 in 2011, white British accounted for 76.06 per cent of the city's people in 2001; 63.86 in 2011. The Asian communities came out at 19.09 per cent in 2001; 26.83 in 2011. Birmingham, England's second city, had a similar percentage of ethnically Asian citizens in 2011 – 26.6 per cent: the white British, 53.1 per cent in 2011 and will be a minority by 2021, as they already were in London in 2011.

Politicians from ethnic minorities are much more visible in the Westminster parliament than in the Scots one, as they were in the Cabinet in 2019. Boris Johnson's three most senior colleagues were children of ethnic minorities who came to the UK: Sajid Javid, Chancellor, son of Pakistani immigrants; Priti Patel, Home Secretary, daughter of Gujurati Indians who moved to the UK from Uganda; and Dominic Raab, the Foreign Secretary, whose Jewish father came to the UK from Czechoslovakia in 1938, aged six. Ashok Sharma, the International Development Secretary, was born in India and moved to the UK with his family when five: James Cleverly, the Conservative Party Chairman, was born to a Sierra Leone mother and a British father. In the Scottish cabinet, Humza Yousaf, the Justice Secretary, is the son of a Nigerian mother and a Pakistani father, who came to the UK in the 1960s.

Rapid change is evident in what had been, and still often is seen as the two countries' traditional strengths and weaknesses. Glasgow had been the 'murder capital of Europe' – with a knife being the weapon of choice, and with a reputation stretching back centuries for violent crime. A Violence Reduction Unit was created in 2005, and, taking some of its cues from the US, the murder rate in both Glasgow and Scotland has been more than halved. London, suffering an epidemic of knife crime from 2017, now tries to copy Glasgow's success.

By contrast, improvements in education in London have, in the past few years, made the city into an 'education superpower' – even as London has by far the highest level of immigrant families in the UK, many of whom have limited English language skills. Reasons given include higher standards in the semi-independent academies and free schools; the Teach First programme, which puts top graduates into tough schools; ambitious immigrant parents, many of whose children now surpass white working-class boys and even in some cases every-one else; and rapid intervention to tackle underperformance. Scotland, which had long prided itself on its good, egalitarian schools, has a system now (in the 2000s) mired in mediocrity. The rest of England lags behind most other countries in Europe in the core subjects of math-ematics, science and reading but is still graded better than Scotland.[7]

The fact is that both nations can learn from each other: and have, through centuries. The fact also is, that strengths and weaknesses, though culturally affected, are not fate.

One difference which appears incontestable, because it has been so clearly shown, is the two countries' attitudes to the European Union in the 2016 referendum. England voted for Brexit by 53.5 per cent, while Scotland's Brexit vote was only 38 per cent (Wales was close to England's level, at 52.5 per cent for Brexit: Northern Ireland between them, with a minority Brexit vote of 44.2 per cent). Why? Adam Ramsay, the editor of Open Democracy UK, gives a battery of reasons, many of them self-serving for Scots: Scotland is better educated than England (more university graduates); the English political power centres on the concept of the 'Queen in parliament', while the Scots believe power lies with the people; with a different legal system, a history of emigration,

Scotland is accustomed to political rule from outside of the country.[8]

It's hard to say if these, and other differences, explain the large difference in the vote between the two nations: indeed, some of them seem unlikely to explain anything. The Scots, like the English, have been governed by the convention of the 'Queen in parliament' for over three centuries, without, until recently, major complaint. The Brexit 'revolution' has been presented by Brexiteers as a people's rising: and the subsequent debate over Brexit, by both Remainer and Brexiteer sides, is cast all but exclusively in terms of 'what the people really want'. This can become a little ridiculous, as the Remainers' call for a second referendum, described as a 'People's Vote', raises the question of what they believe the first exercise to be. But it is a further demonstration that, deeply divided as the two groups are, they agree that they draw their mandate from the people. Finally, Scots education is no longer the world-leading, or even England-leading, system which it, until recently, was: the universities remain high in national and world ratings: the schools do not.

The SNP line on the EU changed radically. In the 1970s, the party leader, William Wolfe, saw continued membership of the EU as 'a political dark age of remote control and undemocratic government', a position strongly endorsed by the rising star, Alex Salmond. But the modernizers, by then including Salmond, saw the rising Euroscepticism among English politicians, and secured a shift to 'Scotland in Europe' in the 1980s. They understood that if Scotland was to leave one Union, it had better find another to join in order to reassure prospective voters.

This has seemed to be the settled will of around two-thirds of the Scots people, to judge from the outcome of the 2016 referendum on the EU. Yet the lack of any credible Leave figure in Scotland, which Ramsay, in his Open Democracy article, sees as a positive feature, an indication of the solid support of Scots, but instead demonstrates rather the lack of debate and clash of ideas. Where the main political parties – the ruling SNP, the Conservatives, Labour, Liberal Democrats and Greens, and with those the Scots-based news media, the business and trade union confederations – all called for a 'remain' vote, the fact that over a third of Scots voted Brexit, including about a third of the SNP supporters, is a more surprising result than it has usually been presented.

The larger question is the state of the EU itself. It is a very large question for Scotland, since its nationalist government is bent on leaving one Union – of the UK – for another, reassuring people that the European Union is the better bet and the safer haven. But the EU is not safe, in large part because its currency is not: one of the reasons why the British Labour government decided not to join the Euro, and the SNP decided to retain sterling.

Three centuries of Union have created a Union which has, until the last few decades, worked largely uncontroversially, as most unified democratic states do: as one which allocates, through the common tax system, larger subsidies and aid to the poorer, harder-hit, more rapidly ageing and more scantily populated (as the Highlands and Islands of Scotland) parts of the country than to the richer ones. Grumbles about the 'Robin Hood' side of national economic management – using the taxes of richer areas to assist the poor – are everywhere in democratic states. In Italy, a major political party, the Lega Nord, was founded in 1991 and drew considerable support for its policy of separation from the south of Italy, which it held to be an area of shiftless people living off northern taxes. Its direct descendant, the Lega, became in 2019 the dominant part of the governing coalition.

But, more often, a state's efforts to, in some measure, equalize the inevitably differing economies of its constituent parts have been passively supported, even by the wealthier regions. The Union has accomplished what the creators of the European Union wished to create, but which now looks unlikely to be realized, at least not for the present political generations: a state able to treat all those on its territory as equal citizens.

The fact that Britain is such a state and that Britishness has a real meaning makes the decision to secede from the Union by a marginal vote in a referendum doubly absurd. Every citizen in Britain will be affected by secession because it will fundamentally change the make-up of the state. The Scots nationalists' position, that the vote belongs to everyone resident in Scotland at the time of a referendum, means that a recent immigrant with little or no knowledge of the stakes involved is privileged over Scots living elsewhere in the UK, and over all other British. The immigrant, if s/he intends to become a permanent resident, *should* have a vote: but so should first-generation Scots living in

England, Wales or Northern Ireland, while British citizens as a whole should be included – with a voice rather than a vote (since it is right that Scots should decide the future of their nation). There is a proposal for a way of dealing with this later in this book, designed to meet the objection made by the former Supreme Court judge Jonathan Sumption in one of his 2019 Reith lectures, that a democratic polity 'cannot operate on the basis that a bare majority takes one hundred per cent of the spoils'.[9]

The very large advantage the nationalists have had in Scotland, once they crossed over the credibility bar at some point in the 1980s, is that they were able both to redefine, and take a grip on Scottish patriotism. Scots patriotism has been, for most of the Union period, a widely accepted, widely adopted but mainly cultural matter: in song, dance, humour; in literature; in sport; in the various forms of Protestantism; and in military prowess. Official patriotism was expressed in loyalty to the British king or queen and country, and in pride in empire.

The twentieth century progressively thinned this out. Culture had been expressed in localities, woven round differing dialects and forms of labour, where most concerns were bounded within rural or urban communities: these are less compelling and, especially for the young, much more globally connected. Political allegiance, when it was occasionally required to be made overt or celebrated, was for most a reflexive gesture of British loyalty.

This was not absent in the generation born soon after the war but it was dying. The ceremonies observed in my birthplace, the fishing village of Anstruther on the East Fife coast, as parading through the streets on old year's night; gathering on the harbour to see the fleet leave; the fishermen's ball; the kirks unaccustomedly full for harvest festivals (this was a fishing *and* farming area) and a local assumption, not welcome among the children, that all adults could take a hand (and sometimes it *was* a hand) in disciplining your behaviour: most of these have gone, now, or leave faint traces. Local was most important; but many families got and sent airmail letters to Australia, Canada, New Zealand and the United States: sometimes relatives came back to look about and say: *that* wasn't there before! My grandfather's two younger sisters came back to Fife as women in late middle age, on a visit as much dutiful as sentimental: born in the later Victorian time, when our part of Scotland was relatively poor, they emigrated and successfully integrated into a booming America, in accent, habits and expectation American.

Michael Fry writes a threnody to the age gone in his fine, ultimately elegiac *A New Race of Men*,[10] contrasting Scotland's 'coherent culture' at the beginning of the nineteenth century, when Scots felt themselves 'a new race of men' with a more diverse, but more divided twentieth century, 'ill-equipped to resist influences that were provincializing it, as Scots seized the great opportunities open to them (elsewhere) . . . and as all sorts of British authorities and social forces tightened their grip on Scotland. The culture, in the broadest sense, suffered the most from this. Not only did it become too weak to defend itself, but the Scots people grew increasingly unsure if it was worth defending.'

This is in part true: the centralizing of government and the strengthening of the state during and after the Second World War was hard on localism, though welcomed by those who voted for, and in large measure received, a level of healthcare and modest financial security, which were not available to them from the state, even when they had been called, indeed compelled, to defend that state. And Scots had seized opportunities open to them elsewhere in large numbers from medieval times: perhaps most of all in the nineteenth century, when empire was their oyster and North America provided a welcome warmer than for most other Europeans.

It is the Scots nationalists' proudest achievement, that they have provided a vocabulary and a mission for an aggressive assertion of a re-established Scottishness, which must rest on the framework of an independent state in order to preserve itself for the future. But it is by some way the opposite of the old British patriotism, which promoted a common identity and pride. Scots patriotism now has relied heavily not on a commonality, a comradeship, with the English, but on a distrust, a dislike, most strongly expressed by some of Scotland's most prominent writers, furthered by the nationalist leadership through a relentless depiction of British political and governing class as chronically out of touch, London-centred and determined to impoverish Scotland with policies of austerity.

The argument here is that the huge dislocations which secession will bring, most of all to Scotland, are not worth the effort because independence will be, at the very least in the short and medium term, materially impoverishing; the politics necessarily configured round a shrunken economy and constrained to be 'neo-liberal', unless embarking on a difficult, contested, perhaps impossible process of widespread nationalization in the pursuit of a more socialist state, while the culture remains roughly the same. I argue that even before devolution, indeed through much of the twentieth century (and of course before), Scotland managed to retain a distinctive culture which, though less locally bounded, was and is still vibrant enough to produce people following the arts, the sciences and entertainment, who enrich the society and the locality in which they were born and, frequently, beyond, as the country has done for centuries. The former Prime Minister, Gordon Brown (2007–2010) argued that 'we should make clear and explicit that the benefits we receive from the Union reflect a fundamental moral purpose – that no matter where you reside and what your background is, every citizen enjoys the dignity of not just equal civil and political rights, but the same social and economic rights too'.[11]

This is written to refute the view that secession is necessary for this to be preserved and furthered: and to argue that continued, if necessarily reformed, Union will best preserve the freedoms it was designed to enshrine.

1

THE OTHER UNION

The competing possibilities and constraints of globalization and nationalism are central to the way in which the twenty-first-century world is framed and experienced. In this still youthful century, what had seemed to be a bountiful gift from the previous one – a world, and above all a Europe, committed, willy-nilly, to ever-closer and ever more fruitful engagement, in trade, in immigration, in culture, in education across national borders – has been submitted, in times grimmer than foreseen, to ever-closer inspection by those who benefit little from these engagements, and often find them wanting.

The new nationalists of Europe have taken up the cause of the many who now feel, for different reasons, that their country has let them down by letting too much of the rest of the world in. Their parties claim they can protect their people from much of this. From mass immigration in the first instance; from trade so free it destroys national industries; from the rule, more or less opaque to most, of supra-national institutions, among which the European Union is presented as the darkest, looming shadow.

The nationalists of Scotland, though, are of a different stripe. The many European movements which would claim nationalism as their political home – the French Rassemblement National (previously Front National), the German Alternativ für Deutschland, the Italian Lega, the Swedish Democrats, the Spanish Vox, the two Dutch far-right groups, the Forum for Democracy and the Freedom Party – are not the Scottish National Party's allies. All have a different goal from the SNP: they wish to win a dominant position in their nation's politics which will allow them to radically shift policies on the economy, on Europe and above all on immigration. Their common aim is to protect: protect the economy from the malign effects of globalization, protect the state from the interventions of the EU and protect the people from the flows of immigrants, especially those coming from Middle Eastern and African states, and also from the poorer EU states, such as the Central European, former communist countries. Muslims are seen as particularly dangerous, represented as hostile to the religious and ethical values of Europe and providing incubation cells for terrorism.

By contrast, the SNP places itself as social democratic, civic, welcoming of immigration, enthusiastically pro-EU and with no plans for trade barriers, quotas or tariffs. The nationalists with whom it has the closest ties are the Catalans, who, like the Scots are part of a larger state, but also see themselves as an ancient nation, wishing to get out of the one which enfolds them, Spain. Relations are cordial rather than close: the Catalans are further to the left than the Scots nationalists: their militancy and willingness to confront the Spanish state is witness to the fact that Spain will not allow secession to be the subject of a campaign, let alone succeed. The Scots Nats, for all their rhetorical exuberance, are allowed to be within the law in their efforts to leave the British state and strive to remain legal.

The SNP argues, in effect, that Scotland must leave the UK to be much the same as it was within it: its politics moderate, its economy firmly market-based. With these as its guiding lights, it argues that Scotland must leave the port in which it has been berthed for over three centuries – the United Kingdom – and become, as nationalists would see it, a vessel free to seek a welcome in another Union, which it believes will serve it better from now on. It is presented as an easy move, with the reassurance of the same currency and the same monarch as now, with continued membership of Nato. For everything to stay the same or, where not the same, get better, everything must change.

But change will be wrenching. If unpicking the UK from the EU after less than half a century of membership will be hard, unpicking

Scotland from a more than 300-year-plus Union will be just as contested, and much harder. The prospect, for all their public confidence,
must be, in reflective moments, terrifying for the party leaders. Even if
they believe their vastly overconfident economic forecasts, they cannot
know if Scotland, alone, can provide for its citizens the standard of
living available when it is part of the sixth or seventh largest economy
in the world. The prospect is also clearly fearful for many of the Scots
whom nationalists seek to convince to take the voyage; a large reason
why, so far, they have refused to be loosed from the British state, even
as they continue to return the SNP as the largest party in the Scottish
parliament, with a significant representation in Westminster.

The post-war, liberal era in the wealthy Western states was increasingly
closely aligned with globalization, and Francis Fukuyama will forever
be aligned with the declaration that 'we may be witnessing . . . the end
of history as such, the end point of mankind's ideological evolution and
the universalization of Western liberal democracy as the final forms of
government . . . the struggle is now over'.[1] The thesis was controversial
as soon as it appeared, and grew more so, to the point that Fukuyama
himself recanted. History had not closed its book, and liberal democracy did not become a politics of choice of most for the dictators in the
world: insofar as it spread, in the 1980s and 1990s, the new century saw
it shrink again. So confident was Russian president Vladimir Putin that
the claim of a liberal democratic future was now truly discarded that
he told *The Financial Times* in June 2019 that liberalism was dead.[2] But
a common view did spread – Russia is, in fact, part of it – that at least
economic globalization was now dominant, and could not be defied
except at increasing national cost. Economic nationalism was stupidity.
    The general consensus on this illuminates the singular position of
the Scots (and the Catalan) nationalists. Where the national populists of
Europe strive to turn their countries into less open societies, nationalist
Scotland enters into the current whirlpool of European nationalisms
as a movement which sees the people it wishes both to represent and
liberate as confident globalists, well able to fend for themselves in the
world's market place, requiring to be protected from no peoples other
than the English. It accepts the main tenets of the economics of globalization even as its century-long quest is to create a new international

border between itself and the rest of the UK, precisely the opposite of what the globalizers think appropriate.

This conviction that nationalism is no longer a long-term option in today's world, and that borders are now unnecessary and irrational, has powerful arguments behind it, and powerful proponents, including US President Bill Clinton (1993–2001) and UK Prime Minister Tony Blair (1997–2007), both of whose convictions were sharpened by arguing with those on the left of their own parties. Among the most influential of the arguments deployed was that made in a 1997 essay 'Power Shift' by Jessica T. Matthews, a former head of the Carnegie Endowment for International Peace,[3] one of the world's most prestigious NGOs and one of the best endowed (by a nineteenth-century Scots industrialist, who combined ruthless management in his business life with huge charitable giving towards the end of it).

Matthews argued that a complex of developments – the Internet, the spread and growth of NGOs, the power of global financial markets and the increasing influence of the global financial institutions, globally integrated crime, increased intervention in national affairs (as the monitoring of elections), the growing grasp and scope of the European Union, together with that of sub-state actors, as regions with their own international representation – were all coming together to create a 'global civil society', to thereby threaten the nation states' freedom of action and cramp their nineteenth and early twentieth-century style. This change was often for the best, Matthews believed, since 'nation-states may simply no longer be the natural problem-solving unit'.

She did not ignore the dangers of the new globalism: indeed, she warned of them in stark terms, 'with citizens already feeling that their national governments do not hear individual voices, the trend could well provoke deeper and more dangerous alienations'. But her advice was not to strengthen nations or their institutions: the global trends running against that were largely unstoppable, the nation states already rendered too incompetent. Rapid social innovations were thus essential, and new 'adaptations' had to be made urgently – including 'a business sector that can shoulder a broader policy role, NGOs that are less parochial and better able to operate on a large scale, international institutions that can efficiently serve the dual masters of states and citizenry, and, above all, new institutions and political entities that match the transnational scope of today's challenges while meeting citizens' demands for accountable democratic governance'.

In her mind, the antidotes to the political earthquake in the nation states were not to make nation states stronger, but to make them weaker. She proposed larger and more capable global institutions which could somehow provide 'accountable democratic government', while being, implicitly, quite different from the present efforts to provide such government. NGOs and the EU were the most likely replacements: whatever their usefulness, neither are democratic, except, in the latter case, very distantly and obscurely. The very brevity and vagueness of Matthews' suggestions betray the great difficulty in imagining global alternatives to national institutions.

They were difficult to imagine because the consensus among policy makers, democratic politicians, commentators and senior officials was so complete, the dissent so much regarded as old school, even reactionary. The global economic institutions were certain of it, including the World Trade Organization, which, according to the US economist Dani Rodrik, 'not only made it harder for countries to shield themselves from international competition but also reached into policy areas that international trade rules had not previously touched: agriculture, services, intellectual property, industrial policy, and health and sanitary regulations. Even more ambitious regional trade deals, such as the North American Free Trade Agreement, took off around the same time.' Rodrik wrote that it was in the 1990s 'when policy makers set the world on its current, hyperglobalist path, requiring domestic economies to be put in the service of the world economy instead of the other way around'.[4] The Scots, on this account, would break with the UK to put themselves 'in the service', as a small and at least initially weak economy, of a world economy ultimately ruthless in making decisions as between these old-fashioned nations, in which high productivity and low cost of labour were paramount.

The conviction that nationalism is a plague upon the planet, best removed, reaches its public apogee in the European Union, founded, in part, to combat nationalism and, in the early decades of the twenty-first century, still with many leaders who continued the federalist ideals of the early founders, or were at least enthusiasts for greater integration, which could only lead, if continued, to something like a federal state.

French President Emmanuel Macron has called nationalism 'a betrayal of patriotism': President Steinmeyer of Germany, 'an ideological poison'; Jean-Claude Juncker, president of the European Commission, said that 'unchecked nationalism is riddled with both poison and deceit'. Chancellor Angela Merkel of Germany told the European parliament that 'Solidarity is based on tolerance and this is Europe's strength. It is part of our common European DNA and it means overcoming national egoisms.'

All of the choices for the main posts in the EU government made in June 2019 were men and women who were convinced integrationists: the former German Defence Minister, Ursula von der Leyen, chosen for the EU's top job of President of the Commission, had proclaimed that she was a federalist. Though she seemed to retreat a little from that in later public statements, it is likely to remain her position: she is, according to the German weekly Der Spiegel, 'passionate about Europe'.[5] Part of her childhood was spent in Brussels, where her father was director general of the Competition Directorate, later a long-serving (1976–1990) Christian Democrat President of Lower Saxony.

She secured the job through a series of deals among Europe's major political leaders, especially French President Emmanuel Macron, her most enthusiastic backer, and German Chancellor Angela Merkel. She was, again according to Spiegel, 'handpicked by European leaders in a confidential meeting to be installed as the leader of the EU's executive body', her nomination being 'a last second solution to a deadlock'. The manner of her coming to power was not strange – all such appointments in the EU are deals between the leaders – except that it was more opaque and unexpected than usual. At the same time as the EU and the more integrationist-leaning national leaders proclaim their commitment to making it more democratic, its most important moves are closed-door events. It is to this Union that the Scots nationalists, strongly sensitive to anything which smacks of undemocratic behaviour on the part of the Westminster government, propose to commit Scotland.

The EU has two large problems with this anti-nationalist, pro-globalist rhetoric. Federalists and integrationists condemn what they wish Europe to become. Macron, in his speeches, talks of a 'sovereign Europe'. Those who believe most passionately in the EU do not wish to ban nation states: they wish to ban the some thirty states who can claim to be European, and create one: the Federal States of Europe. To operate as such a state, it must be sovereign: it must acquire a Finance Ministry with fiscal and other powers, upgrade the Central Bank into an institution that dominates and regulates an integrated European banking sector, create foreign and defence ministries, which develop policies and legislation that can gain support throughout the Union and, as in all democracies, claim that the parliament represents the will of the people. It must be *obeyed:* a necessity even more pressing in a democracy than in authoritarian states, which can resort to coercion more easily.

This is not to make Europe seem like a nightmare super state (it could become one, but all states have the potential to turn into oppressors rather than servants of their people): it is to understand the logic of its creation. To go beyond the present political swamp in which it is stuck, it must create executive centres that can give support to the currency and the EU-wide systems and institutions, which now lack both integration and democratic validity. In order to spread soft power, it must have centres of hard power. It must transform the present parliament, little regarded and attracting low electoral turnouts, into a legislature that demonstrates both its independence, its competence and its ability to attract the trust of a Europe-wide electorate. These are very high goals. If it succeeds in pursuing what for it is a necessary closer integration (a large 'if'), it must greatly strengthen its power over the member states, taking into its institutions decisions that previously resided in the treasuries and ministries and central banks of the member states. Scots politics, both when run through a Scottish Secretary of State and the Scottish Office, and when run through a devolved government and parliament, accustomed themselves to a relationship with Westminster that has, broadly, benefited Scotland. Shorn of that, it will face one whose new leadership will strive to take away, or dilute, the independent powers held, by the nationalists, to be the Scots' birthright.

It's hard, however, as of 2020, to see the integrationists succeeding in drawing the nation states more closely together. The most developed Central European states – Czech Republic and Slovakia, with Hungary and Poland in the lead, are cold or even hostile towards the EU, and in all cases determined not to take any migrants. A group of northern states, under Dutch leadership and including Denmark, Estonia, Finland, Ireland, Latvia, Lithuania and Sweden, have made it clear they wish powers to be returned to them, not further centralized. Wopke Hoekstra, the Dutch Finance Minister, told the *FT* in November 2018 that 'I am a realist. My job is to do what is in the best interests of the Netherlands, and of course I keep an eye of what is in the interests of Europe as a whole.'[6] The 'best interests' for every member state's government, of any persuasion, always trumps the 'best interests' of the EU, at least when defined as closer integration.

How does Scotland navigate these waters? When independent, it will need all the help it can get from the EU Commission. But it became increasingly hard for an outsider to the EU's internal debates to understand in which way it is likely to go, and what its view of nationhood is. At best, an outsider must conclude that the EU's objection to nations is thus a very partial one, since most of the existing nation states of Europe remain largely unmoved by calls to shift more powers to the EU in Brussels.

At the centre of concern about the EU's longer term is the Euro, to which nineteen of the EU's twenty-eight states (before the exit of the UK) belong. Helen Thompson, the Professor of Political Economy at the University of Cambridge, illuminates the problem – one which has its roots in the 'creation of a currency union without an accompanying political and fiscal union . . . stuck with an unworkable currency union, the EU can neither accommodate democracy in its member states nor suppress it. The result is likely to be the continuation of the pattern over the last decade: crisis after crisis with no lasting solution.'[7]

Thompson's belief that democracy, especially in its British form, and a proper monetary union are incompatible would, sooner or later, require to be faced by the independent Scots. The position in which Scotland could find itself, if independent in a continued downturn in the European and world economies, with a currency it cannot control and an insistence that the new member must adopt the Euro, would be a difficult one indeed.

The European Union, preferred by the Scots nationalists to the Union of which they are a part, was, when the SNP was at its highest point in the 2010s, showing the most obvious signs of weakness. The Euro remained too little protected. The most vigorous call, from

Macron, for a new spurt of integration had been shuffled away, first, into rhetorical agreement, then increasingly replaced by frank refusal to countenance the radical implications of his proposals.

The European Union has projected itself, in the years following the collapse of the Soviet Union, as both the antidote to nationalism and the template for a new kind of nation – absorbing nation states while preserving their cultures, creating a non-imperial centre which could, however, regulate the Euro currency, protect Europe's borders, ensure the continent's security and provide a framework for a functioning democratic assembly. It has succeeded in little of that.

In the 2010s, nationalist populist movements, in some states (Italy, Hungary, Poland) governments, directly hostile to its public ethos and its long-term plans for integration, grew stronger. These movements liked to present the EU as the opposite of its self-image – as an imperialist bully, choking off national independent action, and as an agent of the destructive globalism that many in these states had come to blame for their stagnation. It was in many ways flat wrong: the EU had done and continues to do much to rein back the potentially damaging projects of large corporations, including the ravenous US communication giants. And its embrace of the former Communist states of Central Europe has been a generous one, as the many projects built with its money (and the as-yet-uncalculated amount of its subsidies illegally squirrelled away in bank accounts of the new post-Communist elites) testify. But, for the national populists, it was ranged on the globalist side: and thus an enemy.

The surge of support for the nation, extreme, in some of the nationalist–populist rhetoric: more measured, in more centrist politics, is perceived as one that is disproportionately produced by those who feel excluded. Excluded, that is, as much from decent wages and good jobs as from the kind of status and attention given by political and moneyed elites to the global over the national, and the local. The Columbia University Professor of International Relations, Jack Snyder, writes that 'over the past thirty years liberalism has become disembedded. Elites in the United States and Europe have steadily dismantled the political controls that once allowed national governments to manage capitalism. They have constrained democratic politics to fit the logic of international markets and shifted policy making to unaccountable bureaucracies or supranational institutions such as the EU. This has created the conditions for the present surge of populist nationalism.'[8]

In the UK, the journalist David Goodhart drew many progressives' reflexive contempt, then gradually gained – not universally – recognition of the strength of his judgement, with his *Road to Somewhere*, arguing that 'successful societies are actually existing things based on habits of cooperation, familiarity and trust and on bonds of language, history and culture' . . . if our European societies – a magnet to millions of refugees – are to continue flourishing they need to retain some sense of mutual regard between anonymous citizens, which means keeping inflows to levels that allow people to be absorbed into that hard-to-define thing we call a 'national culture' or 'way of life'.[9]

Nationalism, on these thinkers' evidence, is not the brutish tyranny conjured by the leaders of the EU, but a necessary framework for both communal support and individual growth. People also – this had been a Fukuyama theme, borrowed from the Hegelian interpreter Alexander Kojeve – craved recognition. They needed others' acknowledgement of their worth in order to feel that they were autonomous individuals. The major beneficiaries were the rich and the very rich, among whom the celebrities were showered with minute-by-minute recognition. Yet even those who did well enough felt, often, that the familiar world was changing too quickly, too incomprehensibly.

As these movements grew stronger, the advocates of globalism were forced to adjust their positions, retaining a belief that globalization benefited states, but recognizing that it also produced victims. The *FT*'s Martin Wolf had written that globalism was a choice 'made to enhance a nation's economic well-being – indeed, experience suggests that the opening of trade and of most capital flows enriches most citizens in the short run and virtually all citizens in the long run'.[10] In later writing, however, Wolf recognized the downside of the choice, understanding that it not only produced winners, and many who felt themselves as more victim than winner: these included both working and middle classes who saw their own economic and social positions stall, or fall. He came to a nuanced view of globalism: that, as evidence showed, it was good for nations' economy and thus their populations: but that it had to be constrained by and subservient to the democratic choices of national electorates: 'states function because they create identities and loyalties. These are necessary if states, especially democratic states, are to function successfully ... policies must also be judged in terms of their domestic legitimacy. In some cases, immigration being among the most important, that balance was lost. Control over who lives within a country is a fundamental aspect of sovereignty. Globalism does not mean a world without borders. That would be unworkable: without borders, there would be no states. Without states, there would be no order, domestic or global.'[11]

The Scots nationalists occupy a singular position in these arguments. They would agree with the Hungarian Prime Minister Viktor Orban that large states made up of different nations work to cause the distinctive nationhood of their members to disappear, or at least diminish: England is constantly charged with just such an intent. But they are in the opposite camp to Orban and the other Central Europeans on immigration. The latter adamantly refuse to allow in more than a trickle; Scotland broadcasts a welcome.

The nationalists' leadership is strongly attached to the European Union. Yet the material generated by the party, and its supporters, is almost all polemical or propagandist: a relatively balanced analysis of the EU, of Scotland's ability to join it and its position once in it, hardly exists. They can count on the large majority of Scots who voted to Remain in the 2016 referendum to be on their side in this issue: but not enthusiastically so.

The EU does not excite Scots any more than it does the English, except when made a bone of strong contention, as it has been since 2016. The former SNP minister Marco Biagi wrote, in 2017, that 'the Scottish Social Attitudes Surveys have consistently, over years, found little widespread evidence of a gut attachment to European identity. In-depth focus groups conducted by the Institute of Public Policy Research Scotland and Ipsos-Mori ahead of the Brexit referendum concurred. Scotland's EU membership is not, in and of itself, of definitive importance to more than a small number of citizens, certainly much fewer than intrinsically value a sense of attachment to the UK, its identity, traditions and flag. A new independence referendum that came to be a choice between pure emotional attachment to the EU or the UK would be a disaster for the Yes side.' (Biagi is unusually free from automatic obeisance to his Party's established positions: one reason, perhaps, why he preferred, in 2016, to pursue doctoral research at Yale University than remain an SNP minister of Local Government and Community Empowerment.)[12]

It's true, as Biagi writes, that the EU does become important when the UK's decision is to exit: its consequences for Scots business, politics and society are as large as for any other part of the UK. Graver: for if and when the UK exits and if and when Scotland, having received a majority for independence, joins the European Union, it will face the same problem as Northern Ireland and the Irish Republic: a hard border. To argue, as nationalists do, that the European market is much larger and will remain open to it after independence is to ignore the large differential between trade with the rest of the UK, and that with the EU. Since 2002, the value of Scottish trade with the UK has grown by 74 per cent, from $28.6bn to £49.8bn in 2017. Trade with the EU in the same period has also grown, but in percentage terms much less, by eight per cent, from £11.4bn to £12.3bn. Companies from the rest of the UK, numbering 2,790, employed 340,000 workers in 2017 in Scotland, 17.7 per cent of the Scots workforce, while 1,000 EU-based companies employed 127,000, or 6.6 per cent of workers.

As economists who had seen in globalization a system that could both help integrate the world's states and raise incomes in both the developed and developing countries, so pro-globalization politicians, more exposed to choices and frustrations of voters, struggled to adjust. One such is now an ex-politician: Michael Ignatieff is a former leader of the Canadian Liberal Party: he is now (2020) the director of the Central European University – unlike most such posts, a politically turbulent one. His university was forced out of its home, Hungary's capital Budapest, by the Hungarian government, largely, it seems, because the CEU is funded by George Soros, a native Hungarian and a figure of hate all over the former communist world, whose new institutions he did, and gave, much to help.

For Ignatieff, the state is not just a port in a storm but an essential element of democracy. Speaking in London in 2014, he said: 'I think a progressive politics is deeply connected to the idea of sovereignty. And by sovereignty I mean something very simple: the idea that the people should be masters of their own house. It's very hard to have a viable democracy unless it is sovereign . . .

'The sovereignty I care about is the belief that citizens ought to feel that they're masters of the terms and conditions of their life, that they're not flotsam tossed on the waves of global forces, that power is not elsewhere, that power is in their society, to be fought for, to be controlled, to be managed well . . . You can't have any kind of democratic politics at all unless the people feel that voting and public life actually matter, that consequential decisions are made in the political arena. Otherwise politics is nothing more than a Punch and Judy show.'[13]

The trend towards the nation state as protector, as a house in which a citizen could feel a master, would seem to benefit the Scots nationalists, as well as other, less liberal nationalist groups, most of whom wish to shift the politics of the state they are in to the exclusionary right, not leave it. But, in Scotland's case, statehood is a choice: continued adhesion to the British state, or a break with it. As a small, economically and financially precarious new state, Scotland would be much more like 'flotsam tossed on the waves of global forces', more exposed than in a Union which, for it, has been a success. Understanding that nation states function, in Martin Wolf's words, because 'they create identities and loyalties . . . necessary if states, especially democratic states, are to function successfully' is not to cede the terrain to the Scots nationalists, nor to relieve Scots of a choice of to which nation state they wish to be loyal. And that is a matter of reason more than sentiment.

The best-known excerpt from 'Qu'est ce qu'une nation?',[14] the French philosopher Ernest Renan's famous 1882 lecture, is that a nation is a 'daily plebiscite'; part of his belief that a nation is also a 'large-scale solidarity', one which requires at least passive participation: it has, of course, a past, but 'it is summarized . . . in the present by a tangible fact, namely, consent, the clearly expressed desire to continue a common life'. Scots nationalists believe that the desire to continue a common life is best rooted in the nation that was once a state, and that those Scots, presently reluctant to part with the Union, will come to believe this.

The 'clearly expressed desire to continue a common life' speaks directly to the British–Scottish question. In that, as in other claims for secession from a state of which the nation is, or claims to be, a dissatisfied part – as the Basque, the Catalan, the Flemish, the Quebecois – are embedded the questions: what is or should be the nature of a 'clearly expressed desire'? How should the desire for security, which tends to favour continued enfolding in the already existing nation state, be balanced against the desire for, as Scots and Catalan nationalists often put it, 'freedom', defined as the ability to be ruled by one's own people, Scots, or Catalans? What is the national forum within which politics should be conducted: that of the state which has enfolded separate nations for centuries, or that which can be created if and when the nation achieves independence, and itself becomes an autonomous state?

States are artificial creations, or, as Benedict Anderson put it, 'imagined'.[15] He believed that any group so large that all the members of it could not be known to any one of them had, in some way, to be imagined in order to be a coherent and manageable whole. Imagining can be both open to constant change, and highly restrictive. The first accepts, within rules, cultural diversity, even rejoices in it, since it implicitly accepts that what humans can create is a flexible institution capable of transforming itself continually. The second privileges the irreducible core of the national, or racial, community, which dictates separation.

Nationalisms locate themselves along the axis between these poles – and beyond. Further out than the cosmopolitan pole is the idealist view that states should cease to exist, to be replaced by a globally organized order, as Jessica Matthews and other strong globalists believe: at the other extreme and murderous end is the Nazi belief in the dominance of the Aryan race and the organized extermination or forced submission of races and classes of humanity deemed unfit to live in Aryan-led nations. The first has become a liberal belief – liberal in both the economic, and in the social and cultural sense. The second had been seen as largely, though not wholly, driven underground by the destruction of the Nazi, fascist and other regimes and the revelation of their atrocities: nationalism, in over-excited liberal or leftist rhetoric, is sometimes mistaken for 'fascism'.

Unionism in the British Isles was sealed in the 1707 Treaty of Union between England and Scotland, the only agreement that implicitly recognized a non-English people as a nation, conceding control over religion, justice and education to the Scots. England had absorbed, without a treaty and through conquest, the Welsh nation in the fifteenth century after the final defeat of Owen Glendower: it ruled Ireland indirectly through a nominally autonomous parliament, controlled by English settlers from the 1530s, then, by a Treaty of Union in 1800, absorbed Ireland into the UK, with representation in the Westminster parliament, until the successful nationalist struggle culminated in independence in 1923. England's relationship with Wales, though often touchy on the Welsh side, has been peaceful: nationalism, now expressed through the Plaid Cymru Party, has been and remains a minority strain, though, paradoxically, the Welsh language is more widely spoken than any other non-English tongue or dialect in the British Isles, including the Republic of Ireland. The Irish nationalists won independence for the larger part of the island, but the Protestant–Unionist dominated north-east – Ulster – threatened revolt and civil war, and remains part of the UK.

The struggle between Protestantism and Catholicism was largely ended at different times in the states of France, Italy, Portugal and Spain with the victory of Catholicism, where Church and state used mass murder, torture, executions and banishment to drive out the various forms of Protestantism, which had grown into large communities. In pre-independent Ireland, the Protestant ruling class did not attempt mass slaughter on a group, almost wholly Catholic, which was in the large majority: but they were deprived of rights and political agency, which gave the long-smouldering nationalist resistance a powerful religious underpinning.

On the British mainland, the Catholic–Protestant feud was coupled with a long-drawn-out attempt by Catholics and others to return a Stuart to the throne. The 'Jacobites' were so called after the Latin name for James: James II of England and VII of Scotland lost his throne to the Protestant William and Mary, placed on it in 1688 by the dominant Protestant faction to secure the Protestant succession. A Jacobite army, largely composed of Scots and assisted by the French, came near to threatening London in 1745 but were harried back to the north of Scotland, where they were defeated in a final battle, at Culloden Moor near Inverness, in 1746. Catholicism, as in England and Northern Ireland, was not stamped out, but was discouraged. The victory of the nationalists in Ireland in the early 1920s in securing a republic encouraged nationalists in the north-east of the island, usually from Catholic backgrounds, to coerce Ulster into the Republic of Ireland through terror campaigns. These were largely ended by the Belfast Agreement of 1998, which diverted Irish republicanism into often fraught political means. In Scotland, Catholicism was held in check by the powerful Presbyterian Church of Scotland in the eighteenth and nineteenth centuries: as discrimination softened into the twentieth century and the Church of Scotland declined, Catholicism, often rooted in Irish immigrants in the west coast, grew and, relatively, prospered, though sectarian insults and blows (occasionally murderous violence) are still traded by gangs.

The 1707 Treaty was thus seen in Scotland as a protection against the return of Stuart (Catholic) rule, by Union with another, and powerful, Protestant state, one with which they already shared a monarch. 'Richer' was also an important spur, since the last decade of the seventeenth century was ruinous for Scotland, with the collapse of its imperial hopes in Central America, to link with a richer state. The Act of Union laid down that taxes, duties, the currency and rights should be equal across the new state, Great Britain: and that Scots, though retaining a distinct legal system, should enjoy the same rights and liberties as the English and Welsh. It also meant the end of a Scots parliament, and the incorporation of Scots representative political life, rudimentary as it was in a democratic sense, into the parliament of Westminster, where English members were in the large majority.

It was a Union which, through becoming part of English polity, inherited a government explicitly committed to observing a series of rights laid out in the 1689 Bill of Rights, to which the new monarchs, William and Mary, had to agree before being crowned. It was thus a limited monarchy, infused with the ideas of the English political philosopher John Locke – a quite different tradition from the absolutism to which the Stuarts had clung, and which they were finally forced to renounce only in the failure of the Jacobite rising. A Claim of Right was passed in the Scots parliament, also in 1689, accepting William and Mary as joint monarchs of Scotland and reiterating many of the same demands as the English Bill.

The 1707 Union thus brought to Scotland the practical experience of an early shift towards what became, slowly, a parliamentary democracy. Through the centuries to the present, the nations developed not just an efficient common market but also democratic and civil habits, which increasingly underpinned and extended the freedoms that had, in embryo, been contained within the Union settlement. These centuries included what was also in embryo in the early eighteenth century – the imperial expansion of Britain, ultimately to the furthest bounds an empire had ever reached: while at the same time the 'internal empire', in Ireland, failed. In the course of the centuries, however, a multinational and multicultural state was created, in which all, in principle, could 'bow to the same law, speak the same language, support the same Government, enjoy the same liberty, vibrate with the same national enthusiasm, and seek the same national ends': the hopeful description the former slave, abolitionist and orator Frederick Douglass gave the United States,[16] one which remains a work in progress in the US, as elsewhere.

The organized attempts of nations within Western-democratic states to secede is a phenomenon of the post-war period, but with roots centuries old. These efforts differ greatly: common to all, however, is something akin to the Scots feeling of superiority over the other citizens of the state which enfolds them; and with that, a strong strain of historic resentment because of the nations' submission to the powers that forced, or negotiated, their submission, and which usually still rule the state of which they became a part. The indignity is keenly felt among nationalists: that they, once constituted as an independent nation, must bow to another state in perpetuity. Where the Brexiteers in the UK wished to 'take back control' of the political process after a few decades of increasing intervention of the various institutions of the European Union into British governance, nationalists wish to 'take back control' after, in many cases, several centuries of losing it, or never being allowed it.

Resentment over past indignities is in vogue in these times. Anand Giridharadas writes that 'we are living in an era in which the sense of being dismissed, rather than material interest, is the locomotive of human affairs. The rulers of Russia, Hungary and China are driven by past national humiliations. Osama bin Laden was driven by the treatment of Palestinians. Black Lives Matter has been driven by the fatal disrespect of the police. And a large swathe of the American right, which claims to loathe identity politics, is driven by its own perception of being dissed.'[17] The most passionate rhetoric of Scots nationalist leaders is directed to telling the Scots people that they have been and are being dissed and will continue to be, unless they follow the beat of the nationalist drum (see Chapter 5 for the power this view enjoys over the Scots cultural scene).

In his landmark lecture, Renan counselled forgetfulness, and a belief in false history, as a necessary element in nation-building ('L'oubli, et je dirai même l'erreur historique, sont un facteur essentiel de la création d'une nation'). And most citizens of nations *do* forget, or never know, the history that brought them to the present in which they live. The nationalist secessionists, however, don't forget (though they may well indulge in historic mistakes, even deliberate distortions); and part of their duty, as they perceive it, is to stir up their co-nationals into a righteous rage at what their 'foreign' rulers did to them in the past, which for them is also the present.

The most vengeful of nationalist impulses can take terrorist forms, spanning decades in Northern Ireland in the UK, in the Basque Country in Spain, and briefly in Quebec in Canada and Corsica in France. For the rest, in Belgium's Flanders, the UK's Scotland, Spain's Catalonia, Italy's 'Padania' (northern Italy), the campaign to secede remains within the boundaries of peaceful protest, even if it is, as in Catalonia, passionate and militant on the streets and in assemblies.

The list of all would-be secessionist movements in the world, or even in Europe, is long, and many seem, at least for the present, hopeless and tiny minority cases: Bavaria in Germany (the Bayenpartei had 0.9 per cent of the vote in the 2013 Bundestag election, 1.7 per cent in the regional assembly in 2017); Cornwall in Britain (Mebyon Kernow, the main independence party, had 1.9 per cent in the 2015 general election, four per cent in the Cornwall Council elections of 2017); and Brittany in France (the Parti Breton has no representatives: its candidates poll no higher than four per cent in any election). Even if one of these (non-British) movements sought to win the support of their fellow countrymen, they would, in most European states, be stopped: an application of a Bavarian citizen to the German Constitutional Court to overturn the decision in a lower court banning a referendum on independence was brusquely dismissed. The judges reasoned that Germany is a national state whose constituent power derives from the people: a region, or land, cannot usurp the power of the national state and thus secessionist movements are illegitimate.

For all that, the relative weakness of many of the continental European secessionist movements could be a false comfort. Scots nationalism had seemed weak, even eccentric, until the 1960s. 'Padania' secession in the north of Italy did not exist until the 1990s. Contemporary secessionism in democratic states is a new kind of phenomenon: no longer a rising of the oppressed against the oppressors, but a revolt of the comfortable against the comfortable. A common feature of the contemporary secessionist movements is their shallowness, when set against past movements, as those for Greek, or Irish, or Polish independence; the struggles for decolonialization in the British, French and other empires; the tragic fates of tens of thousands of Baltic, Georgian, Ukrainian and other nationalists trapped inside the Soviet Union in Stalin's time. These contemporary movements are not of suppressed peoples, denied statehood over decades or centuries, enclosed in dictatorial regimes: they are regions within democratic states, and generally wealthy ones. They have the right, I believe (not being a continental European constitutionalist) to organize movements and parties for independence: but they usually find it hard to convince a majority of their co-nationals that the cause is worth it, because the stakes are so low.

Catalonia, in north-eastern Spain, in the first decades of the twenty-first century, is, beside Scotland, the nation most actively seeking a separate statehood. The Basque Country, Navarre and Galicia also have similar claims for an independent existence but became, in the 2010s, relatively quiescent. The Basque Country, based on a people spread across both Spanish north-west and French south-west borders, now has the most advanced autonomous status of any of Spain's regions/nations and Basque parties play a large role in the politics of neighbouring Navarre. Galicia, bordering northern Portugal. also has autonomous nation status, and some of its minor parties claim independence from Spain.

A territory within the twelfth-century Crown of Aragon, Catalonia was incorporated into the Spanish monarchy in the fifteenth century, with a large degree of self-government. In the early eighteenth century, following a war of succession in which Catalonia supported the losing side, it, with the other Spanish regions, was incorporated into a highly centralizing and modernizing national state. In the early nineteenth century, Catalonia, with the Basque Country and Navarre, fought a series of battles over the loss of their *fueros*, or local institutions and rules: in the first decades of the twentieth century, Catalonia won back some of these *fueros*, and even some autonomy, granted by the Madrid government. The rule of General Franco (1939–1975) abolished all such devolutionary concessions: when, after Franco's death, democracy was restored, political decentralization and a measure of self government were a consequence.

This produced two types of regions. One, including Catalonia, the Basque Country, Galicia and (in a slightly different form) Navarre – all in the country's north – are regarded as 'nationalities' and have autonomous status. The other type were regions: Miguel Beltran de Felipe, a legal scholar, argues that nationalist feeling had been relatively weak, and rarely widely popular.[18] These regions had a lower order of rights, though could become autonomous states but only after a referendum approving the change. As the Catalan secessionists have learned, a referendum on independence was against the law.

In 2003/4, a socialist government was elected, both in Catalonia, and in Madrid: the national administration decided to grant Catalonia more autonomy. The legislation passed through parliament over the strong opposition of the right, which objected that this was the first time such a major change had not been the subject of agreement among the main parties. Separately, the constitutional court, after four years of deliberation, announced that a declaration of nationhood had no legal basis.

In the 2010s, this, with other delays and disappointed expectations, produced a mounting demand for independence and the radicalization of several of the Catalan parties, which culminated in a declaration of independence by the Catalan parliament, based on a 90 per cent result for secession in a referendum from which, however, over half the population abstained (most polls had shown a small majority for remaining within Spain): voting was attended by several occasions of violent attacks by the police on demonstrators, and on voters. Both the referendum and the parliamentary vote were judged illegal, the former leader of the independence movement, Carles Puigdemont, fled the country and twelve Catalan nationalist politicians were given sentences of up to thirteen years. An irony of Scots nationalism in this context is that they seek, enthusiastically, to join a Union, most of whose members also ban secession or attempts to secede. In Spain's case, the state put leaders of the movement in jail, then hand down vicious sentences for peaceful political protest. In the United Kingdom, organization in favour of secession is protected.

Scotland is the model for the Catalan nationalists and for other regions wishing to recover a long-lost independence. It is squarely in the Catalan mould: relatively wealthy; with storied histories of fighting for independence; both claiming they would be better off ruling them-selves, as historically separate peoples; with pro-independence parties, which dominate their politics. Scotland's claim to be the lodestar of Europe's nationalist restlessness is in part its widely publicized climb from eccentricity to power: it shows that leaders who both use passion to frame the demand for independence and demonstrate an ability to master at least some of the complexities of government can have a powerful effect on those who had not thought of voting for a nationalist party: the passion inspires, and the appearance of efficiency reassures.

Scotland's nationalists are lucky to be in the UK. The fact that Britain has no constitution beyond the sovereign will of the Westminster gov-ernment means there is no constitutional bar; and successive British prime ministers have not sought to stop campaigns by the SNP (nor Plaid Cymru for Welsh independence, nor *Sinn Fein* for Irish unity). David Cameron, then Conservative Prime Minister, did not attempt to forbid a referendum organized by the SNP in 2014: indeed, he agreed with the then SNP leader on the way in which it should be held.

Others, especially the Catalans, must contend with the workings of laws that have put several leaders in jail: that would be near unthink-able in the UK. Quim Tora, the pro-independence Catalan president elected in 2018, said on a visit to First Minister Nicola Sturgeon in July that year that he greatly admired the Scottish model, and saw the 2014 referendum as 'an example for the world . . . (the Scots nationalists) have built a very big movement, and we see the SNP as a very strong party that unites different points of view. The experience of the SNP is very important for us right now, how they have been able to go to demographics that are key for us, the working class, etc. In Catalonia we have a very strong civil movement that pushes the politicians but the combination of both is a very good [template].'[19]

Scotland's 'brand' – placid lochs and towering bens, *Braveheart*, whisky, Burns' songs, traditional highland dress – is, however stereo-typical, useful in providing the backdrop for the image of a distinctive nation. It allows the movement to be popularly recognized, and popularly supported. If Scotland were to succeed as a nation which had lost its statehood for over three centuries and found it again while remaining modern, relatively wealthy and culturally rich, it would greatly encourage others to follow suit. The principle of being freed from the decisions, sometimes unwelcome, taken in a distant capital and 'being governed by our own people', dear to the Scots nationalists, would have been given a living existence. Where the Scots went, others could follow.

A successful achievement of what Scots nationalists call 'freedom', in imitation of the cry of William Wallace from 1995 Hollywood film *Braveheart*, will likely cause a chain reaction. The Catalonian, Flemish, Venetian and perhaps other nationalists would be on their mettle to follow suit – well-positioned as the richest parts of their nation states, each with a major seaport: Barcelona in Catalonia, Antwerp in Flanders, and Venice in Veneto: Scotland itself has Glasgow, once the centre of world shipbuilding and, with Liverpool, a major Atlantic port.

The two leaders of the SNP in its gilded age – the first two decades of the twenty-first century – both gather golden opinions from all sorts of people, including, often, English admirers. This is partly to be explained by a lurid period in English/British politics: the debacle of the Iraq war; the forced ending of the Blair premiership in 2007; the partly unsuccessful premiership of Gordon Brown; the David Cameron term of office crashing, with the 2016 referendum result to leave the EU; and the torrid political scene as the government of Theresa May, then that of Boris Johnson, struggled to get parliamentary agreement on a plan to leave the Union, one which has blanked out most other politics. In this time, especially in the latter part of the 2010s, Scots politics looked good, happy to be contrasted, and to contrast itself, with 'chaos' south of the border. But even allowing for poor competition, the nationalists, who had specialized in eccentricity and worse in their leaders for much of their existence, produced two energetic and politi-cally astute figures capable of heading both the party and the Scottish government. Both were tightly focused on achieving independence – at once their strength, and at the same time their weakness.

Leadership in politics is more important than in most other fields, since the leader must both dominate the party and inspire the people. The more that politics is determined by the media, including the social media, and the less it is by the movements that have been the base, the more crucial becomes the leader's ability to take and keep power and to enthuse audiences. In nationalist politics of the kind practised in Scotland and elsewhere in Europe, the reliance on leadership becomes still more acute. The leader must make the break with the long-established system credible, even imperative: and must rouse and prolong an emotional attachment to the cause, and a belief in its capacity to transform the society.

Alex Salmond, leader of the nationalists from 1990 to 2000 and again from 2004 to 2014 in which time he was First Minister of Scotland (2007–2014) was described by Murray Ritchie, a former political editor of *The Herald* (Glasgow), as 'arguably the most effective politician in the United Kingdom'.[20] Yet he made fundamental mistakes, which have done his party little good: he caused to be published a description of Scotland's economy in 2013, with hugely exaggerated claims for its future, which sapped its credibility; he misread the mood of Scots by taking the Party into a referendum on independence in 2014, and in the event lost by a significant margin of 55:45; on resigning from the leadership and later losing his seat, he took a post as a presenter on RT (Russia Today), the Russian propaganda channel. As this is written, he faces fourteen charges: nine charges of sexual assault, two of attempted rape, two of indecent assault and one of breach of the peace, while in office: he has denied all of them.

His claim to justify Ritchie's judgement is his building of the SNP into the dominant party in Scotland: in itself, an impressive piece of political work over more than a decade. But his legacy is a mixed one: not because all political lives end in defeat, but because he used his position to peddle false claims on his country's economy and, while still a public figure, aligned himself publicly with an authoritarian regime. Indeed, he has shown himself through his career as one drawn to such authoritarian and/or wealthy figures as Rupert Murdoch, Donald Trump (briefly), Vladimir Putin (at a distance) and Fred Goodwin, the former CEO of the Royal Bank of Scotland.

At the height of his power, however, he was able to dominate the

SNP in and out of government; to (twice) choose his own successor, in John Swinney (in 2004) and Nicola Sturgeon (in 2014). He was a powerful, witty and nimble speaker; an excellent campaigner, with a demotic and optimistic style.

He could handle, indeed enjoy, power, and passed his leadership to another who could do the same. Nicola Sturgeon, forty-four when she assumed the leadership, took a law degree at the University of Glasgow, practised law for a few years before being elected, after several failed bids, to the Scots parliament in 1999. Seen early as a future leader, she considered standing for the post in 2004, but agreed to a deal with Salmond under which she would be his running mate, then deputy, with the health portfolio as her own; she also became responsible for investment, and the constitution. Childless, like Salmond – in her case, she revealed she had had a miscarriage in 2011 – her work rate is said to be formidable, while her husband, Peter Murrell, is the SNP's chief executive. The quest for Scots independence is wholly her world.

Both she and Salmond leaned to the left: and, though Salmond had, in his first years in the Party, been on its 'far' left (indeed was suspended from the SNP because of it) their natural position came to be social democratic, which the Party itself took as its official ideology. It has meant that both, especially Sturgeon, emphasize the social benefits that nationalist rule has brought – courtesy of a large subsidy from Westminster, a fact never mentioned. Social democracy, co-existing as it does with some form of capitalism, can only be as generous in its provisions in measure to the success of privately owned companies. Salmond, and with lesser enthusiasm Sturgeon, have both boosted Scottish enterprise: Salmond's warmth in supporting the 2007 takeover by the Royal Bank of Scotland of the Dutch bank ABN-Amro – judged one of the worst takeovers in history, executed with minimum oversight or interrogation by a highly paid board – must have embarrassed even him, though hardly affected his party's rise.

Salmond had, early in his leadership, fought and won a battle for an explicit social democratic stance working within an enterprising, free market – Scotland. David Torrance, the most insightful and inde-fatigable chronicler of Scots politics over the two decades of its most turbulent period, quotes Salmond telling the journalist Ian Dale that 'We have a very competitive economic agenda. Many business people have warmed to the SNP. We need a competitive edge, a competitive advantage: get on with it, get things done, speed up decision making, reduce bureaucracy': the comment of a free marketeer.[21] That approach has ruled the party's economic stance since the 1990s: but if it has pushed aside hazy notions about independence issuing in socialism, it has also in practice dictated greatly overstated optimism about an independent country's prospects.

The party Salmond built and Sturgeon inherited was, until the latter part of the 2010s, one used to success and growth, and to humiliation of the parties that had ruled Scotland for most of the twentieth century, the Conservatives and Labour. Salmond saw the country's 800,000 Catholics, generally Labour voters but feeling still discriminated against in Scots society, as untapped resource. Through a strong relationship with the Scots Cardinal Winning, who revealed that he had become a nationalist, Salmond presented his party as one opposed to bigotry and discrimination. Winning, who died in 2001, much criticized for arguing that it was the responsibility of one abused by a priest to report the incident to the police, not the duty of the Catholic Church, described the SNP, in a speech in Brussels in 1998, as 'mature, respectful of democracy and international in outlook', and quoted polls suggesting Scotland could be independent within a decade.[22]

Salmond's courtship had been necessary: the nationalists had recent form as anti-Catholics. In 1982 John Paul II had scheduled a visit to Scotland: the then SNP President, and former leader, William Wolfe, wrote a letter to the Church of Scotland's magazine *Life and Work*, objecting to the visit on the grounds that the Vatican was 'not a state' and thus not able to send a diplomatic representative to the UK. Refusing to back down as a row gathered force about him, Wolfe wrote privately to his successor as leader, Gordon Wilson, that 'If the slogan "Home Rule is Rome Rule" becomes widely current again, it will become impossible for us to get a really significant and secure support out of the 80% of the population who are non-RCs.'[23]

Wolfe was invoking a political past that had organized itself round religious boundaries: though these still had force, that force was fading, as Salmond saw. His gentle wooing of Winning and his flock was successful, and was a model of later outreaches by the party to the small, but growing immigrant communities, especially of Glasgow. He also had a more particular sympathy for Catholicism – seeing it as 'the anchor, the rock of the independence movement in the days of Wallace and Bruce . . . it was the only institutional force that could be relied upon – certainly not the nobles'.[24]

The positioning of the SNP as the decent, nice party as well as one militant for independence is one of the triumphs of its leadership, one which goes hand in hand with the careful boosting of a cult of leadership. Seeing the SNP in full conference for the first time, in Aberdeen in March 2017, was to witness a party whose senior officials came to the microphone to say that 'I am fantastically proud of the leadership of First Minister Nicola Sturgeon' (Angus Robertson, then deputy leader): and 'Nicola Sturgeon and Alex Salmond! We are proud of them' (Fiona Hyslop, then Cabinet member for External Affairs).

Much of the rest of the two-day event was taken up, on the stage, by people who were in one way or another grateful to the SNP government for helping them. One, a mother with three children, and 'no confidence', said that once she had joined the SNP, her confidence picked up and she was standing in local elections as a councillor. A woman with multiple sclerosis said that the Tory government and the media had made 'our lives much worse', and that the SNP would get disabled people elected. A debate on prostitution featured 'sex trade survivors' who called for the adoption of the Nordic model, which reduced demand for prostitution: a motion on the adoption of the model was passed, though several sex trade workers said surveys had shown it made the trade worse, and more dangerous. A young man said he had come out as gay at 22, and said he had been caused great pain by being called a 'poof' and a 'faggot': he broke down in tears. A woman said her daughter had been saved by the mental health system brought in by the SNP, after she had slashed her wrists: 'other mothers shouldn't have to see their daughter standing in a school corridor dripping in blood', she said, and also broke down. A debate on immigration was largely taken up with justifying the government's encouragement to migrants and calling out the UK government for barring entry.

The individual stories appeared wholly sincere, and were affecting. But what the conference was not, was a debate between rival positions and proposals, usually the stuff of political parties' gatherings. A rare, brief example of this came when an SNP Westminster MP, Tommy

Sheppard, proposed a motion condemning Israel 'for the longest military occupation in the world': a delegate opposed the motion, saying it sent the message that the party was one-sided on the issue. The motion was overwhelmingly passed, without further debate.

The party has retained unity, a formidable unity, by making its conferences and rallies into entirely self-serving events, marginalizing all dissent, including that of its left, a large part of which is represented by Common Weal, whose website publishes sharp critiques of party positions. Common Weal was particularly critical of the Growth Commission report, published by the Party in 2018, and aimed at providing a rational and responsible account of the economics of an independent Scotland in its crucial, early, years. The group charged the report with replacing Westminster-imposed austerity by Scots-imposed austerity, a criticism with some basis (see Chapter 4).

The SNP's success is in part due to strong leadership, identification and skilful manipulation of a politics that is emotionally vibrant as well as policies which claim to make the nation, once it becomes an independent state, richer. But it would not have been possible, nor would the growth of the other independence movements have been possible, had there not been real disillusionment with the politics of the state of which the nation is part.

Scotland saw the decline of the Conservative Party to insignificance in the 1980s and 1990s, even as it remained strongly ahead in England, and thus in the UK. The claim that Scotland was being governed against its will, especially in the Thatcher premierships, carried real weight. New Labour found a response in Scotland as well as England, and the first Blair Cabinets had strong – over-strong, for the English – Scots representation. But after the death of the popular Labour Cabinet Minister Donald Dewar, elected as First Minister at the start of the new parliament, no one figure could be produced who could articulate a unionist politics as well as Salmond could paint the picture of independence. Indeed, Labour was hobbled by its recent past: during the long premiership of Margaret Thatcher, it encouraged the belief that the English majority that sustained Thatcher was ruining Scotland. The nationalists were thus able to argue that, this being the case, Labour was in part to blame for failing to win a Westminster majority, and that the only true defence was to form an independent nation.

Independence may be Scotland's fate: a revulsion against the chaos of the Theresa May years and an inability to see Boris Johnson as one who could represent the Scots, might allow a stable majority of Scots willing to brave the perils of an independent existence. If an independence fever, stoked by greater indignation and even fear of a Brexit-ed future than was the unsuccessful attempt to break away in the 2014 referendum, took hold, there may be little unionists could do to hold back the flood, especially if Scots 'émigrés' in the UK continue to have a vote denied to them, and there is no vehicle for the rest of the UK having a voice in a decision which would end the United Kingdom. Canada, a country whose nineteenth-century consolidation as a state owes much to Scots, may offer a helpful example. It is to be found in the experience of Québec. Independence, almost approved in 1995, now all but off the agenda. A fuller argument for the Canadian experience and the lessons drawn from it forms part of the conclusion: I believe some approach similar to that introduced by the Canadian government to be essential for British democratic life, and not just in the context of Scotland.

Nothing in the twentieth and twenty-first centuries was so damaging to Britain's politicians than the closing years of this century's second decade. Nothing so assisted Scotland's nationalists to achieve their ends. But they have not done so. Nor need they do so. More, the evidence to date points to the UK achieving what the European Union aspires to, but cannot reach: a gathering of separate nations into one state.

2

THE ENGLISH SPEAK

The United Kingdom of Great Britain and Northern Ireland, which took its present shape only after Irish independence, has never been, until the very end of the twentieth century, anything other than a multinational state with a government, and a parliament politically sovereign over all of the UK, based in London. It is not a federation: it has been held, by most constitutional experts and politicians, that it cannot be. They think that England, with some 85 per cent of the population of the UK, just cannot co-exist with three small 'Celtic' nations in the nominal equality of a federation: construction of an English parliament would run against the settled view that a British federation would be so unbalanced that it would topple over. This would be more the case since, as the contemporary *Don* of constitutional expertise, Vernon Bogdanor, writes, 'the formation of the United Kingdom came about largely as the result of the expansion of England through a process of conquest, treaty and negotiation'.[1]

England has both expressed and lost itself in 'Britain' – a form which the Scots nationalists detest, since it implies political amity in a single national body. That hasn't ended: yet there's a strengthening movement for England to express itself nationally, within the framework of the United Kingdom. Devolution to Scotland, and the incessant demands of the nationalists for independence and a (second) referendum to secure it, have roused the English from their constitutional slumber-land to roar (or mildly object): what about *our* nation? Shouldn't *we* have grievances too? Indeed, shouldn't *we* have what the others have: an assembly, in which to debate English issues and from which an English administration will be drawn?

The calculation that England must sink itself into Britain was akin to that taken by the rulers of the Soviet Union: that Russia had to sink itself into the USSR. It had no separate parliament, nor a separate KGB (the latter having real power, the former only a formal one). The canny playing on Russians' many resentments of the other fourteen Soviet republics by Boris Yeltsin in his ascent to the Russian presidency was a major reason for the collapse of the Soviet Union itself. Russia, as the Soviet Union collapsed, accounted for a little over 50 per cent, at 147.4m of the total Soviet population, at 286.7m: since the fifteen republics went their separate ways in 1991, Russia has continued to dominate them in various guises, sometimes more or less welcome, as in Armenia and the Central Asian states, sometimes as a hostile force, as in Ukraine, where conflict continues between Ukrainian forces and Russian-sponsored rebels in the Donbass, Ukraine's eastern region. Only the three small Baltic states of Estonia, Latvia and Lithuania have fully broken with Russia, and are members of Nato and of the EU: though even they are constantly threatened by Russian military exercises on the border, and by cyber attacks.

No other country is like the UK. Moscow, the largest federal subject in Russia, is, at 11.5m, around one twelfth of the Russian population of 144.5m. California, in the US, has a 40m population out of a national tally of nearly 326m, that is around one eighth. North Rhine-Westphalia, at 17.9m, is a little over a fifth of Germany, which has a population of 82.5m. Ontario, in Canada, comes the closest the Western world has to match the imbalance of England within the UK: the province has a population of 13.5m, more than one third of a population of around 35.2m and, like England, contains both the capital (Ottawa), and the largest city (Toronto), though London unites size, political and financial power.

It is true that great disparities of population size can co-exist in federal states: California co-exists in the same constitutional structure and has the same number (2) of senators as every other state , as for example,

Vermont, with 600,000, one of whose senators, Bernie Sanders (since 2007), became internationally famed in 2016/17 because of his run for presidency as a socialist, a run repeated for the 2020 election. If the US can tolerate such large differences, as in this case the US has, there is an argument that very large disparities may work well enough, given time and restraint.

But none of the states of the United States enfolds the capital, as England does London. The US solution to the dilemma of one state receiving the advantage of hosting the national capital was the creation of 'Washington, District of Columbia', a relatively small area created in 1790 expressly to house the Presidency and federal administration, often referred to as simply 'DC'. No one says California to mean the US, or Ontario to mean Canada. For the very large majority of British citizens, England *is* the UK, and many of them use the former to mean the latter, as do most foreigners.

When I correct English and foreigners on England–Britain, they are usually apologetic, but also often puzzled. Most foreigners and the English themselves take the Bogdanor view of the UK: that 'the formation of the United Kingdom came about largely as the result of the expansion of England through a process of conquest, treaty and negotiation'. Since that is the case, why not call it all England? What's the fuss? After all, don't you Scots insist on your national status?

A country which is so much England must express English priorities, and these will tend to be more important within a lop-sided Union. English customs, turns of speech, views of the world, will be more powerfully present for most British and for most foreigners than any other, as will English voices and personalities on the UK-wide media. This is more the case since the historic and contemporary symbols and institutions of British power and reach – the Westminster parliament, the government departments, Westminster Abbey, the Tower of London, the monarchy's main site at Buckingham Palace, the great national galleries, the City, most of the BBC – are mostly in London, both Britain and England's capital. Wales, Northern Ireland and Scotland all market themselves to tourists energetically and with some success, but largely for scenery, for historic buildings, for adventures by land and sea and for hospitality. London is the state's executive centre, and has the buildings and cultural objects of power. The Westminster parliament, with the Big Ben clock tower, the statue of Richard I ('Lionheart') in front of the Lords and Oliver Cromwell before the Commons is promoted as a symbol not just of British democracy, but of democracy itself.

An English observer might say that the small nations have large opportunities to give voice to their needs and complaints, and have all, recently if at different times and to different degrees, been granted substantial self-government. Northern Ireland has had a separate parliament for a century. Scotland and Wales have had referenda on devolved government and, with some hesitation, chosen to have it. As this is written, the Scots still reject independence, and may continue to do so.

In the UK, a sovereign parliament *is*, de facto, the constitution: and at least until the last few decades of the twentieth century, that was in the main accepted throughout the state. Before devolution, Scots, Welsh and Northern Irish were represented, even (the Scots), over-represented: Scots MPs routinely ascend to the Cabinet, and to the premiership. Government has not been wholly dominated by the English, and those at its apex have often reflected the multinationality of the UK.

Since the Second World War, however, this has been fully true only of the Scots. The Welsh and especially the Northern Irish have strong grounds for complaint of very minor representation in the Cabinet and in many other power centres, and a complete absence of tenure of No. 10 Downing Street. Where it would be unthinkable to have a Secretary of State for Scotland who was not Scots, it's quite common for the Secretary of State for Wales not to be Welsh, as Labour's South African born Peter Hain (2002–2010), and the Conservative, South Yorkshire born, William Hague (1995–1997). It's true, however, that Hain represented a Welsh constituency, Neath, between 1991 and 2015: while Michael Foot, leader of the Labour Party (1980–1983) represented Ebbw Vale from 1960 to 1983; and James Callaghan, Labour Prime Minister from 1976 to 1979, represented differently named constituencies in Cardiff from 1945 to 1987. None, however, were Welsh. The Northern Irish Secretary – the post was created in 1972, when the Scots-born Conservative William Whitelaw took the office – is customarily *not* Irish, and few Northern Irish-born politicians have reached senior positions in mainland British politics since the last world war: this largely because Northern Irish politics are conducted among parties which organize only in the province: the Conservative Party has had a section, NI Conservatives, in Northern Ireland since 2012, but has so far managed to obtain only a tiny vote in both provincial and UK elections. Of the non-English nations, only the Scots have a strong grip on UK-wide politics.

Of the fifteen prime ministers since the 1939–1945 war, seven (Clement Attlee, Anthony Eden, Edward Heath, Harold Wilson, Margaret Thatcher, John Major and Theresa May) are 'pure' English, with no near-ancestor being other than English. Four (Harold Macmillan, Alec Douglas-Home, Tony Blair and David Cameron) have strong Scots connections: Macmillan, whose mother was American, was descended from a crofter (great grandfather) on the Isle of Arran, off the mouth of the Clyde: he and Blair, who had a Scots father and a Northern Irish mother, both at times called themselves Scots.

Douglas-Home and Cameron were scions of the Anglo-Scots aristocracy-cum-upper middle class and the former's main home, when he inherited his full title, was in the Scottish borders. Cameron had forebears in both the Scots and English aristocracy: his great grand-father, Sir Ewen Cameron (1841–1908), rose from a clerkship in an accounts department to be chairman of the Hong Kong and Shanghai Bank in London. James Callaghan was English with Irish and Jewish forebears; Winston Churchill was English with, like Macmillan, an American mother; and Gordon Brown is 'pure' Scots; indeed, as one of the three sons of a Presbyterian minister, is from the old religious heart of Scotland. Boris Johnson (2019–) has a Turkish great-grandfather, the journalist and liberal politician Ali Kemal Bey, whose strong con-demnation of the Turkish massacres of Armenians in the First World War and support for British protectorate status for Turkey led to his bloody murder by nationalists in 1922.

Calling the UK 'England' is, for most English, no slight: it is an implicit folding of the 'Celts' into 'Anglo Saxonia' (a distinction with little meaning now: we are quite mixed up). To be reminded that there is another way of expressing that is a (literal) 'political correctness' which, unlike other such common references, which have been erected into taboos, few mind ignoring. To be corrected just seems a little aggravating. When living in Moscow, a visiting merchant banker came to talk to me, and in the course of the conversation called the UK 'England'. Mildly, I said: 'You mean Britain.' He smiled, wagged his finger and said: 'Now now, none of your Scots nationalism!' Daft, irritating, but understandable.

This trivial mis-naming points to one of the largest issues now facing the UK. How is it to continue as a Union, when devolution, especially to Scotland, has so strained its no-constitution constitution to the point where much academic and political commentary believes it to be no longer functional? In the early decades of the twenty-first century, a nation state, or better, a state of nations, regarded as among the most successful and liberal of the past two centuries faces a disintegration, and thus a sharp diminution of its power, just at the time when it faces a transition from being a member of the European Union to not being one, a major aggravating factor in the Union's integrity. The easy, even affectionate, assumption by many English that the surrounding nations are, albeit with some grouches, loyal (with the exception of many among the nationalist minority in Northern Ireland) to a Union that still benefits them, appears to be passing. For unionists, the most pressing issue is how to revive a Union they feel, and the majority in all of the small nations feel, should be retained and even strengthened.

Since the SNP took over government in Scotland, unionists have been on the defensive. The nationalists have the best tunes: literally, since so many Scots songs, still familiar, are still sung, often adapted, and many are Jacobite in inspiration. They are also sure of the kind of country they want: an independent one. But what kind of state, Scotland or the UK, does the unionist majority think they're in? They can't muster the fierce attachment to a future liberation that many nationalists manifest: displays of patriotic enthusiasm were common in the nineteenth century, and in and after the two world wars of the twentieth century, but the default position was taking the Union for granted, at times striving to popularize Britishness. James Thomson, a Presbyterian minister's son from Roxburghshire, wrote 'Rule Britannia' for a masque about Alfred the Great in 1740, still sung at the end of the Proms classical music season. David Wilkie, another minister's son, from Fife, painted the hugely popular 'The Chelsea Pensioners reading the Waterloo Dispatch' in 1822, the painting showed Scots and Irish soldiers as well as English, while a kilted piper plays in the background.

Nationalists think the anti-independence majority is living in a state of false consciousness, or ignorance about the British state. They just don't get how bad it is, and therefore don't muster the energy and courage to change it. The highly regarded Glasgow writer, William McIlvanney wrote a poem about such people, 'The Cowardly Lion' branding them as faint hearted. McIlvanney's poem pictured a lion in a zoo's cage, whose keepers opened his door to allow him to pace about a defined, enclosed space: it was a metaphor for the proposed devolution of power to a Scots parliament, which failed on its first attempt, in 1979, to attract sufficient votes in a referendum. McIlvanney, disgusted by his fellow Scots' rejection of the proposed assembly, wrote that, having sniffed the air of limited freedom, 'the lion had turned to its cage and slunk away / and lives among the stinking straw today' . The writer, an enthusiastic nationalist, thought the Scots naively believed they were living in a relatively free country, and thus couldn't recognize true freedom when they sniffed it. He may have had in mind the cowardly lion who was one of Dorothy's three companions in her trip to see the Wonderful Wizard of Oz: a journey one of whose outcomes was to show the lion that his fears, which made him shrink from challenge, were groundless. A trip to devolution, and beyond to independence, would produce the same effect: remaining in the Union was to live in one's own stink, and funk.

When the Scots folded up their own parliament, they entered into a state already more centralized and more insistent on the all-embracing power of its legislature than most: it was a state with no written constitution then, nor since. British government certainly has features of the 'elective dictatorship', the description the Tory Cabinet minister Lord Hailsham (Quintin Hogg) gave it in 1976. For all of the period since the 1707 Union, it's been a unitary state in which the dominance of the Westminster parliament is absolute. The great eighteenth and nineteenth-century writers on the constitution, William Blackstone (1723–1780), Walter Bagehot (1826–1877) and Albert Venn Dicey (1835–1922) all stressed this: indeed, they regarded it as an all-but sacred mechanism. Blackstone wrote that the 'Crown in parliament', the merger of the monarchy into a representative legislature, can 'do everything that is not naturally impossible'. Bagehot made a celebrated distinction between the 'dignified' part of the constitution, and the 'efficient part': the first, the monarchy, on which the attention of the populace is naturally focused because the monarch's rule is simple to understand, and to venerate; while the efficient part – government, laws, the workings of parliament, the party system, all of which is complex and tedious to follow – rules, its power derived from the throne, but separately wielded. The monarch, then Queen Victoria, was 'the fountainhead of honour': but the Treasury, the money, was 'the spring of business'. Shorn of the obeisance, it can be read as the monarch's job being to distract the population from what government really does: a tradition still strong.

Dicey followed Blackstone in his endorsement of the absolute nature of parliamentary power 'under the English constitution the Crown (in parliament has) the right to make or unmake any law whatsoever . . . no person or body is recognized . . . as having the right to override or set aside the legislation of parliament'. But, in two further principles of governance, he argued for the supremacy of the law, and equality before it; and for a large role granted to conventions, which, though not laws, should be universally recognized, and acted on in a spirit of freedom.

In his *The British Constitution: A Very Short Introduction*, Martin Laughlin writes that 'some Scots jurists have argued that the Treaty of Union is fundamental law and takes the form of a modern constitutional settlement. These arguments have only been made in the last fifty or so years, before which no one seemed to question that fact that this was an incorporating Union founded on parliamentary sovereignty. Following the Treaty, 45 Scottish MPs and 16 representative peers simply joined the Westminster parliament without even a general election being held, making the point unequivocally that Scotland had been incorporated into an Anglo-centric British state.'[2]

Laughlin's observation has been the Scots nationalists' strongest ground for attack. The Union, and England's place in it, has been for decades the target of their criticism, designed to render both Union and England distasteful to Scots (and to everyone else). The most influential have concentrated on two themes: that England is a state that has been unable to modernize, to become a 'proper' nation, and thus is an incubus on the rest of the UK: Britishness is no more than Englishness with a cosmetic dusting of multinationality, now archaic.

Second, and closely allied, it is in thrall, still, to the memory of empire, and to its glory, which, though long gone, imprisons it in a wholly reactionary view of what it is, and a wildly unrealistic idea of what is possible. That last is not the preserve only of the nationalists: it's been a much-used trope by many foreign commentators, writing about the Brexit manoeuvres of 2016 to 2019.

In his relatively brief premiership, Gordon Brown, by birth and upbringing, education and habits of mind a Scots intellectual, strove to push back the rising attraction of nationalism in his home nation. In one of his massive and complex speeches in February 2007, the fruit of late-night and early-morning reading and reflection, he argued that values held the United Kingdom together: 'when people are also asked what they admire about Britain, more usually they say it is our values: British tolerance, the British belief in liberty and the British sense of fair play. Even before America said in its constitution it was the land of liberty and erected the Statue of Liberty, I think Britain can lay claim to the idea of liberty. Out of the necessity of finding a way to live together in a multinational state came the practice of tolerance, then the pursuit of liberty and the principle of fairness to all.'[3]

This was both fair and foul. The nations that formed Britain had produced, before and after unification, a longer line of individuals and movements dedicated to extending liberty in some form than any other nation on earth, providing inspiration to those yearning to breathe freely everywhere, including to the peoples who were, or had been, imperial subjects. And, at the same time, imperial Britain exploited, enslaved and slaughtered across the world: and, in its home territory, so alienated the Irish by refusing to tolerate their Catholicism that it lost the largest part of the island of Ireland. At the same time, one of the finest historians of empire, acknowledging the horrors of the slave trade and the opium wars, wrote that the more imperial Britain became, the more it acknowledged its duty to those it ruled: 'British rule in India or West Africa at the beginning of the twentieth century was both more unequivocally imperial and often possessed a genuine sense of responsibility and ethics.'[4] As I write below, there's a powerful school of thought in Britain and abroad which believes that the English have not lost their habits of mind, or anyway their nostalgia, for empire. Among the many faults in this view is a lack of recognition of how rapidly changes of national mood can happen and how complex and internally ethically riven the British empire was in the late nineteenth and twentieth centuries.

Nationalists speak too easily of 'the Scots', as if they were referring to a united national phalanx solidly behind their campaign to leave the Union. In 2014, after a pro-independence campaign widely described in the Scots and British news media as more creative and more positive than the 'No' side could mount, 55 per cent of Scots decided to remain in the UK. Nationalists had described the Nos as running 'a politics of fear', by which they meant that they questioned the shamelessly over-optimistic economic forecasts published by First Minister Alex Salmond in 2013; a criticism which, by implication, derided the caution individuals and families had in trusting their future livelihoods to a party that would be unlikely to be able to deliver on the utopia it had painted.

One of the most popular tropes, which has been copied, or individually sourced, by those wishing to fix England as out of touch both with its own Union and the European Union, is that it remains in thrall to imperialist myths and dreams. It is a handy theme, and is hugely useful when describing English politicians who want Scotland to stay in the UK, and/or wish the UK to leave the EU, as upper-class idiots. By implication, their followers must also be idiots for being fooled by idiots, though this is rarely spelled out publicly: it would seem so condescending. It is voiced privately. Though I had heard much of his private contempt on various occasions, I was still shocked to hear a highly regarded Irish historian say, at a social occasion, that those who had voted for Brexit were 'scum'. I objected to the description: he re-affirmed it. We both turned away from each other.

The aim of those who believe that imperialist motives and reflexes still govern the English spirit is to show that this reactionary temper still deeply colours English views on the European Union, and its wholly unrealistic expectations for a successful future outside of the EU. This culminated in the 2016 vote for Brexit, and has been a, or even *the* major theme in England's relationship with Scotland, the best explanation for its reluctance to let Scotland go. It points to a continuing attachment, in speeches or actions or planning, to imperial glory, seeing it as something which can, in some measure, be re-established, or is, at the least, part of the mindset which sees Europe as too narrow a field for a country with Britain's glorious past to tolerate.

A standard example, distinguished only by its vehemence, is a column by the *Independent*'s Matthew Norman, on Jacob Rees-Mogg, a leader of the movement to leave the EU, a founder and chairman of the European Research Group, an anti-EU lobbyist. Norman wrote that Rees-Mogg, an ardent Brexiter and an MP for north-east Somerset appealed strongly to 'the dwindling band of old, white, rural, mostly male party members who pick Tory leaders [which] is cocooned within the demented fantasy bubble of a post-Brexit imperial renaissance. No one, not Michael Gove or even Boris (Johnson) , is as expert at locating their G-spot.'[5]

The phrase 'post-Brexit imperial renaissance' points to what Norman, and other imperialist-watchers, mean. The leading Brexiters all seek to boost the UK's chances of succeeding out of the EU, in the wider world: for those on the lookout for imperial reflexes, this means attempting to re-assemble the British empire. Rees-Mogg, a successful and very wealthy financial entrepreneur, has been particularly eloquent on Britain succeeding in the wider, non-European world. With a few years at Rothschild Bank in London and Hong Kong after Oxford, he left to found Somerset Capital Management: he was elected MP the same year. But he isn't an imperialist: he's a free marketeer. Like many who share his uncompromising view that Britain must leave, he thinks that Europe is declining and much of the rest of the world booming: and the UK should be with the latter. In being so, it should again show the world, not its power as an imperial bully but the value of its attachment to free trade.

In January 2018, he gave a speech, widely praised in Brexit circles, which argued that since the EU accounted for only ten per cent of world trade and was declining, while the other 90 per cent was growing, Brexit was, economically, a no-brainer. The speech, at the private Churcher's College school in Hampshire, was aimed to rouse: 'Despite our relatively small geographic size we are still the second biggest exporter of services and one of the largest foreign investors . . . such a nation should take responsibility for its own future and become a role model for the rest of the world . . . if the UK is to execute an independent trade policy then it can play a role in ensuring that there is an injection of wealth into the global economy. This will improve the lot of all mankind and we, the British people, will be propelled forward on this rising tide . . . it can become a rule-setter in the world . . . its future can be true to its history . . . Britain's success as a nation . . . has been translated through free trade and free markets and has allowed people to come together to meet each other's needs in voluntary exchange . . . Britain has been called on to be a shaper not only of our destiny but that of the whole world. The next great economic revolution should be made in Britain for the benefit of the world.'

There is much that a liberal or leftist will find to criticize in Rees-Mogg's financial and political career. Somerset Capital Management, the Panama Papers show, is managed through subsidiaries in the tax-evading Cayman Islands and Singapore: Rees-Mogg has defended tax havens.[6] He called the growth of food banks 'uplifting': a stupid description of an institution which points to growing poverty. The forecasts of growing British exports in his Churcher's College speech are likely to be over-optimistic at least in the short term, and give no nod to the export success of Germany.

However, the speech, given in an eighteenth-century foundation, has no trace of imperial invocations. Imperialism is the control of peoples outside of the imperial states' borders, for purposes of economic gain, military domination and, in Britain's and France's cases particularly, the export of a culture and religion considered superior. Like the other leading politicians who are Brexiteers, as Liam Fox and Michael Gove, Rees-Mogg is squarely in the Thatcherite, free-market tradition: in some ways, the opposite of an imperialist. His Britain of the future will flourish by being faster, sharper and better educated than the competition. That which Rees-Mogg confidently predicts may well fail and is, in any case, a very large risk: the world into which Brexit plunges the UK cannot be controlled as the British empire controlled large parts of the world: it is a Darwinian one, where what Christopher Coker calls the 'civilizational states', as Russia and China, are the active imperialists of the twenty-first century.[7] But it isn't a call for a return of empire, or a lament for its loss.

The lack of contemporary examples of British imperialism isn't just the easy resort of columnists, but also of serious writers, including the scholar Danny Dorling, a professor of geography at Oxford, and a visiting professor at Goldsmiths, University of London; a visiting professor at the University of Bristol and a visiting fellow at the Institute of Public Policy Research. From 2007 to 2017 he was honorary president of the Society of Cartographers and much else. From 2010, he had published often, two books a year, three in 2011 and 2013. Most of his work is on equality and inequality, where he has established a high reputation as a severe critic of the large and growing inequalities in British society, mapping the very wide differences in income in both the UK and the world.

His 2018 book, *Rule Britannia: Brexit and the End of Empire*, written with Sally Tomlinson, a senior research fellow at Oxford's Department of Education is, however, of a quite different standard. It's a polemic, often shapeless, full of assumptions and unsupported claims, where the 'proof' of the imperial ivy throttling British souls is often centuries old. This, even though 'rather than never (never, never) being slaves, as the chorus of "Rule Britannia" implies, many ancient Britons were slaves of the Romans, the Vikings and the Danes and then for many centuries they were vassals of the feudal Normans'. So what? In any case, the text says 'never *shall* be'.

Dorling and Tomlinson write that Britain's education on empire 'is still mainly stuck in a mythical past, especially in its history and geography teaching': Michael Gove, when Education Secretary, by contrast, charged the teaching of the empire as being 'negative and anti-British'. Yet a 2016 full-length study of teaching on the empire by Terry Haydn, a professor of education at East Anglia University, 'finds that textbooks and websites used by teachers take a balanced approach, examining positive and negative historical sources, opinion and commentary'.[8]

As to the cruelty and exploitation of the British empire, there's no doubt. It is also true that much in which the British take pride, including many of its fine universities, were funded by exploitation of the colonies. But to make the case that Britain now remains in thrall to the grandeur that was Britannia, while insisting that the UK is uniquely arrogant and uncaring about its imperial past is both to ignore the experiences of France, Japan and Italy and the present policies of China and Russia, and to display a sour-minded parochialism surprising in two scholars whose work, especially that of Tomlinson in Africa, has been so extensive.

Critics routinely conflate pride in being British with 'imperial nationalism'. In a survey by the academics Magne Flemmen and Mike Savage based on interviews, one respondent said: 'I watch the Olympics and things, more recently, I've been very pleased to see the British coming out well . . . I think we're the best, personally [Feeling British . . .] is important . . . watching [daughter] on the podium . . . and them playing the national anthem . . . it sends shivers down your spine, you know, it's just –, and it's nice to –, to be British. Yeah . . . I'm quite proud to be British . . . there is –, good things about British culture . . .'[9]

Another interviewee said: 'I think it's generally still a very polite and ordered and fairly homogenous society, with some things I think people can be proud of being British for. We've done a lot of good things as a country . . .' Others in the survey made comments that could be interpreted, on a strict reading, as racist, as, for example: 'I do believe that we should not be giving in to some of the minorities who want us to change our way. And I don't mean that disrespectfully to any individual, but I do think we have traditions and standards in British life . . .' Another said: 'My friend's married to a girl from Africa. I think that that has gone a bit serious, I think it's too serious'; a puzzling remark, but certainly one that implies disapproval. Flemmen and Savage quote respondents as expressing pride in being British and characterize their views as imperialist. But pride in one's country is a common emotion, as much among citizens of states which have never been imperialist as those who have.

The most determined labeller of imperialism as a major factor in the vote for Brexit is a columnist of Ireland's newspaper of record, *The Irish Times*, Fintan O'Toole, whose distinction as a journalist at home and abroad lends resonance to his arguments, but doesn't improve them. His book, *Heroic Failure* is a sustained attempt to fix on Britain or, as he more precisely defines it, England – a grand debilitating delusion, the state in the iron mask of imperial nostalgia.[10] His is a 'not unfriendly' endeavour: 'when your neighbour is going mad it is only reasonable to want to understand the source of their distress'. It is a project of pity: the approach of a wholly sane man in a white coat pointing out, regretfully, the mental dysfunction of a gibbering idiot.

He has no trouble in finding examples of British pride, and of 'innate moral superiority', proof of the imperial mood. They are, however, in the past, if not so far in the past as the example quoted from Dorling and Tomlinson. The bohemian-inclined Cyril Connolly (1903–1974) is quoted as seeing the post-war order as one in which 'the English would play a part of 'supreme importance . . . and take on the cares of a confused, impoverished and reactionary . . . Europe'. Joan Robinson (1903–1983), the left-wing Cambridge economist, believed that the British empire 'was not discreditable' and that Britain should 'try to show the world how to preserve some elements of civilization and decency'.

Fair enough for O'Toole to highlight the Anglo-Saxon attitudes, though these were post-Second World War reflections, when a certain amount of national self-regard after the defeat of the Nazis is understandable: besides, neither Connolly nor Robinson were advocating imperialism. Stranger is a quite sustained passage, designed to show that the English are wallowing in the self-pitying delusion that Brussels controls them. For this, the fantasy of submission and dominance which is E. L. James' *Fifty Shades of Grey* (2011) is pressed into the imperial service.

O'Toole sees it as not seeming 'entirely beside the point' that the book was published in the lead-up to Brexit, with the dominant Christian Grey a proxy for the EU, and the submissive Anastasia Steele 'an innocent England seduced into entering into his Red Room of Pain' . . . like England in the sadomasochistic hallucinations of the Brexiteers, she cannot resist the 'sweet agonizing torture' of playing submissive to Brussels dominant.

I thought, for the first few paragraphs, that O'Toole would turn about and say something like: 'Just joking!' But he seemed to mean it as a valuable insight: similarly lengthy tours of duty are ordered for the Len Deighton novel *SS-GB* (2009) and Robert Harris' *Fatherland* (2012): their themes of a Nazi-occupied Britain serve as revealing the 'deep structure of feeling' in England – fear of the Germans' primacy in the EU.

He's anxious to point out that Britain was a racist place in the 1960s, and so it was: Enoch Powell's 'Rivers of Blood' speech was an explicitly racist augury of racial strife caused by the influx of West Indian families, and it was widely popular. Houses with rooms to let had notices in the windows: 'No Negroes, No Irish'. And so it still can be: Stephen

Lawrence, a black teenager, was murdered by a group of young white men in south London in 1993 because of his colour.

But racial accommodation comes slowly, especially for those who fear cultural change in their community, or competition in the labour market. Ireland, all but entirely white while the UK was growing steadily more multicultural, has rapidly changed in attitudes to both sexual and racial minorities: the Taoiseach, Leo Varadkar, openly gay and of part-Indian descent, is a prominent example.

England – Britain – voted Brexit not because those who did so regretted the loss of empire, thought it could be re-assembled, believed that the Commonwealth could take its place or saw the EU as a sado-masochistic monster. They wished to be governed by a parliament and an administration that they understand, and on which they have a direct influence through their vote. They resented an influx of immigrants, both from Eastern Europe and from further afield, having been promised, falsely, that the numbers would be radically cut.

Nor were their impulses those of the 1960s, nor indeed 2010s, racists. Lisa Nandy, the Labour MP for Wigan and a Remainer, wrote in the *New York Review of Books* that her 'leave-voting constituents have been called stupid, racist little Englanders. The truth is nothing of the sort . . . when people were asked if they wanted to leave the EU, it was an opportunity to push back against one of the most vivid symbols of a political system that is faceless, unresponsive and unaccountable, where decisions are made by people hundreds of miles away.'

I voted, reluctantly, for Remain: though in large part I share Nandy's view that the EU's political system is 'faceless, unresponsive and unaccountable'. Brexit will damage both Britain's and Ireland's economies and, to a lesser degree, that of the rest of the EU. The EU has done much good, especially in the former Communist states of Central Europe, and in the expansion of student exchanges. It overreached itself, in seeking to integrate all member states as a preparation for some form of federalism. Britain had, potentially, been best placed to initiate a reform which would see its will to integrate confined to those states which explicitly wish to cede more elements of their sovereignty to the Union: while forming an alternative circle of those which wish to retain the single market and the practice of cooperation. Its deep problems have been illuminated by Brexit: the response in the longer term must be a radical re-evaluation of its role and its potential, one that should involve the UK.

The 1707 treaty gave Scotland, uniquely among the surrounding nations, the standing of one state united with another much larger state through, as it developed, equal (based on population) parliamentary representation. For most of the period since Union, till the middle of the last century, the official, though not always the popular, assumption on both sides of the Anglo-Scots border was that the more integration, and the fewer special bureaucratic, representative or constitutional arrangements, the better. Everyone knew the Scots were different, but they were British: the north British. It is a term, scarcely used in the past few decades, invented, ironically, by a Scot, King James VI of Scotland and I of Britain, a strong if ineffective proponent of complete Union between the two countries. Its most evident use for much of the twentieth century was the name of the large railway hotel at one end of Edinburgh's Princes Street, which had served the North British Railway company, retaining the name after the railway folded in the 1920s. It was re-named the Balmoral (Gaelic: great dwelling) in 1991 by the film star Sir Sean Connery, a strong nationalist and financial supporter of the SNP.

Scotland had no separate representation in the British government until the post of Secretary for Scotland was created in 1885 (or re-created, since there had been such a post from 1707–1746), upgraded to a full Secretary of State for Scotland in 1926, permanently in the Cabinet. It had no national assembly till 1999 when a Scottish parliament was legislated into existence: the parliament, at first sitting in the building of the General Assembly of the Church of Scotland in Edinburgh, moved in 2004 to a new and striking building. It was strikingly late in completion (three years) and still more strikingly over budget (at £414m, more than ten times the original estimation of £40m). Still, it was greeted with enthusiasm as a design masterpiece, the main architect being Enric Miralles, appropriately Catalonian, who died in 2000, before his work was completed.

It was presented by nationalists not just as a complement to Westminster democracy but as an antidote to it: its debating chamber was, like the later Welsh chamber, set in a semi-circle, not in two rows of starkly opposing benches. It did, as could have been imagined, nothing to reduce the strength of opposing views, nor should it: compromise and agreement comes not through the geography of a debating chamber but through political will and the possibility of compromise – and the opposition of nationalism and unionism is fundamental. For the nationalists, the seed which was the Miralles parliament would surely flower into a thistle, to overmaster the English rose within its own patch – the thirsty thistle sucking in the loyalty of the Scots while the rose, deprived of sustenance, less needy, faded and died.

The SNP had for many years seen a devolved parliament as an irrelevance on the road to independence. William Wolfe, the former leader, brought the party round to the view that a devolved assembly was in its interests, as a stepping stone to a fully independent legislature. The Labour and Conservative parties had for much of the twentieth century agreed that devolution was not required: the exception was a vague commitment to devolution by Edward Heath in the 1968 'Declaration of Perth', set aside in his 1970–1974 government, as the nationalist threat appeared to recede and the economic and industrial struggles took centre stage.

England was slow to manifest real resentment over devolution to Scotland. But it was foreseen, and New Labour did try to address the anomalous shape of the multinational state whose reforms, to the Lords as well as in devolution, were doing so much to change the working constitution of the UK. The main idea was to federate England so that the subjects of the federation would be nearer to the population size of Scotland and Wales. The Blair-led government tried to bring in federalism through the north-east of England in a 2004 referendum, but it was soundly defeated, with the support failing to reach even a quarter of votes cast. John Tomeney, the academic who chaired the Yes 4 The North East campaign, said in the aftermath of defeat that there was 'a growing breakdown in the belief that political institutions can affect people's lives for the better'. Yet to the north, over the nearby border with Scotland, nearly half the electorate apparently deeply believed that the political institution that was the nationalist party *could* affect people's lives greatly, and for the better. If only it could rip Scotland out of Britain.

In the latter part of the 2010s, support for regional assemblies rose modestly, though the only putative new subject of a federation showing substantial support was Cornwall. A Yorkshire Party and a Northern Party both appeared in the 2010s, though so far with only a few per cent for their candidates in elections.

Devolution, under the Cameron and the May premierships, took the form of creating city regions, as, in early examples centring on Manchester and Liverpool with elected mayors, which enjoyed increased powers and funding. An agreement to create a 'city region' in 2018 won the assent of the councils of Newcastle, Durham and north Tyneside. South of the River Tyne, in Gateshead, the council balked: the city's council leader, Martin Gannon, refused to take part, reviving the previous view that 'so many public bodies' were getting in the way of real progress by merely multiplying the number of politicians.

One of the purposes of the devolution of powers to city regions is a way of changing the constitutional subject. It recognizes that England doesn't want to federalize, at least not yet, if ever. Devolution has to be grounded in existing councils and city areas, with these picking up responsibility for practical issues such as skills training, but not higher politics. Britain has long been criticized for being an over-centralized state: it seems that England, at least, likes it that way. But the campaigns to shift that mindset, masked by the monopoly of Brexit over the political process and debate, have only begun to limber up. It is from these lines of thought and activism that a re-working of the Union must come.

Largely unobserved, the nationalism of England is moving to the centre of the political stage. Discussions and plans now flower: many on the left, conflating far-right groups with English nationalism, believe, with little evidence, that it's a racist, far-rightist endeavour. In fact, it's diverse politically. It has its own store of resentment: of a state whose long subsidy of the 'Celtic' nations is ignored or denied; whose instincts and political orientation are caricatured as tending to backward, imperialist nostalgia; whose civil society is held to be both less morally engaged and less intellectually rich than the Scots' equivalents; whose attitudes to immigrants are declared to be suspicious and grudging at best; and whose culture has largely disappeared. All of these themes find expression in Scots nationalist discourse, and are repeated with little examination of their solidity in fact.

Granting a devolved parliament to Scotland was undertaken not so much in a fit of absence of mind (as the acquisition of empire, in the phrase of the historian Sir John Seeley) as in a mood of resignation, at least by the part-Scots Prime Minister of the period. In Tony Blair's memoir, the Scot who gets most attention is not the land, but Gordon Brown, Chancellor from 1997 to 2007, Prime Minister till 2010, whose feuding with Blair and whose growing determination to take his place was a volcanic rumbling throughout Blair's decade of office, punctuated with eruptions. Scottish devolution gets a few pages, prefaced by the observation that he was never 'passionate' for it but 'thought it inevitable': since nations were 'having to combine with others in pushing power upwards in multinational organizations to meet global challenges, so there would be inexorable pressure to devolve power downwards to where people felt greater connection'.

In this and in other passages, Blair makes it clear enough that the constitutional issue that most engaged his imagination, even passion, was the building up of the European Union. A legislature, even one actually or potentially subordinate in every action to the UK government, was unattractive. The threat that nationalists would succeed in making it again a state, was a large risk. And the Scots were, as he notes, 'notoriously prickly', especially the Scots journalists, 'a PhD dissertation on prickliness all to themselves'. He gave an example, where a remark he made in an interview: 'If even a parish council can [have tax-raising powers], why shouldn't the Scottish parliament?', meant to underline its importance, was given a headline: 'BLAIR COMPARES PARLIAMENT TO PARISH COUNCIL.'

The most substantial section on Scots devolution was concerned very largely with these issues, with little on the nature of the devolution, the powers devolved and those reserved, the effect on England. He calls devolution 'a central part of our programme for Scotland' – and leaves it there. He did not appear concerned that it would annoy, or even interest, the English: perhaps because it didn't interest him. Yet there were no fewer than eleven Scots in a Cabinet of around forty-one (including the Prime Minister) in Blair's first ministry (1997–2001), and several in the most crucial departments: Gordon Brown, as Chancellor of the Exchequer; with Alistair Darling, later Chancellor in Brown's premiership, as his Chief Secretary; Lord Derry Irvine, Lord Chancellor; Robin

Cook, Foreign Secretary; George Robertson, Defence Secretary. That is, those who oversaw the economy, the legal system, foreign affairs and defence of a country four-fifths English, were Scots. That would have been largely uncontentious in a past when politicians from every part of the UK could be assumed to be solidly British first, at least in their office. By the late 1990s and more strongly in the 2000s, the attention and money paid to Scots who were increasingly identified with a party that called for urgent separation from a despised Britain ended that assumption.

For Scots politicians, raised in a party where arguments for and against devolution had raged, and where nationalism was eating away at Labour's hegemonic grip on Scotland's politics, devolution was an issue central to their politics. Yet, even among them, at least officially, discussion was inhibited. Donald Dewar told me in 1998, the year before he took over as First Minister, head of a Labour majority in the Scots parliament, that large stretches of what should have been discussed in Cabinet or in committees were banned from the agenda, for fear of leaks. The leaks, said Dewar, whose death in October 2000 deprived the country of one with both a fine brain and a fine character, popular beyond his party, were feared because they might arouse alarm and opposition among the English, both the electorate and in the House of Commons, including in the Labour Party.

New Labour spent much time on the small nations. In Northern Ireland, a Blair-led initiative to build on work done by John Major secured a deal from the IRA that it would cease terrorist acts: the Belfast, or Good Friday agreement came into force in December 1999. In the same year, a devolution of powers was agreed, the Scots parliament opened in 1999 and moved to its sumptuous new building. In Wales, devolution was also agreed, with fewer powers than in Scotland, and an assembly, or sennedd, architecturally and financially much more modest, was opened in 2006, at a cost of £70m. Of the three, only Wales continued to return a majority of Labour MPs into the 2010s. Labour had never contested Northern Irish seats; in Scotland, its vote, once dominant, collapsed into third place behind the nationalists and the Conservatives, the last of these often talked of as having been permanently expelled from the Scots body politic.

The new developments in the Celtic nations were felt by many of the

English as marginalization. England lacked the national recognition and the devolved administrations that the three others had. In spite of the customary conflation of 'Britain' with 'England', English nationalism, as a separate expression, was suppressed, most of all by themselves. One part of the Englishman's burden of the three Celtic statelets was to eschew a patriotism that was other than British, or a flag that was other than the Union Jack, designed by James VI and I. Until the last few decades of the twentieth century, to fly the red cross on a white background, flag of St George, was to advertise one's adherence to the right wing of the working class, a group that polite society thought deplorable.

This view was illuminated in a very English way. Emily Thornberry, Shadow Foreign Minister (from 2017) tweeted a picture of a house in Chatham where, in 2014, she had been canvassing for a Labour candidate, which was covered in English flags, with a white van in front of it. Thornberry had been a barrister, and is married to another, titled, barrister (she has the right to call herself Lady Thornberry, but doesn't), living in the London Borough of Islington. Though it has large tracts of low-income public and private housing as well as expensive enclaves, Islington had become a shorthand for wealth, leftist politics and political correctness.

The message that accompanied the tweet, 'Image from Chatham', was a neutral one: English understatement, but interpreted as a sneer at proletarian patriotism. The assumption that it *was* a sneer was general, shared by the then leader of the Labour Party, Ed Miliband, who was reportedly furious. Thornberry apparently accepted the general assumption, apologized and resigned from the Shadow Cabinet, to be re-appointed in a higher position by the next Labour leader, Jeremy Corbyn. Some foreign journalists, reasonably enough, expressed confusion as to why a photograph of a house which, after all, was asking to be noticed, and a neutral comment, should be so reviled. You had to be English.

England could be evoked, often sentimentally and quite frequently, by giving lists of subjects that were 'typically English'. George Orwell's list was consciously lower class: 'the clatter of clogs in the Lancashire mill-towns, the to and fro of the lorries on the Great North Road, the queues outside the labour exchanges, the rattle of pin tables in the Soho pubs, the old maids biking to Holy Communion through the mists of the autumn morning', the last of these appropriated for an April 1993 speech by Prime Minister John Major, together with warm beer. The poet John Betjeman was more bourgeois, and strongly Anglican: 'England stands for the Church of England, eccentric incumbents, oil-lit churches, Women's Institutes, modest village inns, arguments about cow parsley on the altar, the noise of mowing machines on Saturday afternoons, local newspapers, local auctions, the poetry of Tennyson, Crabbe, Hardy and Matthew Arnold, local talent, local concerts, a visit to the cinema, branch-line trains, light railways, leaning on gates and looking across fields.'

The TV presenter Jeremy Paxman spanned high and low society, conjured up (in part): 'David Hare and William Cobbett, drinking to excess, Women's Institutes, fish and chips, curry, Christmas Eve at King's College Cambridge, indifference to food, civility and crude language, fell-running, ugly caravan sites on beautiful cliff tops, crumpets, Bentleys and Reliant Robins and so on.' His book, *The English* (1998) was a best seller: its conversational style and unflashy erudition, as well as its ('typically English') self-deprecation in the service of covert self-congratulation, commended it to a large audience. Constrained by his BBC persona, he could not agitate for an English parliament (he may or may not have thought it a good idea): but he dared the thought that 'the red white and blue (Union Jack) is no longer relevant and (the English) are returning to the green of England'. And he could sound a note of regret at the disappearing elements of Englishness, with the prescient thought, for the late 1990s, that: 'in their everyday lives, the English metropolitan elite (of which he was an outstanding example) now has more in common with Parisians or New Yorkers than it does with rural or suburban England': an insight that was to be greatly developed in the new millennium, and not just in the UK. All three of these list-makers were public-school boys – Orwell at Eton, Betjeman at Marlborough, Paxman at Malvern: it may be that a sentimental view of England is more attuned to one so educated.

Mere regret for the passing of an age has taken a sharper edge. England's powerlessness, and its enforced enfolding into 'Britain' found no more full-throated threnodist than the philosopher Roger Scruton, who died in January 2020 and who himself a farmer, evoked the soil, the village and the church, and tried to see off the many, mostly leftist critics of England with a determined (though of course self-deprecating) celebration of its modest eccentricities: 'they [the English] collect stamps, butterflies or biscuit tins; they grow vegetables so large that nobody could eat them, and breed dogs so ugly that only an Englishman could look them in what might charitably be called the face . . . [this] is the way of people who are at home, and who refuse to be bossed around by those whom they regard as outsiders'.[11]

He was angered that the New Labour government of the time was composed 'largely' of Scots. They weren't, as he suggests, in the majority, merely disproportionately represented. Scruton lamented that, in the Britain where powers had been devolved to the small nations, 'there simply is no English part . . . England has finally been disposed of'.

The Scots are the target and the progenitor of the swell of English feeling. Scilla Cullen is the chairwoman of the Campaign for an English Parliament, a fringe group coming in, if so far modestly, from indifference. At a conference in Winchester in January 2019 she testified to the abuse the Campaign attracted, saying there is 'a deep-seated animosity to "the English"; we [in the Campaign] are often thought to be far right. We have been barred from two university campuses, and stopped from singing "Jerusalem"' (ironically, a favourite hymn of the left).

In a short essay she sent me, she too calls to mind villages, quiet country lanes, the sound of wood on leather and pubs (the importance pubs have in such pictures shows why the creator and one-time leader of the United Kingdom Independence Party, then the leader of the Brexit Party, the victor in the May 2019 European elections, Nigel Farage, strives to pose in or near one, with a pint of beer in his hand). She writes that she admired the Scots regiments' courage in the Second World War and agrees with the Scots that they reject (not all do) being called British, since 'so do I'. But she's dismissive of any Scot's attempt to claim co-authorship of British democracy: 'England was the origin of the mother of parliaments, Magna Carta and the Bill of Rights. These are English, not British achievements, despite what Gordon Brown, the British Prime Minister elected in Scotland, has said. England ceased to be a constitutional entity after 1707 . . .'

The dislike of the 'pro-Scottish' (or 'anti-English') Blair government is pronounced in those who seek to revive English national feeling: Scruton, in his *England: An Elegy*, saw the Blair governments as 'inherit[ing] from Old Labour an anti-English stance', one dramatized, as far as he was concerned, by its 2005 legislation against fox hunting; though the law, according to (mainly English) environmental groups, is largely ignored, and few convictions have been brought.

He believes, with many others, that the whole concept of Britain has been thrown into disarray. 'It has become quite apparent that there is no such cultural entity any more.'[12] What historian Michael Kenny describes as Scruton's 'elegiac characterization of an England at the mercy of the interlocking processes of globalization, immigration and Europeanization'[13] inclines the latter to pessimism, the more since for present English generations 'the factors that shaped that [English] identity of the past, the Anglican church and its non-conformist constellation, the empire, the common law, the monarchy and parliament, are all in a state of retrenchment, or decline'. Scruton saw few in high politics who were sympathetic to his views, and increasingly saw the mass of the English as ignorant of the foundation elements and sinews of English life, seeing, for example, 'English literature surviv[ing] only in TV adaptations'.

Scruton's laments, Scilla Cullen's Campaign, and the increase in English patriotism, are routinely seen as of a piece with the far-right groups. This attests less to the content of their views, more to a far-left desire to see the right as shading easily into fascism. Yet this is usually unfair. The best-known 'Progressive Patriot' is the popular left-wing singer Billy Bragg, whose book of the same name (2007) charted his conversion from a distaste for the Union Jack when waved by far-right groups, to a realization, through reading and reflection, that there was a strong radical stream through English life – the levellers, Tom Paine, the Chartists and the post-war creation of the welfare state that had shaped his life. Patriotic themes appeared in his work: after singing in one song of a love of country, a leftist friend asked him: 'You're being ironic, right?' But, he said, he wasn't: he had discovered a love of country, which he compared to the love he had for his son: intense, though not uncritical of faults and mistakes. Michael Kenny writes of him: 'that an Englishness (which) can be engaged in progressive terms and might even . . . "belong" to the left, established an important reference point for a growing number of advocates of the merits of English patriotism'.[14]

Both Scruton and Bragg are, in their different ways, preachers – Scruton preferring the post of a lonely prophet in a cultural wilderness that was once England, Bragg the engaging iconoclast in a leftist, post-modern showbiz culture in which patriotism has long been beyond belief.

At the end of the millennium's second decade, English nationalism now acquires some organization, coming in from easily dismissible fringes, led by figures with some heft in the political world, who believe it worth their time and effort to lay down foundations for a development which could be serious because, in their view, the construction of a new politics, English politics, which is thus the construction of a new British politics, cannot be avoided. It's clear, too, that the main spur for this is devolution, and by far the most important element is devolution to Scotland. The long, often dramatic growth of the SNP, with two high-octane leaders in Alex Salmond and Nicola Sturgeon, and an insistent demand for the break-up of Britain, began to push some in England to question why, of all the four nations, England had neither representation nor a voice. When it became clear that New Labour, taking office in 1997, was determined to devolve, resistance began.

The Campaign for an English Parliament grew out of these twin prompts: a small group, Harry Bottom, Terry Brown, Guy Green, Pearl Linsell, Tony Linsell and Cyning Meadowcroft, several of these members of the Labour Party, came together in 1998 to discuss the large shifts in the British constitutional landscape: and came to the view that Britishness itself could no longer be preserved through the self-denying submersion of the English identity. The group grew quickly and, though it never attained mass membership, it has maintained a constant pressure, now finding a more encouraging atmosphere surrounding its central demand.

Its inclination towards the far right is asserted, with no factual backing, by many Scots commentators. Robert Crawford, in an astonishing observation (for one both a scholar and poet) in an essay on 'England's Scotland' writes that 'In England . . . a resurgent English nationalism very different from the Scottish civic nationalism of recent decades has led not just to "Brexit" but to heightened xenophobia and even, in the

2016 stabbing of Labour MP Jo Cox, to political assassination',[15] as if campaigns for an English parliament and waving the St George's Cross flag led directly to Thomas Mair, Cox's killer in May 2018. Mair, a Scot from Kilmarnock, raised for much of his life in Birstall, West Yorkshire by his grandmother, was neither English nor an English nationalist. Evidence from his home and his computer showed him as a classic neo-Nazi, with a swastika-badged golden eagle on his bookshelf on which were books on Nazi racial theory and other far-right literature. As he shot and stabbed Cox, he was heard to shout 'This is for Britain', 'Keep Britain independent', and 'Britain first'.

Scilla Cullen says that from the start, the Campaign group, in part because so many had been in the Labour Party, was intensely conscious of the possibility of entryism, the practice, much used by Trotskyists, of joining Labour in order to take it to the left from within. The form of membership dictates several layers of approval before full membership: even so, she says, 'some still think of us as on the far right. My sister joined after she heard a woman journalist from the *Guardian* say on the radio that the Campaign was a racist organization: she was angered by that'. Cullen agreed that immigrants, and their descendants, shied away from 'English' and preferred 'British', but said that, too, is changing: 'football has meant that immigrants and the second and third generations are accepted as English. They play for the teams, in the national team. When England has its own identity it will, and it would be a good thing, if they saw themselves generally as English.'

Some small groups do carry the taint of racism or have racism as their main business. Cullen said a few members of the Campaign had joined the English Democrats, a group also campaigning for a parliament, but with many allegations of racism, and with a membership policy which reportedly did not screen out British National Party applicants for membership.[16] In July 2016, the *Liverpool Echo* ran a brief interview with Paul Rimmer, an English Democrat candidate for mayor in Liverpool, who had left 'vile racist and homophobic remarks' (which it did not quote) on a Facebook page. Asked about these, Rimmer said: 'No group or religion is beyond satire. What I say is in the cause of freedom of speech.' The English Defence League and the British National Party are both explicitly racist groups, though small and constantly consumed by internal wars. Tommy Robinson, otherwise Stephen Yaxley-Lennon, a member of the EDL, was retained in 2018 by the then leader of the UK Independence Party, Gerard Batten, as an adviser – a move which sparked the resignation of several prominent members of the party, including its former leader and best-known member, Nigel Farage.

In liberal societies, it is true that no group or religion is or should be beyond satire. It is one of many challenges from the extremes in both mainline and cultural politics to the prevailing liberal norms. The dispute between those who cleave to these norms and thus defend the right, within wide limits, to insult and demean, and those who would ban or 'no-platform' some of such speech is one of the main cultural conflicts in the West of the early 2000s.

The late 1990s and the early 2000s marked a decisive shift. Blair and Brown are the two demons, but also credited with (or blamed for) being the co-creators of the current English national movement. Gareth Young, a former Campaign member (who remains a nationalist, but became 'fed up by all the attacks on me from the English Democrats for being too liberal') told me that Brown's insistence on Britain and Britishness in the three years of his premiership and his speeches on these themes, designed to draw the Union together under a common identity spanning the various nations and including immigrants and their descendants, had the reverse effect on the growing nationalism of England. 'It highlighted the fact that the other three nations had an identity separate from Britain, and the English didn't.' Young admires the SNP government for its active encouragement of immigration and refusal to play the ethnic card: and says that the Campaign 'must continue to offer a civic nationalism', which he believes it always has.

English nationalism now attracts the left more than the right – not the far left, but the centre left, including the group which calls itself Blue Labour. These are Labour MPs and others who believed that the state should be more active in combating the effects of globalization on the low paid and which took up the cause of the English in calling for their identity to be recognized and some form of separate representation developed. The adherents to the group agree with Gareth Young that the 'pro British' campaign of Gordon Brown did not calm the rising dissatisfaction in English quarters, but rather exacerbated it.

John Denham was in the Brown Cabinet: he had resigned once, when Minister of State at the Home Office in 2003, in protest against the Iraq war: he stayed in the Brown government, but announced that he would relinquish his Southampton seat in 2015. He had started a blog called 'the Optimistic Patriot', with his own and other thoughts on bringing together social democratic politics with English nationalism. In an entry in January 2016, he wrote that Labour's decisive defeat in 2015 and its loss of nearly all its seats in Scotland was an indication that it had lost touch with both its Scots and English supporters: 'Labour in Scotland didn't just lose to any old political party; it lost to one that successfully framed its politics in the language of popular nationalism. It's a mistake to lump popular nationalism together with all other forms of populism. Nationalism can be populist in irresponsibly evoking simplistic and emotive solutions to complex problems, but it is not necessarily so. Nationalism can be a way of expressing a common sense of identity, direction and purpose . . . the election confirmed the emergence of large groups of English voters who now see elections in terms of 'what is in the English interest'. The idea that there is an English interest, distinct from and possibly threatened by the interests of other parts of the UK is new: 'the "English" are more likely to vote to the right and more likely to be anti-EU. Put this together with the upward rise in English identity, and it's clear Labour has a problem.'

Denham, sixty-five in 2019, had studied chemistry at Southampton University and worked in a succession of NGOs, while sitting as a councillor in Hampshire County and in Southampton City. He won the Southampton Itchen seat in 1991 and, like other English MPs in the 1990s and 2000s, he heard the grumbles that the Scots were being privileged by a Scots-heavy government, and then a Scots Prime Minister and that shipbuilding, once Southampton's major industry, had been sacrificed for Scotland's sake.

This last complaint was largely true. Vosper Thorneycroft, the last major shipbuilder in Southampton, closed in 2000: the 1,200 workers were mostly moved to Portsmouth, where a large new shipbuilding facility was being built. In 2013, however, the BAE yard in Portsmouth closed, losing the competition for three patrol boats and type-26 frigates to the Govan and Scotstoun yards on the Clyde. Responding to the news, Denham said that 'southern England had been sold down the river while the government looked elsewhere': he shared the view of other MPs in the area, Labour and Conservative, that the decision to locate the contract in Scotland was driven by the need to shore up the unionist vote in the referendum on Scottish independence the following year.

Soon after resigning his seat in 2015, he founded three organizations: an academic institute in the University of Southampton, called the Centre for English Identity and Politics; a political group, the English Labour Network; and a think tank and lobbying centre called the Southern (England) Policy Centre. The last of these is concerned largely with economic and social issues such as immigration, rural deprivation and pockets of poverty within one of the richest areas in the UK. The Labour Network, claiming some fifty MPs in membership, campaigns for a greater public salience of England in Labour politics and for the creation of an English Labour Party. The Centre for English Identity and Politics, as Denham admits, made up of him with part-time secretarial help, is the intellectual wing of his activity, a place where he and invited speakers throw out lines of speculation and reflection on Englishness, to see what attention and assent they can catch.

The idea that the English interest in a separate parliament was prima facie evidence of racism was tightly held by many politicians who saw themselves as progressive. In a Demos pamphlet on multiple identities published in 2005, Vince Cable, later the leader of the Liberal Party (2017–2019), wrote that 'the threat to harmonious social relations in Britain comes from those who insist that multiple identity is not possible: white supremacists, English nationalists, Islamic fundamentalists' – even then, an extraordinary conflation of those who wished to recognize England as a nation with white racists and Islamist extremists. Will Hutton, in the *Observer* on 28 April 2019, asked 'Is Labour to be the party of Europe in uncompromising opposition to the rise of an ugly, hard-right, English nationalism? Or will it continue to temporise over Europe, so enabling the centre of political gravity to shift towards the English nationalist right?' Scots nationalists, soon to win control of the Scottish parliament, were implicitly put in the democratic camp (where, indeed, they belong). For those awakened to England's subaltern position in the politics of the late 1990s/2000s, the easy portrayal of their concerns as in the crazies' camp is galling.

To lay some foundations for his story, Denham invited the Cambridge history professor Robert Tombs, a scholar of France who, in 2014, had published a near 1,000-page survey of *The English and their History*, to give a speech to mark the launch of the . One of Tombs' main discoveries in a long labour was that there was no single English characteristic which one could pin on the nation and its people: writing of Margaret Thatcher that: 'it had long been commonplace to assert that party differences were disappearing in a morass of centrism, but Thatcher's death showed that in terms of emotion, if not of policy, England retained two antagonistic political sensibilities with historical roots stretching back at least two centuries'.

Tombs compared a number of views of past writers on England, including the French François Guizot, Flora Tristan and Élie Halévy, the Irish Edmund Burke and the Scot David Hume. The core views of these ranged from Hume's conviction that progress came not through growing political freedom but through autocratic Elizabethan rule per-mitting rapid economic development, contrasting with Guizot's sense that the Glorious Revolution of 1688 had been an example of liberal-ism for the world, abolishing 'absolute power in the political sphere and the intellectual sphere', through Tristan's vision of an industrial revolution as 'a dystopia of injustice, exploitation and vice' (similar to that of Friedrich Engels in his *Condition of the Working Class in England*, though written before), with Burke's praise for 'England's embrace of continuity' and revulsion at France's destructive and oppressive revolu-tion, while Halévy saw Methodism as both radical and respectable, favourably compared to the French revolution Burke so hated.

Tombs wrote that 'these incomplete insights are not wrong': to be first to industrialize did entail brutality and the stunting of lives of hun-dreds of thousands; Methodism was radical but also respectable (in the mid twentieth century, it was the religious passion of the lower middle-class Thatchers of Grantham); autocratic government could and did aid economic breakthroughs and high growth (see China today); and England's history is replete with struggles for liberty. He took from this that 'Englishness is composed of "conformity and eccentricity, blunt-ness and reticence, deference and assertiveness, honesty and hypocrisy, community spirit and hypocrisy"' . . . perhaps these contradictory characteristics are indeed all 'typically English' (actually, they seem quite applicable in some degree to all societies where conformity or submission to authority is not imposed).

Tombs' judgement also lays waste to the reductive narrative of England peddled by the Scots nationalists: the more, since the 'contradictory characteristics' could fit the Scots national character as much as they can to England (or Ireland; or Wales). Perhaps England, in this case Britain is more apposite, is less coherent as a state than, say, France or Germany, since it contains both the hyper-capitalist City of London and the strongly socialist National Health Service, the taxes from the first doing much to sustain the second.

Denham himself did a programmatic speech on his Centre as one in the Speakers' Lecture series, in the ornate Speaker's House in Westminster, in 2018. It was forthright: it posed England as a neglected giant, while around its feet small nations were spoiled by attention, special treatment and public spending: 'We cannot overcome our national divisions unless Englishness is allowed its proper place as an accepted, legitimate and celebrated identity within the multiple identities of modern Britain.' Slightly more people polled said they felt more English than British (this strongest in the over sixty-fives) but many said they also felt strongly British.

England had not been able to develop a politics of its own, said Denham: forced to merge its identity with the rest of the UK, give privileged places and funding to the small nations and see what are and were English events and successes being absorbed into British achievements, while those of the three small nations were granted national status. Against the many arguments that the rise of English nationalism was responsible for the Brexit vote, Denham argued that the reason was the *lack* of nationalism: 'In the absence of that national debate, in the absence of any English political institutions, and with the widespread marginalization of English identity, it should not be a surprise that the English more than anyone else wanted to "take back control".' He resisted calling for an English parliament, though he pointed out that a BBC poll showed 62 per cent of the English supported it, but left it dangling as a possibility.

He saw the process of devolution as one exposing the fissures in the nation, insisting that Englishness, long buried, is now important. Far from a complacent, middle of the road polity, 'it is here that the forces that have torn us apart over Brexit are the most violent'. Violent, and miserable: the country 'believes that its best years were in the past, while other parts of the union believe the best lies in the future. Not a single demographic in the published (BBC/YouGov) poll had future optimism ahead of nostalgic pessimism. Confidence in Westminster's ability to represent people where they live is catastrophically low, as is their ability to influence their local council.' Yet those identifying themselves as 'English' rather than 'British' are increasing greatly, especially the older: and the more they did so, the more they tended to vote for Brexit, and for the Conservatives.

They wanted an identity, stronger than in the past: saw 'British' as no longer enough to assuage the need for an emotional identity, a patriotic staff on which to lean. The fire of the Irish, from both religious communities; the steady insistence of the Scots nationalists in power that escape from the incubus of Britain was salvation, even the less pronounced, but now audible, nationalism of the Welsh – all had seemed to be accepted phlegmatically, even humorously – but now were not. They were now, in varying ways, from the flag of St George to a substantial (within England) rejection of the EU, seeking their own nationalism, as a counterbalance.

A BBC/YouGov survey, Denham told his audience in the Speaker's chamber, found that two-thirds of the 'English' identifiers 'believe we are tolerant, welcoming, friendly and generous. Just under half the 'British' see the English in this positive light . . . the survey at least hints at the emergence of minority among British identifiers who are not just "not English", but positively antipathetic to the English.' In a later speech, in September 2019, Denham argued that 'Brexit was made in England, in a divided nation lacking its own institutions, democracy and sovereignty, unable to tackle its divisions. No possible outcome of Brexit will, of itself, heal those divisions. They will continue to disrupt politics in unpredictable and disruptive ways.' Had the 2016 referendum been taken when England had recognized its own separate nationality within a state of nations, he said, it would likely have voted against Brexit, since it would not have felt the deficit of sovereignty with Scotland, with a devolved assembly, did. 'Brexit', he said, 'must be England's democratic moment.'

In an interview (while we were having a meal in Winchester, in a restaurant which is part of the Maison Blanc chain, founded by the French chef Raymond Blanc) he said that 'the view that "English" equals fascism still exists in a certain section of the country, almost always people on the left, in politics, in the media: not huge numbers, but in powerful and influential positions: in some ways it's getting worse. People especially on the left look at Tommy Robinson and think he's indicative of Englishness.'

'You don't have to be white to be British. And there's very little evidence that the English are hanging on to their imperial past. Instead there are the issues of loss, dispossession, not having a voice. They want a chance to work out, to re-imagine, who we want to be. For the moment, there is no story about England.'

Another player of the English card has been still more precise on what was needed. The Marquess of Salisbury is one of the greatest aristocrats of England, and certainly among the most politically engaged. His ancestors had been at or near the pinnacle of English, then British, political power for centuries: the first, Robert Cecil, First Earl of Salisbury, was Elizabeth the First's closest, and highly influential, adviser. The third Marquess served as Prime Minister three times, between 1885 and 1902, coining the phrase 'splendid isolation' to refer to his preferred strategy of keeping out of European affairs. The latest, seventh, Marquess of Salisbury, agreed with Prime Minister Blair that only ninety-two 'hereditaries' should remain in the Lords on its reform: he was then fired from the Shadow Cabinet for not informing the Conservative Party leader, William Hague, of the negotiations, a sentence he received with a repentant demeanour. He took advantage of the moment, however, to flash his aristocratic ambience, saying that he had behaved like 'an ill-trained spaniel', conjuring up a brief excerpt from aristocratic country life, of over-excited Cockers frolicking about the space before the great house, as the shooting party sets off at dawn.

He never, however, lost a passion for politics, to which his eminence and wealth gave him ready access. As the English awoke from their doze of insouciance over Scotland's aggressive demands for more and more devolutionary concessions, he put together a cross-party group, which produced a plan for a new Act of Union to 'guarantee the rights and autonomy of each constituent nation and region within a reformed UK under a new Act of Union'.

The plan, 'The Act of Union Bill', introduced, by a first reading, in the House of Lords in October 2018, deals with the preponderance of England within the UK by ignoring it. It gives each of the four nations an assembly, or parliament, while a much slimmed-down federal government takes responsibility for foreign affairs, relations with the European Union, immigration and macroeconomic issues. It proposes two possible constructions for the new English parliament: either a parliament which starts de novo, or one which is embedded in the present UK parliament but deals only with English affairs, at times separate from UK parliament business. In the latter case, a member would in effect have a dual mandate. There is no provision for federation within England following the creation of an English parliament: Daniel Greenberg, a barrister and a former parliamentary legal counsel, a member of Salisbury's steering committee who drafted the Bill, told me that 'we're not claiming to meet the needs of English regionalism. We want to address a more pervasive feeling: that the present system isn't quite right.'

At a seminar in St Andrews in October 2018, Salisbury said he was neutral as to whether the House of Lords should be abolished, or kept as a revising chamber like the German Bundesrat, containing as it does representatives of the sixteen Bundesländer. Greenberg says he believes that Salisbury thinks that 'the House of Lords should just go': a remarkable evolution for the head of a family for centuries so deeply implanted in networks of land ownership, wealth and political power, so dedicated to using these large advantages in public service at high levels. It stands as a signal of the depth of the political restructuring in Britain.

Membership of the European Union, devolution to Northern Ireland, Scotland and Wales and the reform of the House of Lords have introduced a new element into the no-constitution constitution – a fact which, Vernon Bogdanor argues, has been 'little noticed because the various reforms have been legislated piecemeal, and because they seem without internal coherence'.[17] Though the Westminster parliament theoretically remains supreme, it's hard to believe it could abolish, or radically change contrary to their wishes, any of the three present devolved assemblies. They have virtual constitutional security. Salisbury's plan, or something like it, would legally embed that virtual status, though it may not become a written constitution. The group behind the putative Act believes there is no need to reform many existing constitutional arrangements, such as the courts, which work well, confining itself to 'those parts of the constitution which appear to be present sources of difficulty'. It believes the four nations 'is each entitled to its own internal sovereignty' – the use of that last word itself marking a very large shift.

The four nations' plan is dependent, as any plan for the future shape of the Union must be, on the desire of England, expressed in a clear and democratically arrived at form. So far, such a wish has been either small, regionally confined (as to Cornwall) or the product of a sporadic resentment that the surrounding nations, especially Scotland, get a better deal.

Scots nationalists insist that the English problem has the status of a permanent crisis, which cannot be solved, and thus Scotland, if not all three of the small nations, must become independent. The word is overused: it isn't a crisis, though it is a problem. A new settlement for England, which will have consequences for the other three nations, should and can be found: but it must gain broad assent, which will take time. Like much else in British public life, the English problem was parked while Brexit consumed more and more of government time and of media attention.

There's an unspoken assumption here. It is that England, more likely England and Wales, may itself go independent. Scotland may achieve independence: *Sinn Fein* may win a majority in Northern Ireland and mount a referendum, which would give assent to a merger into the Republic – two developments that would bring social unrest in strongly divided nations, especially in Northern Ireland, with a recent history of terrorist violence. In such a case, the English and Welsh might think themselves well out of it.

Denham says that 'there still is a strong case for the Union to stay together – it lies in the intertwining of the nations and the solidarity among them'. Tombs, saying of himself that he remained a hopeful unionist, nevertheless wrote in *The English and their History* that, as the drumbeat of devolution continues to sound, perhaps growing still louder, there would 'surely be greater English self-consciousness and more debate about what kind of country England was and wanted to be'. Many recalled G. K. Chesterton's ominous line (from his 1908 poem, 'The Secret People'): 'But we are the people of England, and we have not spoken yet.' No one had the faintest idea of what they might say.

J. G. A. Pocock, in a review of Tom Nairn's book *After Britain* (see Chapter 5), reflects that the nation is a way of allowing people to 'come together and say "this is who we are and will do, or be, next"'.[18] But there exists also 'a plurality of nations, seeking to affirm themselves as states, [which] have existed and modified each other's history, by means not necessarily fair or just or continually satisfactory. If they possess ways of continuing to make and examine their own and others' history, they will possess a joint political structure, since in this formation politics is a way of making and managing history and this, in turn, is capable of being examined and re-made . . . if they have been making one another's history, they need multiple, or many-sided, membership in the history they have made together.'

The nations of these islands have 'been making one another's history' for centuries: the twenty-first century has brought the largest challenge to unity, a century after the Republic of Ireland found first qualified, then complete independence. Making history means having made long lines of relationships, of common endeavours and trades, of friendships (and enmities) – and this before we confront the facts of a unified market, a sharing of risks (as bank crises) and the allocation of public expenditure (for some years benefiting Northern Ireland, Scotland and Wales in that order) and tens of thousands of work, academic, cultural and leisure entanglements. 'Independence in a United Kingdom' has been a reality, if a partial one, at least for Scotland, for more than three centuries. It has been, for all three small nations, much reformed, and can and will be further. But it is here, now, a tested solidarity.

3

THE CASH NEXUS

The Union between Scotland and England, argued for more urgently by Scots than by the English in the last decades of the seventeenth and first of the eighteenth century, became in our times, both for national-ists and unionists, a matter largely of money. The nationalists believe that Scotland can be richer if independent, the unionists believe it will become poorer. That was the principal ground on which the 2014 referendum on independence was fought, and, by the nationalists, lost.

Part of the purpose of the argument here is that there is more to the Union than money. Yet it remains central, and has always been so, although, historically, combined with and often overshadowed by other reasons. Certainly for the nationalists, there has always been more to independence than the economic facts of life – much more. And to protect their political offering, there *must* be more, since the economic promise now looks so shaky.

The maintenance of the Protestant religion, an end to wars, the security of a larger and more dynamic economy and the creation of what today we might call 'the UK single market' were the large reasons for the Union, which made the loss of the Edinburgh parliament bearable for a bare majority in it – if violently contested over the next few decades. The historian Brendan Simms wrote that 'it took two major European wars to create the United Kingdom. In 1707, during the struggle against Louis XIV's France over the Spanish Succession, Scotland and England established a parliamentary and defence union, as well as a single market and customs union, in a new state called Great Britain'.[1]

In the course of the next three centuries, war between the two states became unthinkable and religious differences became, in the twentieth century, irrelevant, except where the still very relevant differences in Ireland echoed in Scotland. Once the empire crumbled, and with it the broader horizons for employment, adventure and in some cases wealth available to the Scots, Irish and Welsh, what was left was the money. The small nations were poorer than England and, in the twentieth century, were subsidized in one way or another by it. When, in the early 1920s, the Republic of Ireland became independent, it was markedly poorer than the state it left, a fact that remained till the 1970s, when modern Ireland's rapid growth began. Centuries of English maladministration and a deep cultural and religious divide apparently made the split with the rest of the UK, for most Irish citizens, worth the relative poverty: for some, it was not, and in the north they threatened civil war to keep Ulster British, which it has remained. For those who remained in what became the Irish Republic, they were discouraged from saying so.

The Irish Republic was no example for the two other small nations which made up Great Britain. Independence for Wales and Scotland was, until the latter part of the twentieth century, regarded as plain silly, while for the Northern Irish majority, secession from the UK and merger with the Irish Republic was seen as actively threatening. For most Welsh and Scots, there was enough Welshness or Scottishness where they lived to satisfy them – the more so since, crucially, 'there was no ambition (in England) . . . to create a single nation, or to inculcate a single feeling of British identity obliterating those of the Scots, Welsh, Irish or of course English'.[2]

But there was not enough money in the small nations to sustain a comprehensive welfare state, created by the Attlee-led Labour government after 1945, at the same level as in England, without English assistance. The mechanism which has been, since 1978, used to fund public services in the small nations at or about the same level as in England, so that they enjoy more or less similar levels of public provision, is called the Barnett Formula, created under the aegis of the Chief Secretary to the Treasury (1974–1979) in the then Labour government, Joel Barnett. It assigns spending to the small nations, determining 'changes in the grant paid to Scotland [and Wales and Northern Ireland] as a proportion of changes to the budgets in English departments performing comparable functions'.[3] The proportions are based very largely on the size of the small nations' populations.

Barnett's was an ad hoc initiative: its intent was to prepare for a devolution of political and economic power to Scotland and Wales, expected to come into force in 1979, but which failed in a Commons vote. It was also, as Barnett, by that time ennobled, made clear to a House of Lords Committee in January 2009, a wheeze for reducing a heavy workload. 'I had to negotiate with all secretaries of state and they all wanted more money. It (the formula) relieved me of a little pressure in the sense that . . ., there was a round sum allocated to Scotland, Northern Ireland and Wales and they then decided on the allocation within their territories. I did not have to be involved in that.'[4]

The mechanism has been much criticized, but has never fundamentally changed – largely, according to Barnett himself in his evidence to the committee, because it benefited the small nations so much. Their public services were better funded than those in England – in the case of Northern Ireland and Scotland, much better (the partial exception, in some areas of spending, is Wales). Barnett, from the beginning of his evidence, was concerned about this. The advantage to Scotland in the fiscal year 2007–8, on the latest figures available, he said, was no less than £1,600 per person: 'I was worried that the figures would so upset people in England that they would demand a separation which would be, in my view, hugely damaging because I have no wish to see the UK split into three separate countries. I want to see the UK sustained and I thought it did not seem fair and therefore should be reviewed with a view to seeing whether changes were needed and what those changes should be . . . if something is not done and an astute leader in Scotland uses the extra expenditure in ways that we cannot do in England, as with prescription charges and university fees, then the people of England will get more and more upset and demand the very thing that they cannot get in Scotland.' Scots nationalist leaders are certainly as astute as Barnett feared: prescription charges are free in Scotland, not in England; and university fees are also free to Scots students, and students from the EU, but not to students from England, Wales and Northern Ireland. However, by 2018, increasing concern was being expressed within the Scots government about the rising costs of both these programmes.

The free services are attractive south of the border: why would they not be? A few months before Barnett was sharing his worries with the committee, ITV did a poll of the citizens of Berwick-on-Tweed, a town just over the Scots border in England, which had changed hands between the two nations on different occasions in medieval times, settling in England in 1482. The poll asked the citizens if they wanted Berwick to again become Scots, after a break of half a millennium. By a margin of 60 to 40 per cent, they voted to do so, citing 'better services including free personal care for the elderly, better access to new medicines, the absence of upfront university tuition fees and the promise of free school meals for young children in primary schools'.[5]

The poll was unsurprising. The majority of the respondents did not care if they were formally 'Scottish' or 'English'. They did not have to move house, change doctors and dentists, find new schools for their children, lose friends. The border moved, not they – and that their inclusion in a Scots welfare state was more generous than an English one trumped nationality. They would, after all, still be British, and were taking an economically rational decision.

The attraction of Scotland because of its better-funded public services was the pride of the nationalists: that better funding, however, did not and does not rest on the stable base of a successful economy. Its productivity, among the most crucial determinants of economic growth and thus resources for public spending, is, compared to other OECD states, only middling: the SNP government's pledge to increase it by 20 per cent has not borne fruit. That which more successful and productive economies say is essential, a strong and mutually supportive focus on the problem among government, workers and management, is largely absent. Though it was catching up with the UK average productivity, itself no better than middling, that catch-up ceased in 2015. Economists believe that the main reason for the narrowing of the gap between Scotland and England was because England was creating jobs at a faster rate, which means that productivity, the ratio between labour input and output, goes down unless output rises faster than the hiring of workers, which, in England, it has not. Thus, the apparent greater productivity of Scotland was a function of the reduced productivity of England. The better public services are substantially funded by the Treasury subsidy: Lord Barnett's legacy.

The focus on raising productivity crucially requires a government which privileges and encourages better and more efficient management, and better and less confrontational labour relations. But that has appeared to be lacking: one reason is the bitterness with which the SNP government has encouraged Scots to regard the recent past.

One of the constantly invoked and most popular critical themes in contemporary nationalist – and leftist – rhetoric is that Scotland, once the workshop of the world, had been de-industrialized by Margaret Thatcher and the Conservative governments of 1979–1997. That has large elements of truth: but it excises a still larger one. By 1976, when James Callaghan succeeded Harold Wilson, who had resigned for health reasons, industry was at a low point, taxes had gone up to a standard rate of near 40 per cent, with 98 per cent on un-earned wealth, inflation stood at 25 per cent in 1975 and remained in double figures, sterling fell sharply against the dollar and Denis Healey, the Chancellor, had to negotiate a $3.9bn loan from the IMF (in fact the third, and largest, applied for), granted on condition of £2.5bn cuts in public spending. Callaghan warned the 1976 Labour Party conference that Keynesian measures to improve the economy would no longer work. This was the Britain Thatcher inherited: any government would have been forced into radical action, which would likely mean tax rises, closures, public service cuts or unemployment, perhaps most or even all of these.

Everywhere in Britain, large-scale layoffs caused hardship and dislocation: Scotland was no exception, but because it had such a large cultural and national investment in (especially) engineering and coal mining, and in the workers who made up most of the workforce in these sectors, decline triggered a higher degree of political and moral distaste. Shipbuilding, and other skilled work, gave not just employment, but also status and pride: in the novel *The Shipbuilders* (1935), the Glasgow journalist George Blake captures the inter-war decline well, switching his narrative between the stranded, laid-off workmen and a

well-meaning, but helpless, yard owner, Leslie Pagan. As he sails down
the Clyde, on the last ship his yard would make to be fitted out, passing
the desolate yards, Pagan muses miserably that the shipbuilding crash
'was a tragedy beyond economics. It was not that so many homes lacked
bread and butter. It was that a tradition, a skill, a glory, a passion was
visible in decay, and all the acquired and inherited loveliness of artistry
rotting along the banks of the stream.' Glasgow, with a powerful urban
culture, akin to Chicago, with which its writers often compared it,
depended heavily on craft pride.

A majority of Scots voters had not chosen the Conservatives since
1959: the SNP made much of that, the political force of the argument
most fully accepted during and after the Thatcher period. The SNP
had an instant solution: leave the country which had elected a government that was destroying Scotland's economy and with that, its society.
See it, vote it, sorted.

The legacy of the great workshop years weighed heavily on the Scots
economy from the 1950s. In employment terms, manufacturing peaked
in the UK in the mid 1960s, then began an accelerating decline, boosted
by the faster pace of closures in the late 1970s and into the 1990s, shaping
'a narrative of economic change that was highly climactic or even cata-
strophic, especially in a Scottish context', according to Jim Tomlinson of
Glasgow University.[6] This was what Thatcherism, above all else, meant
in Scotland's political discourse, even in parts of the Scots Conservative
Party, which was not, in the main, Thatcherite. Glasgow, with just over
half of its workforce in manufacturing in 1951, had less than 20 per cent
in 1991: Scotland's equivalent figures fell from 42 to 21 per cent.

Tomlinson, in several essays and in interview, sees a sharp break
between a period from the 1950s and 1970s, when de-industrialization
was strongly under way but when alternative work, some of it supplied
by large plants opened by US corporations wooed by large subsidies,
was available – and 'the 'market fundamentalist approach embedded
in the Thatcher years'.[7] This approach did not only put a great many
workers on the dole: it also destroyed what Tomlinson sees as the
'moral economy', a series of agreements, explicit and tacit, on the part
of the state, management in both public and private companies and
workers represented by trade unions, to proceed with cutbacks and
closures only so long as other jobs were created.

The success of moral economy arguments, which were common in some form across the democratic world in that period, including in the United States, was highly contingent on a favourable economic environment, as well as governments, companies and managements which valued good relations with workforces which were often highly unionized, and even at times shared something of an industrial–social democratic view of society. This meant that those with state and economic power, politicians and employers, had to be willing to accept some diminution in profitability and efficiency, even occasional financial loss, to accommodate demands for near-full employment. When, by the 1970s, market conditions in some sectors turned decisively down, the moral economy was tested, and cracked.

The crack was largest in shipbuilding. By the late 1960s, production had been narrowed to only a few yards. The Labour government, in 1968, brought together a group of these into a new, partially state-owned group, Upper Clyde Shipbuilders. By 1971, with only one of its yards (Yarrow) profitable, it had a desperate need of at least £6m of working capital, which the then Conservative government, led by Edward Heath, would not extend: it was forced to enter liquidation.

The workers had reached a limit, and struck, but not in a conventional way. Led by four shop stewards, Jimmy Reid, Jimmy Airlie and Sammy Barr, members of the Communist Party, and by Sammy Gilmore, a left-wing member of the Labour Party, they came up with the idea not of downing tools, but of picking them up. They did not picket outside the yards, they remained in them, working to complete the orders for ships already under construction. The 'work-in' roused huge support in Glasgow, Scotland and beyond.

Reid especially, a natural orator and leader, was able to frame the struggle in both practical and class terms – and in Scots terms too. 'It is a privilege', Reid told a yard meeting, 'to belong to the Scottish working class.' To another crowd, 'here in this demonstration is the real Scotland: the Scotland of working people'. The marches sang 'We shall not be moved', a song that had its roots in a black slaves' spiritual; and also the jaunty 'Scotland the Brave': the lyrics, by the Glasgow writer Cliff Hanley, suggest the singer is a Highlander, and in the line 'Towering in gallant fame', celebrate martial valour (a quality safely embedded within a British military tradition). The song had been the unofficial Scots anthem for football and rugby teams till the late 1980s, when growing nationalism encouraged its substitution by the more maudlin and English-hostile 'Flower of Scotland'.

That the government was a conservative one, 'the bosses' party', and that the ministers who took the decision to allow the yards to close were all English, gave a nationalist edge to the protests, though none of the leaders of the work-in favoured independence, and most of the workers who voted would have chosen Labour. That for most of the workers there was no other work (certainly not as well paid as the skilled trades had been) gave an urgency and bitterness to the protests, which won their aim, in the short term, as the government backed down and funded the group. Parts of it were later closed, others sold off: one of the largest investments in the 2000s in the land the yards once occupied has been a transport museum, which strongly features ships, finely done and well-resourced, but as always in such cases, doubling as an expensive gravestone for the real thing. Shipbuilding continues on the Clyde, but precariously. Much of the industry, with its attendant research and development base, had moved – by the twenty-first century, this was to the east, where the three main national centres are China, South Korea and Japan.

Jim Philips, another Glasgow University economist, who, with Tomlinson, also deploys moral economy arguments, writes that the politics of devolution took off among working people, away from the Labour Party, which had renounced all interest in it, in the 1960s, when the beginnings of de-industrialization became evident, and when, as the years went by and more plants closed, the London government was seen as incapable or unwilling to intervene. In these years, he writes, agreement on the morality of the economy were put aside, including in the coal industry, which, publicly owned as it had been since the war, was an apparent model of management-union consensus: 'Workers in the UK enjoyed greater collective strength from the 1950s to the 1970s than they did in preceding or following decades but . . . this was based on favourable economic and labour market conditions that enabled miners in Scotland to push their managers and policymakers to accept moral economy approaches to coalfield jobs.'[8] Absent these conditions, labour's strength shrunk.

Scotland had been more globalized in the nineteenth and early twentieth centuries than the UK as a whole: that is, more dependent on world trade and links with foreign countries. It is arguable that Scotland was, in the early decades of the twentieth century, the most globalized nation in the world: my grandfather, who with my mother brought me up, served his apprenticeship on the Clyde (far from his native fishing village in East Fife) then joined the Blue Funnel Line, one of the largest British merchant ship fleets trading in the Far East, as an engineer. He was proud of his skill, of his authority over the lascars, or Asian seamen and of the empire: my mother was irritated by his archaic imperialism, and the racism which went with it.

Poles and other outsiders were brought into the mines after the war (one of whom became my stepfather), disturbing the prevailing local, often father–son, employment patterns in the mining towns and villages, because of a shortage of labour. Their deployment would certainly have been the cause of the enmity between them and the Scots miners, to which my stepfather attested. By the 1960s, accelerating in the 1970s and culminating in a disastrous strike in 1984–1985, the tempo of pit closures quickened, in part because the seams were exhausting but increasingly because they ran at a large loss. The coal available on the world market, much of it from China and India, was far cheaper, even with transport costs.

Before the great management–government–worker confrontation which was the 1984/5 mineworkers' strike, closures had at times caused local strikes but were usually settled. Where there was a national dispute, as in 1973 and 1974, and in 1981, government backed down, a fact which gave the National Union of Mineworkers a natural pride in their power. In a study of the closure of the Michael colliery in Fife in 1967, Jim Phillips shows that the nearly 2,200 workers at the pit largely found other work: over a thousand at other pits, most in Fife, some in pits elsewhere, some going to early retirement, others leaving the industry for other work. Unemployment rose in the area, but not disastrously – to six per cent in Leven and Methil, 7.2 per cent for men.[9]

By contrast, the 250,000 jobs lost in Britain after the 1984–1985 strike left a residue of very high unemployment, reaching 20 per cent in most former mining areas, together with a legacy of ill health and, for those finding new work, lower pay . This was a UK-wide phenomenon: in a decade, deep coal mining had all but disappeared in a country which had, in the nineteenth and early twentieth centuries, built its economic might on it.

The Scots pits suffered with the rest, as in a few years after the strike the pits of Britain were almost all shuttered. The vice president of the NUM and president of the Scottish area of the Union, Mick McGahey, a communist whose father had been a founder member of the party and who had begun work at fourteen in Gateside Colliery, near Glasgow, was loyal in public to the far-left national President, Arthur Scargill, but increasingly distressed by a failure to settle, which meant that the final defeat, un-negotiated, was heavier than it could have been on the mineworkers . In a conversation with me after the strike, he said that 'I am not sure we handled it all correctly. The mass intrusion of pickets into Notts, not just Yorkshiremen; I accept some responsibility for that, and so will the left have to. I think if as an executive we had approached Notts without pickets, it might have been different. Because I reject, I have made this clear since the strike, that 25 or 30,000 Notts miners, their wives and families and communities are scabs and blacklegs. I refuse to accept this. We did alienate them during the strike.'[10]

The excision of that part of the Scots working class who saw themselves, and were seen by others, as the class's most distinguished and militant members, was a further weakening of the material and human base of a leftist social consensus in the nation. Coupled with the gathering view that Thatcherism was a destructive wind against which no socialist shelter could be built, the last great action of the mineworkers weakened Scotland's labour movement and encouraged leaders and voters of the left to look to the nationalists as a bulwark against 'English' politics.

The Scots labour movement, for the first decades after the war more 'labour' than 'Scots' in its political leanings, nevertheless inclined away from the centralism of many of their Scots parliamentary colleagues. The Scottish Trades Union Congress had been suspicious of an assembly, and were scornful of the SNP ('Tartan Tories', was the ever-ready jibe): but the argument for economic powers, and control over the leaping oil revenues, began to win favour by the second half of the 1970s.

Devolution had been scorned by the Labour Party's leaders: but it began to appeal to younger Labour Party members on the left of the party, including Gordon Brown. He, as chairman of Labour's

Devolution Committee, campaigned hard for devolution before the lost parliamentary vote on the issue in 1979, and remained both strongly for the policy and scornful of the SNP. The most powerful of the generation of Scots Labour leaders born soon after the war, Brown characteristically sought to span two different positions and to bring them together, in government, into his own view of British social democracy. An early devolutionist, he was still heir to the centralist–progressive strand in the Labour Party, laid down so firmly in the post-war years by the Attlee governments.

The British road to social democracy was based on a moral approach, shared, if with different degrees of passion, by all the leading members of an often disputatious Party and government. John Bew, in his lucid biography of Clement Attlee, prime minister in the governments of 1945–1950, and the brief government of 1950–1951, writes that 'above all, Attlee set the ethical terms on which Britain's new social contract was founded'. Though Labour inherited an empty treasury, a vastly over-extended defence commitment, ruined city centres and industrial plants, an adverse balance of payments, hundreds of thousands of men and women to demobilize and very large debts to service, its great advantage was that its moral force was, for at least the first five years, in tune with the majority, especially of the working and lower middle classes, whose wartime (and pre-war time) experiences had given them a hunger for both rights and a higher standard of living underpinned both by better wages and by public provision.

The war had fused the nations of the UK into more of a common polity than ever before: its management had greatly increased the numbers and power of the domestic civil service and the centralization of policies. Attlee and his colleagues thus inherited, and found it useful to use, a machine which imposed common standards, services and provision everywhere in the UK – an approach which chimed both with the Party's desire for socialism's fruits to be available and equal for all.

Scots, from whatever background, were little represented in the post-war Labour leadership. None of the Scottish Secretaries: Joseph Westwood, a former miner and miners' union official, 1945–1948; Arthur Woodburn, a former secretary of the Scottish Labour Party, 1947–1950; and Hector McNeil, a former journalist, minister of state in the Foreign Office during the war, 1950–1951, were prominent or influential in the party's leadership. The large figures, apart from Attlee himself, were working class Englishmen: Ernest Bevin, Minister of Labour during the war and Foreign Secretary after; Aneurin Bevan, a back-bencher during the war and Minister of Health after; and Herbert Morrison, Home Secretary during the war, Leader of the Commons and Deputy Prime Minister after.

Labour enjoyed decades of support for its policies, and the very large provision of public-sector housing replacing the slums, especially in Glasgow. The nationalists were able to end that hegemony in the 1990s/2000s, in large part by arguing that the moral underpinning of health, welfare and education policies, which had appealed so widely in the late 1940s (and which continued, if in diluted form, by Conservative Governments until the late 1970s), would be better served by them than the Labour Party. Labour was down and stayed down, though not out, in the 2010s: then, the liveliest challenge to the SNP was a revived Conservative Party, led by a naturally politically brilliant, and relatively young (b. November 1978) politician, Ruth Davidson. Davidson and her colleagues transformed what seemed like a doomed cause into a force once more, especially in its former fiefdoms of eastern Scotland, with even some gains in working-class areas in the West. As a measure of her success in the 2019 European elections, the Conservative vote in Scotland was proportionately higher than anywhere else in the UK, including the south-east of England. She did it, she believes, by emphasizing that she led the Conservative *and Unionist* Party – and thus became a home, at a time of a shrivelled labour movement, for those who wished to mark their disagreement with a vote for the Union. But she had her limits: in mid 2019, disheartened by a vote for Brexit in the UK, not reflected in the strong vote for Remain in Scotland; out of tune with the new Tory Leader, Boris Johnson; and with a son born in October 2018, she resigned the leadership.

The new economic landscape revealed how diminished the red bases had become. Just before the referendum on independence in 2014, the Scots government published a background paper with a chart showing that industry, in 1973, accounted for 29 per cent of Scots output. Adding to that construction at nine per cent, 'other production' (mainly light industries) at eight per cent and farming and fishing at three per cent, economic activity employing mainly manual workers at various skill levels was just under half. In 2009, by contrast, when the UK had been governed for two-thirds of the thirty years between 1979 and 2009 by Conservative governments, industrial output had more than halved, at 12 per cent, with other production at seven per cent, construction at eight per cent and farming and fishing at one per cent, The total, at 28 per cent, was little over a quarter. From 2009 to 2016, manufacturing declined further, to seven per cent.

The two growth sectors were business services and finance, up from 15 to 25 per cent; and government and other services, up from 18 to 26 per cent, together accounting for just over half of Scots output. In his *Grasping the Thistle*,[11] the future SNP minister Michael Russell (with Dennis MacLeod) wrote that 'Scottish government . . . by common consent . . . is far too large': in power (from 2007), his party made it larger.

The sweeping away of most of the red bases – in Glasgow, in the coalfields, in the big plants – and the concomitant decline of a culture which contained strong strands of fundamentalist religion and socialism, cleared the way for an attachment to a nationalism which promotes a patriotism limited to Scotland with a strong anti-English, anti-British undertow, while eschewing, at least so far, a narrow illiberalism common among other nationalist movements and parties.

The strongest nationalist bases in the 2010s, Glasgow and Dundee, had been strongest for Labour. In neither city would large-scale industry return: instead, high-tech investment was wooed, and large investments made in cultural centres, such as, in Dundee in 2018, the northern branch of London's Victoria and Albert Museum, housed in a graceful ship-shaped building designed by the Japanese architect Kengo Kuma. The decision to approve the branch was made by Mark Jones, the then director of the V&A and, though English, a founding director of Edinburgh's Museum of Scotland.

A culture-led revival is certainly welcome – and as certainly fragile. Legacies as malign as those that afflicted both Glasgow and Dundee, the latter once the centre of jute manufacture, which employed a largely female workforce, are hard to overcome. Two other cities were praised for their efforts in recasting themselves in part through developing cultural centres, what he calls the 'cognitive cultural economy', by the British-American sociologist Allen Scott – Manchester and Sheffield.

Manchester, with a new arts complex near its centre (and a huge statue of Friedrich Engels beside it) showed strong growth: Sheffield, with a complex of theatres, galleries, cinemas and studios has raised its game sharply in the arts, but, like Dundee depended on now largely absent industry (in its case steel and cutlery production), has an even higher proportion of workers in the public sector than the Scottish city. A sharp downturn in the Scots economy after independence would hurt the city disproportionately. Those centres and classes whose majorities voted against independence are those who would best cope with economic problems attendant on independence; if it came, they could move to the rest of the UK, or abroad, or stay in relatively well-paid jobs in Scotland. Those in the working and lower middle classes who voted for independence would struggle most. By the late 2010s, this should have been clear to everyone. But the nationalists' steady assurance that independence would solve economic problems and usher in a Scandinavian-like society, with comprehensive social services and high wages, appeared to convince.

That the many centres in the UK which had suffered similar losses of once-dominant industries did not descend into real poverty has been largely due to the British state. Where the major aim of what is called – a term promiscuously used – neo-liberal economic policy, more popularly austerity, has been to hold down inflation, and where regional policy in the UK has fallen into disfavour, subsidies to wages, housing and children have risen, and the public sector has been expanded. Health service, dominated by the National Health Service, is by far the largest employer in late 2010s Scotland. The jobs which most people do are much less dependent on global forces than they were in the later nineteenth and early twentieth centuries. In becoming a more insulated 'economic community of fate' rather than one dependent on the flows and ebbs of world trade, Scotland became more of a nation-in-itself than it had been before, its economy providing a better springboard for nationalism than existed in its imperial glory days. Then, it was dependent on international commerce: now, for the maintenance of its living standard at present levels, it is dependent on the public purse.

The decline of industries proven vulnerable leave different sorts of vulnerabilities. Publicly provided services, as education and health, are devolved to the Scots government but are both part of UK-wide networks and have been funded by the block grant, which favoured the three nations. Both education in schools and parts of the health service have, by the late 2010s, declined in quality and delivery in Scotland: and the shocks that independence will unavoidably deliver will increase pressure on them. The imperial workshop period, where very large profits were made for the heavy engineering companies and very little was done to improve the lives of working-class families living in some of the worst housing in Europe, has been bit-by-bit replaced by a provident state in which relative poverty remains, but lived at a much higher material level, with services available of a higher quality and quantity than ever before.

These services and subsidies cushion the decline of industry. The subsidies could have been set at a higher level still, or more usefully new industries could have been wooed in or assisted to begin, had the expansive oil years continued into an independent Scotland. Now, an independent Scotland, on most forecasts, could continue to provide the level of public provision it has only by raising tax revenues substantially. As more and more responsibility for the economy is devolved to the Scottish government and as the SNP continues to press for independence on a less illusory basis than the 2013 programme for independence, 'Scotland's Future', set out, the Scottish National Party must confront the harder choices of running an economy that has been dependent on its big neighbour for most of three centuries.

The nationalists and leftists were not wrong to blame the Thatcher governments for the rapid decline of industry, and the rapid rise of unemployment. Those born during or soon after the war, the cohorts which were rising to positions of power in every field, knew a post-war world in which, from the late 1940s to the early–mid 1970s, the British economy sustained an average unemployment rate of around two per cent. It rose to several multiples of that in some of the Thatcher years.

The Thatcherite Conservatives were in power, were resistant to public money being used to save ailing industries and thus had to carry the can: it was another matter to believe, as both the left and the nationalists claimed at times to do, that the industrial corporations of the UK, many of them suffering from low productivity, frequent strikes and uncompetitive products, could be supported indefinitely, or saved through nationalization. Production of the Rootes Group's Hillman Imp was directed by the then Labour Government, with grants to sweeten the move, to the heavily unemployed area of Linwood, near Paisley. The Imp, a small car designed for an era of expensive petrol, proved unreliable: while the 5,000 workforce, many reduced from individually skilled shipyard work to production lines, was frequently on strike. Opened in 1963, it closed, finally, in 1981, the second full year of 'Thatcherism'.

Thatcher, impatient of the rites and understandings that her party had carried for many decades, made no exception for Scotland. She scrapped Edward Heath's policy for devolution (never pursued during his premiership) when she was in opposition in 1976, prompting the resignation of Alick Buchanan Smith and Malcolm Rifkind, respectively Shadow Secretary and Shadow Minister of State for Scotland (the latter was to accept the post of Scottish Secretary, 1986–1990). As much as the leaders of the Labour Party, she was a centralist, seeing the country she came to govern as, for the purposes of her core policies, an undifferentiated whole, with the partial exception of Northern Ireland.

Yet her growing attachment to the free market warmed her to a certain idea of Scotland, incarnated in the figure of the Kirkcaldy-born economist, Adam Smith (1723–1790), who anticipated the form and conditions of the industrial society just as the revolution which gave birth to it was beginning. Thatcher was a great fan of Smith, the Scots Enlightenment's most celebrated figure. And Smith was a great fan of the Union with England, not least because it had brought greater freedom to working people: 'By the union with England, the middling and inferior ranks of people in Scotland gained a complete deliverance from the power of an aristocracy which had always before oppressed them.' [12]

The first fully fleshed theory of market societies came from Smith's pen, who observed the first trends of the industrial revolution in England in the early part of the eighteenth century. These included a sustained rise in the productivity of farming, especially as more and more of that land, which had been collectively worked, was enclosed for private farming; a rapidly growing population with some disposable income, prompting a demand for manufactured goods; the appearance of new technologies, as the steam engine, first developed by the English inventor Thomas Newcomen, greatly improved in Smith's time by the Scots engineer James Watt; the growth of cities; fewer barriers to proactive entrepreneurialism and independent money-making, even by a few from the lower classes. Scotland, much poorer and with a more turbulent society, caught up later by a series of adaptations of technology the English had developed, pushing these further (an early model for 1960s Japan), doing so with enthusiasm and real success, displaying both inventive and entrepreneurial flair, especially in the 1800s.

Adam Smith was a reserved, studious man, without family, who lived for much of his life within the walls of universities, or with his mother. In his two major works, the *Theory of Moral Sentiments* (1759) and *The Wealth of Nations* (1776), he set out a description of how what became capitalism was growing, what it was bringing to the world, what it demanded and what it would demand of a new class. This was the industrial proletariat, hardly visible when he wrote the latter book, but destined to be part of an increasingly rigid division of labour which, as Smith saw, would increasingly break down what had been craft work into smaller and smaller, continually repetitive industrial tasks.

A growing understanding of the immense power of the marriage of technology, market demand and the capacity of a disciplined labour force led him to complement his heralding of the new economy with plans for reform. These included education for workers, which Scotland provided, often through Church of Scotland ministers in many communities: England had been more lax in ensuring such study. In *The Theory of Moral Sentiments*, written before *The Wealth of Nations*, he addressed the problem of why human beings should care about others, beyond themselves and their immediate family and friendship circle. He 'solved' the riddle by asserting that in every man 'there are some principles in his nature, which interest him in the fortunes of others, and render their happiness necessary to him, though he derives nothing from it, except the pleasure of seeing it. Of this kind is pity or compassion, the emotion we feel for the misery of others, when we either see it, or are made to conceive it in a very lively manner.' The fact that there are 'some principles' of this kind means that society could function without becoming merely despotic.

The Wealth of Nations, however, asserted a different sort of motor force for men's actions. 'It is not from the benevolence of the butcher, the brewer, or the baker that we expect our dinner, but from their regard to their own self-interest. We address ourselves not to their humanity but to their self-love, and never talk to them of our own necessities, but of their advantages': the much-quoted sentence is often enrolled to prove the uselessness of state intervention into a market where 'self-interest', not state canteens, served up dinners every day.

Smith wanted those who were enriching themselves through the market to feel that they *should* express benevolence. In a deeply religious society, that appeal to benevolence could be backed by the fear that the mere accretion of wealth with no thought for one's fellows could bar one from heaven, the narrow eye of the needle barring the fat camels of business. But the motor force of desire for *more* tends to prove more compelling, especially in largely secular societies (China's historic aversion to transcendent religion and post-Communist adoption of the rational, utilitarian Confucianism helps to fashion it into a formidable capitalist power). The first theorist of market societies sought a soft capitalism: but even when regulated and softened, 'regard . . . for self interest' always ensures a hard inner core. Charitable giving by the very rich is considerable – though by far the most considerable in the US, less elsewhere. But for reliable provision for the poor, the state is essential.

Thatcher was seen in Scotland, and beyond, as cleaving to that hard inner core. She was one who, through her devotion to monetarism, as presented to her by her close colleague, Sir Keith Joseph, used the hard-core approach to discipline the British economy. This, from near the beginning of her premiership in 1979, meant privatizing most of the state-owned manufacturing (as British Steel), transport (as British Airways) and communications (as British Telecom); and allowing or encouraging most of the loss-making industries to close, radically downsize or be sold to a more efficient operator.

Iain Macwhirter, the chief political writer of the Glasgow-based *Herald* and one of the first of the mainstream commentators to come out as a nationalist, wrote in the *New Statesman* (26 February 2009) that 'Thatcher was a sincere Unionist who thought she understood the Scots, and that they would eventually come round.' Macwhirter may be right, that she thought she understood Scots: but if so, it was at a rarefied, intellectual and religious level, rather than a view based on observation and reflection. Her most commented-on effort to bring them round came nearly a decade into her period in office, on 21 May 1988, in what has become known as the Sermon on the Mound: a speech to the General Assembly of the Church of Scotland, whose headquarters is to one side of the short, steep road, known as The Mound, from the New Town's Princes Street to the Old Town's High Street. There, she presented herself to the ministers, she said, as one speaking 'as a Christian as well as a politician'. It was a moment that brilliantly illuminated the clash between the ethical position of Thatcher and the liberal mood of a once-stern Presbyterian Church.

Her 'sermon' was much mocked and derided: how could one whose policies had blighted so many Scots communities, put so many men and women on the dole queue and consigned so many of the young to a workless future claim to share Christian virtues? Yet though it wholly avoided any attempt to grapple with the economic and social dislocations in the country, the 'sermon' was an almost poignant attempt to connect with the Scots character through a shared faith: the Methodism in which she was raised (she had switched to the Church of England on her marriage to Denis Thatcher), with a still more exacting faith, Scots Presbyterianism. Both, however, were in severe decline: and in Scotland, many of the ministers of the established church had become as liberal or leftist in their views as the Church of England.

Thatcher's conversion to Anglicanism was not, she believed, a large step: her temper was formed by the faith of her father, and her early years. Both the Methodists and the Presbyterians place great weight on the scriptures, on grace through faith in Christ, simplicity of worship and the performance of righteous actions. The Prime Minister thought she was speaking to brothers in Christ: instead, she was speaking to men (all men, then) who, especially the younger ministers, in large part shared the view that her worldly policies were wreaking havoc in many communities, which they as ministers served, and beyond them, to a wider Scots audience, who increasingly believed the same, often with more vehemence.

Thatcher had had, three years earlier, a confrontation with the Anglican church when it had published, in the autumn of 1985, a document named 'Faith in the City', a strongly reformist essay which emphasized the plight of inner city areas, 'where economic, physical and social conditions are at their most depressing'. In one passage, which the Prime Minister underlined and queried, it claimed that 'the exclusion of the poor is pervasive and not accidental' – she was well aware that her policies were what was meant by 'not accidental'.

At odds with the liberal wing of the Church of England, whose influence was heavy on the report, she believed that Presbyterianism was more concerned with belief and scriptural guidance than in seeking an end to urban poverty. Thus she felt she could boldly propose to the ministers gathered to hear her that 'Christianity is about spiritual redemption, not social reform . . . we must not profess the Christian faith and go to Church simply because we want social reforms and benefits or a better standard of behaviour; but because we accept the sanctity of life, the responsibility that comes with freedom and the supreme sacrifice of Christ.'

Though she spoke in what she believed was the philosophical and social framework of Adam Smith, she did not mention him. She had, however, invoked Smith the previous year, at a meeting of some 200 Scots party workers, saying that 'much of so-called "Thatcherism" was the philosophy of celebrated Scottish economist Adam Smith, who wrote *The Wealth of Nations*'. On the Mound, she said she had sought and found in the scriptures the underpinning for her belief that self-enrichment is no sin: 'We are told we must work and use our talents to create wealth. "If a man will not work he shall not eat" wrote St Paul to the Thessalonians. Indeed, abundance rather than poverty has a legitimacy which derives from the very nature of Creation.' In this she was in Smith's tradition, but also in that of her faith's founder, John Wesley, who had advised his followers to 'Get all you can, save all you can, give all you can.' She put it less succinctly to the ministers, reminding them that 'the Tenth Commandment – Thou shalt not covet – recognizes that making money and owning things could become selfish activities. But it is not the creation of wealth that is wrong but love of money for its own sake. The spiritual dimension comes in deciding what one does with the wealth.'

The individual of conscience, the family – these were the basic building blocks of a responsible and free society: 'intervention by the State must never become so great that it effectively removes personal responsibility. The same applies to taxation; for while you and I would work extremely hard whatever the circumstances, there are undoubtedly some who would not unless the incentive was there (i.e. low taxation to encourage greater wealth creation).' The 'you and I would work ...' and a concluding 'earnest hope that we all come nearer to that other country whose "ways are ways of gentleness and all her paths are peace"' were pleas for a joint understanding on the basis of common belief in salvation through works. It seemed to resonate with some, mainly older, ministers who applauded her: the bulk of the audience was polite, but restrained: most of the commentary was critical, even mocking.

The Church of Scotland had largely kept pace with the Church of England in moving towards liberal positions: a significant number of ministers, many organized in an evangelical group within the Church, still oppose the liberal slide, but are embattled. A May 2007 article in the monthly *Evangelical Times* lamented that 'if we compare the church in Scotland today with that of the 1950s we see great changes . . . since then, liberal theology has prevailed in Scotland's divinity faculties, and prominent churchmen with heretical views have been tolerated . . . [Evangelicals] failed . . . to take a united stand on the authority of Scripture against the ordination of women and now . . . find themselves fighting a rearguard action against the blessing of civil partnerships'. In May 2018, the General Assembly voted, 345–170, to draft laws allowing ministers to conduct same-sex marriages. By that time, the Methodists, who have no central authority, varied on whether or not to permit pastors to marry same-sex couples: in the UK, several have.

Thatcher's Christianity, conservative even then, was running against the tide in nearly all Protestant churches that were not evangelical: frustrated by contemporary Anglicanism, she found in Immanuel (Lord) Jakobovits, the chief rabbi of mainstream British Judaism a congenial spiritual exemplar. She was, at least for now, the last truly socially conservative Prime Minister – a factor which increased her unpopularity in Scotland, both among those who had ceased to be actively religious, and among the majority of the sometimes-church-going middle class.

She had looked to Scotland to find two virtues with which she was in tune: a stern Church cleaving still to the solid verities of faith, believing in charity of individuals but as concerned as she was with the encroachment of the state. Most Scots were unlikely to know who he was, and even Kirkcaldy had, in most of the period since his death in 1790, little mention of its most distinguished son. Those who did know of him, economists and other academics, shied away from an interpretation of his work which emphasized the free market, especially the benignity of greed. His most famous sentence, on the central place of human greed in the provision of life's necessities, has been taken up with economists of the right, most notably by the American economist Milton Friedman (1912–2006), who laid down that the only responsibility corporations had was to increase their profits.

That other famed son of Kirkcaldy, Gordon Brown, Labour Chancellor 1997–2007, Prime Minister from 2007–2010, wrote of him: 'Adam Smith always believed that the town centre was far more than a marketplace. And when he stood under the banner of freedom, he did not argue for a freedom that gave men immunity from a responsibility to serve their society.'[13]

Thatcher would not have radically dissented, but her emphasis would have been quite different. Her famous phrase 'there is no such thing as society', made in an extremely friendly interview with Douglas Keay, the editor of *Woman's Own* in 1987, after her third election victory, was an attempt to underscore her belief that 'society' was an abstraction, while individuals and families made up its real content. When the phrase was taken out of the interview and given a life of its own as an accusation that she preferred a state of fragmented individuals with no social ties, her office issued a statement saying that 'her approach to society reflects her fundamental belief in personal responsibility and choice. To leave things to "society" is to run away from the real decisions, practical responsibility and effective action.' Both formulations could be drawn from Smith's writings: he was an economic philosopher feeling his way into an adequate theory of an emerging economy and society. Yet the effect of the Thatcher reforms, and the wave of industrial closures, left many communities in the west of Scotland, the north east and north west of England and in south Wales, and mining areas all over the country, quite shattered, sustained by state handouts, but with the central economic purpose of their areas gone, dragging much of the society and culture down with it.

Thatcher's religious beliefs were sincere, and her belief in the free market was sincere. The first were, however, private, not just in the sense that, like all post-war prime ministers, she did not choose to make much of her religion but because she saw the exercise of religion as the private business of the individual. The free market, including on the need to increase profits, was something to make much of, in a society which she believed had lost a belief in the need for it. All other talk she thought of as cant. Milton Friedman wrote if corporate bosses invoked social responsibilities as meaning the bees in the bonnets of the reformers, then they were 'preaching pure and unadulterated socialism. Businessmen who talk this way are unwitting puppets of the intellectual forces that have been undermining the basis of a free society these past decades.' Thatcher did not go to the extreme of calling business leaders who wished to make their plants less polluting, or tackle sexual and racial discrimination within their companies, socialists. But she was some way along the Friedman road out of serfdom, whatever the price.

But she could not feel her way into Scots society of the 1980s. The loss of so many working-class jobs, the shrinking Conservative base in the country and the rise of an increasingly confident nationalism combined to make her unwelcome, even hated. Her high, carefully trained and 'posh' voice, her scorn for any measure of devolution and the portrayal of her by both the left and the nationalists as a ravaging monster laying waste to the nation took over a very large part of Scots attitude to her and her party, which, in Scotland, suffered badly at the polls, though with a time lag, with much higher losses of seats after she left power than during it.

In 1979, when she first won, there were twenty Conservative seats in Scotland: in that year, the SNP dropped from eleven seats to two, raising hopes left and right that its good times were over. In 1983, the Conservatives went up one, to twenty-one seats, while the SNP remained at two. In 1987, the Conservatives lost more than half their seats, holding on to ten, with the SNP at three; in 1992, John Major's first election, the party recovered one seat, to come out at eleven, with the SNP at three. New Labour wiped out the Tories in Scotland in 1997 – they won no seats, while the SNP doubled their number, to six: New Labour was to continue to dominate in Scotland until 2010. The Conservatives clung to one seat after 2001, keeping a single seat, even in 2015, the SNP's *annus mirabilis*, where the nationalists took fifty-six Westminster seats. Then, in 2017, with Davidson at their head – young, centrist, gay in both old and new senses, as unlike

Margaret Thatcher as could be imagined – they soared back up to thirteen.

Thatcher had cemented her reputation among Scots by testing the poll tax, which shifted the local authority base of taxation from property valuation to individuals, in Scotland, where it roused mass protests, and refusal to pay, with the SNP in the van of the protests. She had by that time become almost wholly toxic beyond the depleted right: in an interview comment in 2008, Salmond, then first minister, said that 'the SNP has a strong social conscience, which is very Scottish in itself. One of the reasons Scotland didn't take to Lady Thatcher was because of that. We didn't mind the economic side so much. But we didn't like the social side at all.[14] He was forced to retract the concession that Thatcherite economics might not be wholly objectionable. Even the usually outspoken Ruth Davidson, when asked her view of Thatcher, replied cautiously and neutrally that she 'changed perceptions'.[15] Thus the iron lady proved a good friend of the nationalists, in giving body to their view that only they could supply a defence against the ravages of a figure like her and a government like that which her party had become.

Yet the view has hobbled debate in the country ever since. The economy did well enough in the Major and New Labour period, in line, more or less, with the rest of the economy. In the shock of 2008, Scotland provided more than its share of shocking events with the collapse of its two major banks, Halifax Bank of Scotland, and the Royal Bank of Scotland (see below). But the large issues of an economy were not tackled. Radical economic change was 'Thatcherism', which offended against the vague leftism the SNP professed as it grew, and which played well into much Scots opinion.

The SNP has not campaigned on changes necessary in the Scots economy, nor has it given a convincing sketch of the economy it would want to see after independence. The Scottish TUC official Stephen Boyd has argued that the nationalist government has had little or nothing to say about the UK economic model except to condemn it, giving no pointer towards how an independent model would diverge from the model, in the regulation of finance, in corporate governance reform, in ownership structure, in inequality of income, while accepting that, for a decade after independence, Scotland would use the pound sterling with no influence over the Bank of England, which issues the currency.

Above all, writes Boyd, a commitment to a Scandinavian style social democracy is an empty one: no leading figure 'managed to summon the intellectual honesty to admit that the Nordic society they desire and promote so relentlessly simply cannot and will not be funded on current levels of taxation'.[16] In the same volume, the veteran SNP leftist George Kerevan seeks to 'embed a non-capitalist practice inside the belly of the whale'[17], an approach that has received no encouragement from successive SNP administrations, which, sensibly in a short-run political sense, prefer vague commitments to hard programmes.

The argument often made by SNP members and officials is that the party is there to gain independence: having done so, various political groups on the left and right can be expected to form in order to compete for power. That is disingenuous. The nationalists are bound to offer a picture of a post-independence Scotland and, in their main economic documents, they do: this forms part of the next chapter. To achieve independent statehood having been part of a larger national or economic entity will be a tough and lengthy process. Scotland is a developed market economy with a relatively high GDP per head. But it will not avoid turbulence, and an economic decline. That will be the greater for a lack of will in confronting the real and damaging conservatism in Scots economic behaviour.

4

THE CRUMBLING PILLARS

The collapse of the Halifax Bank of Scotland (HBOS) and the Royal Bank of Scotland (RBS) in 2008, when the first had been one of the most admired banking houses in the world, and the second was, by asset value, briefly the largest bank in the world, was an explicit reproach to the values that Scots tend to claim as their own, and which formed a large part of the image within which foreigners have been encouraged to see them, and they have been encouraged to see themselves. These were values of precision, probity and prudence: the collapse left the stain that the first two letters of these virtues, PR, and often mendacious PR at that, had been one of the guiding principles of both banks for the short twenty-first century. PR can be helpful and clarifying when well used, deceitful when badly used. Both these banks called upon their public relations to be more of the latter than the former.

That their falls did not trigger a recoil from the SNP, the party then in office and one whose leader had both worked for the RBS in his earlier years and encouraged it to expand rapidly, demonstrates how completely the nationalists had taken command of the loyalty of its members and voters. It showed, too, that Labour, which had also been keen to promote the banks' success, was on the back foot. The final irony was that the whole mess, caused by the greed of bankers, was saved by the British government with two relatively frugal Scots politicians: the Prime Minister, Gordon Brown and the Chancellor, Alistair Darling, in command in Downing Street.

The billions of pounds of financial loss illuminated a melancholy fact. Scotland's two principal banks, which bore the national name, had come through an age of enlightenment, of Victorian religiosity and twentieth-century respectability, into a modern world in which banks had been cut, or had cut themselves loose from the conventions and rules, most powerfully those which were not written. Though they were slower than some others to adapt to a new order, they soon did, and did so voraciously – suffering for it and imposing suffering on millions of clients as well as the banks and their staffs themselves.

The Bank of Scotland, the country's oldest (founded 1695, one year after the Bank of England), suffered a complete collapse, so all-embracing that it had little choice but to submit to be taken over by Lloyds Bank to avoid bankruptcy (though it retains a separate name and branch network).

Ray Perman, in his book on the Bank of Scotland crash, notes that, for most of the twentieth century, 'Scottish banks were austere institutions ... a strict ethical code was implicit in the Presbyterian character of each of the banks. Lines were imaginary, but everyone knew where they were and once crossed there was no way back.'[1]

Crossing previously closely observed lines was not a sudden matter. The Bank of Scotland was seen as reliable, even conservative, certainly, but so were other banks: though they competed for accounts, the competition was restrained. London-based banks, for example, wouldn't create a Scots network, nor would the Scots banks do so in England. Oil changed that as, in the late 1960s, the fields were revealed to be substantial and the English banks threw custom aside and came north to be part of the oil financing boom. At the Bank of Scotland, a young man named Bruce Patullo put on an oil conference in London's Savoy Hotel and gained a foothold in financing BP's exploration of the Forties field.

Patullo, at the age of forty-one, became the bank's CEO in 1980 and quickly built on an already changing culture, fending off an attempted acquisition by Barclays and opening branches in English cities, tasked with finding big corporate loan opportunities, while telling his staff they must also speed up the rate of deposits. It still saw itself as an institution in which trust had to be earned by exercising caution along with growth, a 'rectitude bordering on Calvinism', as Perman puts it, once more invoking the religious culture clinging still to the national champions.[2]

The bank acquired a New Zealand building society, then a bank in Western Australia: anxious to increase its size to deter predators, it mounted an audacious bid for National Westminster, a much larger, if reportedly badly managed, bank, but was pipped by RBS. Now more desperate, it jumped at the suggestion it should talk to Halifax, the UK's biggest mortgage lender and, after some haggling, a deal went through, with the two senior executives at Halifax, James Crosby, the CEO and Andy Hornby, head of retail soon taking the top jobs at the renamed HBOS, with their chairman, Dennis Stevenson.

In the 2000s, HBOS developed a markedly and explicitly different culture from that of its past, even its recent, Patullo era. The 'Big Bang' era ushered in by the 1988 liberalizations of the City of London marked the end of fixed commissions, allowing more competition; the end of the separation of dealers and advisers, thus clearing the way for mergers and take-overs; and the end of a bar on foreign ownership, thus opening London's market to international banks. This had roused roaring animal spirits in all the UK banks: HBOS, under new ownership, was to the fore in the hunt.

Selling was everything; profits soared, and fears of overreach from old timers dismissed as, often, they themselves were. Corporate lending, including taking equity stakes in the companies it financed (previously unheard of) made it a force among a new breed of entrepreneurs, like Philip Green, the clothing retail tyro, backed by an HBOS division headed by Peter Cummings, who had worked his way up the bank from the tea trolley. The culture became increasingly like the approach for which Green was famous: make a quick decision after doing your homework, move fast to implement it, no committees, no delays, no inhibitions. Green's success didn't last. In the early summer of 2019, the future existence of Green's Arcadia group of retail brands as Miss Selfridge and Topshop, once high street fixtures and young women's habitual destinations, fell into the hands of its creditors and landlords, who reluctantly agreed to lower their expectations and prices to keep it going.

The bank itself plunged in 2007–2008, in the great crash to which it was cruelly exposed by its debts. Hornby, by then CEO, was reduced to a spectator as HBOS was pushed by the government into the only deal that could save it from destruction – a takeover by Lloyds, which at first celebrated a deal that overnight greatly increased its reach and grasp. It failed, however, to do adequate due diligence and discovered it had embraced a needy invalid. It had to raise £13.5bn in new equity, diluting the holdings of both Lloyds' and HBOS' shareholders, while selling off hundreds of branches.

The bank, and the government, and the regulator, the Financial Services Authority (now the Financial Conduct Authority), had known that the bank was overreaching and was receiving billions of support from the Bank of England, even as, in 2008, it published a £4bn rights issue. The former head of Regulatory Risk at HBOS, Paul Moore, who revealed this, was fired, as he writes in his memoir, for trying to warn his company's leaders that they were flouting their own ethical policy.[3] The bank survives as a wholly owned subsidiary of Lloyds, largely run from England.

Founded in 1724 to provide competition to the Bank of Scotland, then suspected of Jacobite tendencies, the Royal Bank of Scotland was strongly Presbyterian, a religion which stressed a direct relationship with God, personal responsibility and truthful dealings with all. Scots bankers, bold financial innovators in the nineteenth century when the country's economy and engineering prowess grew mightily, introduced the joint stock bank, overdrafts and ensured common procedures throughout the banking industry, including the circulation of uniform banknotes. S. G. Checkland, an historian of the Scots banks, believes that by the end of the century, 'major Scottish banks were now so large, and under such strict management, and perhaps so careful, that none was ever threatened with liquidity problems'.

Making an unwitting parallel with a major cause of the Royal Bank's humiliation in the first decade of the twenty-first century, Checkland observes that the chief executive, or general manager, of a nineteenth-century Scots bank was 'virtually all-powerful . . . with the same kind of authority over his crew as the captain of a ship, for the rank-and-file employees had no trade union or organization of any kind'. It was a profession that came to have the highest opinion of itself: Ian Fraser, in his fine account of the RBS crash, instances a bicentenary celebration (1928) in the North British Hotel (now, reflecting the rejection of an Anglophile past, the Caledonian) in Edinburgh, at which the Duke of Buccleuch, one of a line of aristocrats to take the chairmanship of RBS, as they did of the BoS, said that 'the banking system of Scotland is probably the greatest and most original work which the practical genius of the Scottish people has produced . . .' The conduct of the banks and the innovations they introduced to make banking more secure and responsive to business were 'an evidence of Scotland's more settled outlook, because the principle behind it was faith and trust between man and man.'

Trust between man and man was strongly in evidence when the accountant Fred Goodwin joined RBS in 1998 as Finance Director. George Mathewson had been a largely successful chief executive for five years and, at sixty, was being pressed by the board to name one who could be a credible successor. He had been impressed by Goodwin, then a young (late thirties) CEO of the smaller Clydesdale Bank when they met in comradely gatherings of the Scots bank chiefs. Mathewson was convinced he could trust the younger man with the Bank's future when he retired, as was a board which contained some of the most experienced financial and business people in Scotland. They were prepared to meet his demands for a final pension of two-thirds his final salary and an understanding that he would be Mathewson's successor.

He came, first as Finance Director, already bearing the nickname of 'Fred the Shred', which was to define his reign at RBS as it had at the Clydesdale. In both banks, the name derived from his highly abrasive and obsessively detailed approach, prone to organizing sessions in which he would publicly berate, or 'shred', senior executives. The rumours about his style had not, it seemed, put off the RBS board: at Clydesdale, he had cut costs (mainly by firing staff) and improved profits. Fraser's book's main title, *Shredded*, is an ironic tribute to Goodwin's unaffectionate reputation and nickname.[4]

A complicitous silence was to mark Goodwin's period of leadership (2001–2008) at RBS as much as his autocratic and egoistic manner: there were no major leaks of the leader's bullying style. Two closely reported and highly critical journalistic books on his period in power and the 2008 crash which ended it, Iain Martin's *Making it Happen* (2013) and Fraser's *Shredded*, stress the bank's feverish search for higher growth and profits, its convulsive grasping after new acquisitions with – especially in the case of the Dutch ABN-Amro, the one which helped sink RBS – astoundingly slipshod due diligence.

At all stages till the last, it was cheered on by the leaders of the devolved Scots government. Opening the Bank's new campus-style headquarters at Gogarburn, between Edinburgh and its airport, the then Labour chief minister Jack McConnell said that RBS was 'a perfect realization' of his government's strategy for 'developing a modern and prosperous Scottish economy'. As the bank strove to take over ABN, another first minister, the Scottish Nationalist Party leader Alex Salmond, wrote a 'Dear Fred' letter in which he observed that it was in Scotland's interest for the bank to succeed, and that he offered 'any assistance my office can provide', signing off with a 'Yours for Scotland'. Salmond, who had been an economist, specializing in oil, for RBS in the 1980s, should arguably have been able to guess something of the risks, financial and ethical, which the high act of RBS–Goodwin presented. But, as with the New Labour government in London and the George W. Bush Republican administration in Washington, the booming bank sector was viewed benignly everywhere: the Harvard Business School had RBS as a case study, titled 'Masters of Integration'.

The sheer shamelessness of the PR at RBS seemed able to mute any of the alarms sounded in the news media and among City analysts. In the *London Review of Books*, John Lanchester quotes the report and accounts of February 2017, when the scale of the coming disaster was evident to insiders, as claiming that 'It is the Group's policy to maintain a strong capital base . . . maintaining a prudent relationship between the capital base and the underlying risks of business.'[5] Everything – the fleet of Mercedes limousines, the private jet, the vast, multi-million annual salaries and bonuses, the splurges of more millions on sports events – was kept until the very end of the imperial era. And at the very end, it received £45.5bn to be able to survive, followed by years in which it racked up £63bn of losses, fines for manipulation of the London interbank borrowing rate (the rate at which banks would borrow from other banks) and treatment of its small business customers and a $4.9bn fine in a settlement with the US Department of Justice for sales of toxic mortgage bonds. In October 2018, exactly ten years after the fall, its chairman, Sir Howard Davies, revealed that the Bank's leadership was turning over whether or not to change its name, since the Royal Bank of Scotland name had suffered 'very serious' reputational damage.

The supposed moral advantage which is (still) advertised to Scotland's benefit over England was indeed shredded by RBS, as it was in HBOS. Greed was at least as unrestrained in Edinburgh as in the City of London, against which Scots nationalists still rail. More – it was further hyped by a misplaced patriotism, which came through not just the bank but also politics and the news media – and through Scots society as well. This was Scotland showing the world, once more, how to do banking. Instead, it caused the largest crash in British banking history and was only prevented from ruining Scotland by the fact that Scotland remained within the United Kingdom, and its taxpayers saved it.

The Scots banks, whatever their dourly proper pre-war comportment had been, were from the 1980s as much swept along as the City of London or Wall Street by the potential for massive expansion of banking which the liberal economic reforms of the City of London under the Thatcher government made possible, and which the US-inspired vast lending in the derivatives market turbo-charged.

In her discussion of this in *Fools' Gold*, subtitled *How Unrestrained Greed Corrupted a Dream, Shattered Global Markets and Unleashed a Catastrophe* (2009), Gillian Tett wrote that, on encountering the nascent derivatives' world in the City in the mid 2000s, she was 'startled by the scale of it. By 2005, the credit derivatives world . . . was exploding, with more than $20 trillion contracts in the markets, most of which had been written in London or New York. Yet there was barely a whisper of this activity in public view.' RBS was in the van of the new activity, there with the big boys of Wall Street: Tett writes: 'Lehman Brothers, Citigroup, Bear Sterns, Credit Suisse, UBS and the Royal Bank of Scotland all . . . fiercely ratcheted up their derivative operations. Not only was the competition demanding that they become more aggressive, but low yields on the more traditional credit investments were fuelling the drive for higher returns.'[6]

The silence included that of the Labour Party, then in power, which thought that the City should be granted further liberalization, producing as it did such a large tax contribution to fund the government's social programmes: greed at the service of social democracy, on a scale which Adam Smith, who commended the benign economic effects of greed, could not have conceived. Tett, a PhD in anthropology, had read the French sociologist Pierre Bourdieu, who wrote that the most successful projects and 'ideological effects' are those which are rarely spoken of in public, but 'ask no more than a complicitous silence'.

The self-serving view of Scots practical genius with which the Duke of Buccleuch regaled his guests at the celebrations in 1928 had some basis. It was a Scot, William Paterson, who had the idea for the Bank of England and who was a director of it, till he left in disgust because he couldn't get paid. And it was a Scotsman, John Law, who had the idea for what became the Bank of France. These were men, like the later luminaries of the Scottish enlightenment, who could see how the economy and society were changing: in Paterson's and Law's case, they also had the ambition and boldness to create institutions to serve the needs of the capitalist societies which were developing. But both were ruined by taking their ideas, pursuing imperialist plans, into what turned out to be dangerous territory – in Paterson's case, literally so.

Law persuaded the French government to allow him to issue shares in the Mississippi Company, which drew together the French trading colonies in Louisiana: he greatly exaggerated their potential, and the bubble created in the sale of shares collapsed in 1720. He beat a hasty retreat from Paris, where he had been lionized and, shorn of most of his wealth, he escaped to Brussels, dying of pneumonia in poverty in Venice in 1729.[7]

Paterson went one further, and ruined not just a bank, his family and himself, but also his native country. The Darien Company, 'one of the bitterest and saddest chapters in Scottish history', was dreamed up by him, as a competitor to the many trading companies being developed overseas by European powers (like France) and which all pursued fantasies of boundless, easily obtained wealth.[8] He convinced the Scots parliament to give his company a permanent monopoly on trade with Asia and Africa, and a 31-year monopoly on trade with America.

The project was a complete disaster. Most of the would-be colonists, including Paterson's wife and daughter, died of disease in the swampy area, situated in what is now the borderland between the states of Panama and Colombia. Three of the thirteen ships which set out from

Leith in 1698 returned, laden not with gold, but sick men and women. Half of the country's cash had been sunk in the scheme. Its only benign (or further malign, depending on your view) feature was that it encouraged Scots unionists to hasten Union with England, since the country desperately needed support, though it increased the scepticism of many English about a treaty with such a poor and feckless people.[9]

The two Scotsmen who were the authors of these influential innovations were tremendously creative, but were also wildly over-confident and careless of their own and others' money and lives. In the introduction to his finely done biography, James Buchan quotes Eleanor de Mézières – an Englishwoman married to a French Marquis, an ardent Jacobite and a friend of Law's, who had bought many shares in the Mississippi Company, but sold out before the crash – as saying that 'it's really a shame that he did not curb his boundless imagination, for he is a man of great quality. He was lost because of an exaggerated idea of himself.'[10] The two Scots geniuses of banking were not men to trust with your money or your life: the twenty-first-century leaders of the two great Scots banks showed a narrower recklessness, without the genius.

Yet the Scots banks, which grew and prospered as the advantages of the Union began to come through in the 1740s and 1750s, had been well managed by men who were not geniuses, but were usually honest enough. Their innovations, such as cash credit, the forerunner of overdrafts, and the establishment of branch networks, were practical extensions of the service they gave to individuals and businesses. The bank manager, in the small towns where most Scots lived, was a leading part of the town's establishment and increasingly one on whose judgement personal and civic development and the striving for wealth depended. Expectations of his integrity, and the teaching of a powerful and potentially punitive Church of Scotland, of which he would likely be an active member, would keep him on the straight and narrow if he needed external help to strengthen an inner conviction of carrying a moral as well as a financial duty, and inculcating it in his staff.

A lost world, if one within living memory. But as the world was lost, so was the specialness in which the Duke of Buccleuch, and many others before and after him, deeply believed: that Scots bankers possessed a higher moral standard, especially when charged with high responsibilities. Insofar as it existed, it melted in the heat of a culture of grab-what-you-can. Indeed, the two leading Scots banks became models of how to allow greed and the desire to show the world that they were better and sharper and meaner than the competition: the pay of the most senior executives rose hugely through the 2000s and into the 2010s, with bonuses worth millions added most years. Ninety years after the Duke's encomium, the bank's (English) chairman revealed that a bank called 'Royal' and 'of Scotland' was embarrassed by its name.

In the early 1970s, the SNP was climbing in the polls and, at the same time, the size of the oil fields within the UK's division of the North Sea was becoming common knowledge. The party re-worked its propaganda to emphasize one clear message: 'It's Scotland's Oil!' The insistent claim was that 'there was nothing that could not be done with the enormous revenues, nothing less than the total regeneration of Scottish social, industrial, and cultural life was seen to flow from the oil revenues controlled by an independent Scotland.'[11]

Among the most potent images used was the face of an aged woman, looking straight out of the poster, with an expression that conveyed sadness and loneliness. The slogan was 'It's her oil too.' It was an emotive image which, coupled with other messages affirming that Scotland, and Scotland alone was the true possessor of the oil, conveyed the impression that her plight could be alleviated, if not conjured away, once the oil was in Scots hands. It was a vastly different image of a Scottish widow from the beautiful young woman in a dark cloak favoured by the eponymous insurance company.

Oil greatly fired up themes already present in SNP propaganda and rhetoric, above all emphasizing once again the basic imbalance in the Scots–English relationship, to the latter's benefit. The 1974 Manifesto produced for the election in that year gave oil pride of place, claiming that the fact that the tax revenue from the production was destined for the coffers of the UK's 'weak, incompetent and generally vulnerable' government (at that time the government was run by the Conservative Party, which was, by 1974, indeed in a weak position) was another instance of English robbery: 'Scotland's resources and taxation have made England prosperous with little of that prosperity remaining in Scotland. This . . . continues apace with the drain of tax revenues from

Scotland's oil.' The slogans were crafted to appeal to Scots as consumers: 'How would you like petrol at five bob (25p) a gallon? With 825 million pounds every year from Scotland's Oil, self-government will pay'; as workers: 'How would you like a job in Scotland? With 825 million pounds every year from Scotland's Oil, self-government will pay'; and as caring grandchildren: 'How would you like your granny's pension doubled? With 825 million pounds every year from Scotland's Oil, self-government will pay.'[12]

The growth of the nationalist party greatly frightened the UK government: both the Conservative government of 1970–1974, and, more thoroughly, the Labour governments of 1974–1979, which had to grapple with both the up- and downsides of the discoveries. The latter, led by Harold Wilson from 1974–1976 and by James Callaghan from 1976–1979, was caught in a series of internal and external binds, through which it navigated with difficulty and, in the end, crashed against the rocks of a faltering economy and an aroused and impatient labour movement.

The Labour government received, in 1974, the recommendations of the long-running (established under a Labour government in 1969) Kilbrandon Report. The co-incidence of the report's recommendations for devolution to Scotland and Wales and the realization that the oil in the North Sea was a huge windfall at once opened debate on how the oil wealth was to be managed, and what it would do to politics. Many in the Labour Party, and some in the Cabinet, saw the oil as a means of extending public ownership in the UK's industry, then struggling with low productivity, frequent industrial action and declining markets. A growing number of Scots MPs, most of whom had accepted centralization as their political heritage, began to view devolution as a prophylactic against nationalism. The Treasury was determined to use the tax revenue to reduce debt and pay for rising unemployment, while above all else holding all the power over its deployment – the guardian of the post-war settlement. All were united in their determination not to give encouragement to the nationalists.

Alexander Kemp, in his two-volume *Official History of North Sea Oil*, relaxes a formidably detailed narrative by his descriptions of the debates and manoeuvres within the government.[13] On one occasion, the head of public relations at the Department of Energy (Kemp does not name him, but it was Bernard Ingham, later spokesman for Prime Minister Margaret Thatcher) briefed journalists that the line between Scots and English offshore waters was an extension of the land border, which runs diagonally from the Solway Firth in the west to the mouth of the River Tweed in the east – an indefensible projection, but one which would have brought some oil fields into the English sector.

The SNP, in its greatest surge to date, had taken 30 per cent of the Scots vote in 1974, and had begun to cut into Labour-held areas as well as those held by Conservatives, originally their main victims. Though the devolutionary project recommended by Kilbrandon was formally accepted, ministers and officials were fearful that a devolution to regional assemblies, no matter how restricted their powers, would see elected politicians come together who might, in the case of Scotland, be nationalists and would certainly demand a share of oil revenues, if not all of them. The government's Constitution Unit redoubled its efforts to oppose such an eventuality, arguing that Scotland would be safer in the long term once the oil fever passed, as pass it would, within the larger entity of the UK; and that, if independence were to be won, tariff barriers against Scottish exports to the rest of the UK, which was over 60 per cent of its export market, would be the result.

One of the arguments found to shore up the central control both ministers and officials wished to preserve was that since the rest of the UK had effectively subsidized the Scottish economy for many years, it was unjust to penalize England just when the tide was turning. This was the polar opposite of the SNP's claim that 'Scotland's resources and taxation have made England prosperous' (at Scotland's expense), and closer to reality.

The oil question and the SNP's growing power illuminated the large question which underlay the attacks from the north and the raising of defences in the south. The matter was not just that of 'Whose oil?', but of 'Whose country?' Like all nationalists seeking independence, the Scots nationalists were claiming that a British writ should no longer run across Scotland: that the 'auld sang' of an independent state which had been supposed ended in 1707 could be sung again by men and women who would be, in their view, freed from an English tyranny. To embrace nationalism was to reject unionism and thus, above all, England. It was to commit to the creation of a new state.

Were it to happen, it would come at a most favourable time for Scotland and a terrible time for the rest of the UK. The decade of the 1970s was a turbulent one: the 1970–4 Tory administration had come to power promising to liberalize and supercharge the economy: after a brief boom, opposition, especially from the unions, put paid to both. A turn to seeking an agreement with a powerful and militant labour movement also failed; and a miners' strike finished the job. Benefiting Labour, it also bequeathed the party the same economic problems, and trade unions, which had at first agreed to a wages policy to hold down inflation (reaching 25 per cent in 1975), then broke free from it in a series of damaging public-sector strikes, to help ensure a majority for a Conservative Party led by Margaret Thatcher, who had spent much of her years in opposition honing her economic liberalism.

The discovery of oil was a huge boon: with all of its problems, it could greatly increase any government's choices and flexibility. But had Scotland's nationalists been able to take power, and with power, the oil (disregarding Ingham's re-ordering of the seas), it would have created a rich Scotland and an impoverishing England (and Wales, and Northern Ireland).

The consequences of such an outcome were most clearly, even dramatically (but for years privately) illustrated by a senior Scots civil servant, working in the Scottish Office in Edinburgh, in the early 1970s. Gavin McCrone was the Office's chief economist, whose boss was the powerful Scottish Secretary Willie Ross: with a lively mind, McCrone saw more clearly than most how much the oil would mean to the nationalists rampant and set out to describe it, by means of an exercise of 'let's suppose . . .' He supposed, in a memorandum to ministers that Scotland was independent and the oil was flowing. What would that look like?[14]

He noted that the nationalists' case was not primarily cultural, certainly not blood and soil ethnic separatism, but an insistence that Scotland's economy was lagging badly, and needed the care and attention only an independent government could give. Most Scots, he wrote, had so far preferred to stay in the Union on economic security grounds, believing that Scotland 'gathered more economic advantage than disadvantage from the Union'. Yet the thunderclap of oil was that the wealth it promised 'raises just this issue in a more acute form than at any time since the Act of Union was passed'.

Scotland was dependent for its standard of living on subsidy from England, since its public spending was above the UK average, and its revenue lower. While it remained a region, there was, if the public spending level were to be maintained, nothing to be done about that, since the most effective way of boosting employment and exports, an exchange rate adjustment devaluing the currency, was not possible between regions with the same currency.

The UK government had been charged by the SNP for cutting a bad deal with the oil companies, a charge with which McCrone agreed. And far from exaggerating the oil wealth that independence would capture for Scotland, the SNP had pitched it far too low. Estimates were difficult to make accurate: 'but what is clear is that the balance of payments gained from North Sea oil would easily swamp the existing deficit, whatever its size, and transform Scotland into a country with a substantial and chronic surplus'. Indeed, so 'chronic' (in the sense of constant) would this be that it would be in surplus 'to a quite embarrassing degree and its currency would be the hardest in Europe', a 'haven of security' as reliable as the Swiss franc.

Warming to his theme, the chief economist forecast that real incomes would rise sharply as GDP per head grew and imports cheapened. To be sure, the oil could adversely affect farming and industry, by hardening the currency so much to render much of their produce uncompetitive: but he wrote that the balance of payments surplus could be reduced by large overseas lending. The surplus could then be spent on modernization of manufacturing and of the infrastructure, stimulate the economy and pump assistance into West Central Scotland – Glasgow and its environs, the most depressed part of the country. It would become a development area, while policy would be to move services from an overheating Edinburgh to Glasgow.

The wealth of the country would greatly increase the country's political power in the EU (then the European Economic Community, or EEC), with its commissioners and other countries suitably deferential to its position as the major producer of oil in Western Europe. 'For the first time since the Act of Union was passed', McCrone wrote with a flourish, 'it can be credibly argued that Scotland's economic advantage lies in its repeal.'

Yet nationalist policy is, wrote McCrone, 'extremely selfish', even if some justification could be found for it in the fact of Scotland's relative poverty within Europe, 'one of its worst problem regions'. Its rise would be at the expense of England , which would be 'in dire straits' without the oil revenue, a situation which would 'occasion much bitterness in England, if not an attempt to forcibly prevent it'. Thus, in a throwaway line, McCrone suggests that his vision made flesh could in extremis mean, after more than three centuries, conflict between the two nations.

Oddly, or perhaps not oddly, the landlord-takes-all position of the nationalist party was not shared by the Scots public, which, though believing that Scotland should be privileged in the share-out of oil revenue, didn't think that it should take all. After the 1974 election, surveys of the British Election Study showed that '36.5 per cent believed Scotland should receive a somewhat larger share than the rest of Britain, 31.5 per cent that it should be shared equally, 23 per cent that Scotland should have by far the largest portion, and 8.25 per cent claimed the whole'.[15]

In any case, the Scots, at least to date (2020) have not had to make the choice. The great chance passed when, in the 1970s and 1980s, the SNP hadn't yet claimed the virtual monopoly on Scots political representation that it could for a few years in the 2010s. Indeed, in the 1979 election, perhaps as a reaction to the fact that a referendum on devolution had not secured the required majority, it slumped. It recovered in the Thatcher years, notably *because* of the Thatcher years, which came to be seen as an attack not just on the Scots economy but on the understanding of the 1707 Union itself – that Scotland would retain a separate culture, which had to be recognized and honoured by a London-based administration.

Alex Kemp told me in an interview that the first Labour-led Scottish governments did not seriously seek to upset the status quo on oil revenues. This was perhaps because the Scots economy, which had been so relatively impoverished when McCrone was enjoying his foray into science fiction, had improved greatly because of the boom which the oil caused, most strongly felt in the north east but trickling through even to the south west. Also, though few Scots would be found to admit it even now, the improvement in the British economy in the second half of the 1980s and into the 1990s owed much to the

Thatcher reforms, even if they accelerated the decline of much of British industry.

The nationalists, of course, could not let it go. Their strong growth as they cut away at once rock-solid Labour areas in the 1990s to the 2010s, their increasing confidence that Scotland was with them on the issue of independence, encouraged them to hold a referendum in 2014, in which Alex Salmond, then the party leader, claimed that in the following year, revenue from oil would be much higher than the official estimates from the Office of Budget Responsibility. 'Scotland's Future', the thick White Paper in which the exaggerated claims were made, produced to encourage Scots to vote for independence, showed the importance the party attached to oil and the lengths they were prepared to go to assure Scots that it was their passport to riches. They knew that, since the economic argument was, as McCrone said, the basis of their strategy, it had to be represented as a bonanza rather than, as it was, and still more is now, a steadily wasting asset.

Oil was the game changer which came too early in the game. Its growth, and that of the nationalists' support, were out of sync. Had the political surge come sooner or the oil discoveries later, Scotland, with almost exactly the same population as Norway (5.25m to Norway's 5.35m in 2016) could now, with good government, be rich – if not as rich as Norway, with significantly lower extraction costs. In 2018, the World Bank, using a new basis of calculation of wealth, put Norway as the richest country in the world, beating the previous leader, Qatar: its oil fund was then over $1trln, 1.3 per cent of global stocks and shares. Norway lies some 500 miles away, across the North Sea, a paradise lost.

The need to convince Scots that they would be better off in an independent Scotland than one imprisoned in the UK prompted the SNP to issue, in 2013, 'Scotland's Future' – as a White Paper, that is, a government rather than a party document, covering post-independence economics, some months before the referendum on independence. The lack of realism in that paper prompted it to issue another, this time a party document named the Sustainable Growth Commission, in 2018, whose more or less overt task was to show both a new responsibility and a continuing confidence in independent wealth.

Both documents had a hidden narrative: that is, that nationalism in Scotland was unlike the heroic nationalisms of the past: the American revolution against British rule, achieved in 1783; or the Greek war of independence against the ruling Ottoman empire, succeeding in 1830; or the Irish revolt against Britain, largely won by 1921. This was not just because the colonial oppressor, the Westminster government, lavished earnest affection on Scotland to convince its people they would be greatly missed; nor that devolution, increasingly far-reaching, was readily agreed by Westminster in a series of steps, which meant that by 2019, Scotland's devolution of powers was among the most radical in the world.

It was because, implicitly, the nationalists realized this was not, for most, a very big deal. An Ipsos MORI poll of November 2010 on issues of concern to Scots showed 'Scottish independence, constitution/ devolution bottom equal on six per cent', while the economy (43 per cent), unemployment (29 per cent) and education (26 per cent) lead the issues. A poll by the same company in June 2018 did not have independence/constitution/devolution mentioned at all, though strong concern over EU/Brexit, top of concerns at 53 per cent, would certainly have included a reflection on independence within it. In nearly all such polls, Scots put the economy, education, the health service, unemployment at the top of the hierarchy of what gave them pause for thought, just as the English did.

A realization of this may have lain behind the extraordinarily energetic exercise of persuasion contained in the 650 pages of 'Scotland's Future'. From Salmond's preface to the 387 end notes, the people of Scotland were flattered and seduced, showered with optimism and assured, over and over, that everything – economy, education, democracy, health, civil society, transport, environment, culture, media, social services, and relations with the neighbours – would vastly improve. The first minister told the Scots that theirs is 'an ancient nation, renowned for the ingenuity and creativity of our people, the breath-taking beauty of our land and the brilliance of our scholars. Our national story has been shaped down the generations by values of compassion, equality, an unrivalled commitment to the empowerment of education, and a passion and curiosity for invention that has helped to shape the world around us. Scots have been at the forefront of the great moral, political and economic debates of our times as humanity has searched for progress in the modern age.'

Salmond and the 'Scotland's Future' authors were at pains to stress that, with the receipts from oil, Scotland's GDP per head would be one fifth larger than in the rest of the UK.

Taxes in Scotland would remain at or below the present UK levels and pensions would be increased; 'health inequalities', a shorter life expectancy, especially for men, would be reduced by the creation of a fairer society; money saved by sharply reducing spending on defence and expelling the nuclear submarines and warheads from the base at Faslane, on the Clyde.

There is much else, in this vein. The claims are rarely without some foundation: but they depend on optimistic assumptions – of Scots post-independence capacity, of world economic conditions and of a settlement with Westminster favourable to Scotland. They also depended on a large revenue from oil, estimated for 2016/17 at between £6.8 and 7.9bn: actual revenue was £0.2bn. This was the easiest claim to refute, since it was precisely spelled out; but oil revenue goes up as well as down, and the oil price rose from 2017 onwards, making the estimated revenue to Scotland, had it been independent, to be around £1bn, a modest bonus for an independent Scots Treasury, but on a spend approaching £50bn, no more than that.

The second pass at a description of Scotland's economy after independence was published in May 2018: the Sustainable Growth Commission (SGC) report was authored by Andrew Wilson, a former MSP and head of a successful consultancy, Charlotte Street Partners. The report was overseen by a fourteen-person board, which contained five academic economists: it was by seen by many, not all, as more realistic than 'Scotland's Future'. It remains the SNP's official economic programme for the post-independence state: it was enthusiastically endorsed – with one small reservation – at the Party's spring conference in Edinburgh in 2019 (though its author was not invited to speak to it). The enthusiasm was understandable: the SGC promised that Scotland would, in a decade or a little more, join a group of rich, small Western democracies, such as Denmark, Finland and New Zealand, as an equal in GDP. It would also join the EU and would be able to sustain, or better, the level of social and public service provision the country presently enjoys within the Union.

Yet there was an upset: not major, but telling, in a very rare vote by the delegates against the leadership. Wilson had come down firmly on the need to retain sterling as Scotland's post-independence currency, even though it would have no say in the governance of the currency. The report implied that sterling would have to be used for at least a decade, perhaps considerably longer, while it found its economic feet. The delegates, the Party's enthusiasts, didn't like the idea of being tied to an English currency for so long and put up an amendment, which was carried, to the effect that the pound should be replaced with a new Scots currency 'as soon as practicable'. This still gave a future independent Scots government plenty of room to define what was 'practicable': but it was a warning that for the most active nationalists, a break with all of Britain's institutions should be as far as possible complete.

Within the SNP, Wilson has been a leading moderate and pro-business voice, arguing for the continuation of 'Britishness' as a cultural attachment for Scots even after independence and insisting that an independent Scotland would need to have an unambiguously pro-market economy. More than most other senior SNP figures, he has been for years part of the Scots, even British, establishment: he was head of communications for the Royal Bank of Scotland and took a senior position in the world's largest advertising and PR company WPP, now for tax purposes nominally headquartered in Ireland. He is the opposite, both in person and in past political positions taken, of a shining-eyed zealot: he has written in support of Scots supporting English teams in international matches (except when playing Scotland), an unpopular stance within the SNP, and beyond. He is a fellow of Scotland's Chartered Institute of Bankers as well as the London-based Institute for Fiscal Studies.

The last of these organizations, in commentary on the SGC report, praised its relative moderation and sobriety, but was politely sceptical of its optimism. An 'observation' by David Phillips, an Associate Director, thinks it 'sensible' that the Report bases its projections on the Government Expenditure and Revenue Scotland (GERS), the official description of the country's public finances; commendable that it uses the Office of Budget Responsibility forecasts for public expenditure, quoting its figure of 7.1 per cent as the deficit in 2021–2022; that is, the gap between the receipts and the expenditure of the Scots government: the Barnett Formula presently funds the considerable difference between Scotland's per capita deficit and the UK's average per capital deficit.[16] This would be, were nothing else to change, the deficit Scotland would carry when independent, and shorn of the Barnett money – three times higher than the present UK deficit. The SGC reduces that figure to 5.9 per cent on various assumptions – with which the IFS 'could quibble' – but, taking one thing with another, Phillips concedes that the projections are 'not implausible'.

What is implausible, though the IFS doesn't use such language of its fellow's report, is the report's assertion the deficit would fall to 2.6 per cent in ten years, but would avoid the current 'austerity' visited upon Scotland by the UK government, because public spending would still continue to rise in real terms. Phillips writes that it is 'inconsistent to claim that these plans do not amount to austerity but the UK government's current policy does. While the UK government did reduce total public spending by an average of 0.2% a year in real terms between 2009–2010 and 2016–2017, since then, it has eased off somewhat. Between 2016–2017 and 2022–2023, total public spending excluding debt interest payments is forecast to grow by an average of 0.7% a year in real terms. The Commission's proposals for 0.5% increases per year therefore look remarkably like an extension of current policy in the UK: indeed they imply slightly *slower* real growth in spending than the UK Government is currently implementing.' The IFS didn't say so: but its carefully phrased criticisms suggest that the economic slogan the SNP could most truthfully promote in a future referendum would have to be: 'It's Scotland's austerity.'

Between the lines, the IFS states, the Commission is arguing for greater austerity for Scotland than that planned by the UK government. And though a 2.6 per cent deficit doesn't seem much, and many countries, including the UK, can run one of that size or larger for years, they are able to do so because of their size, their past record and their assumed ability to service the debt. Smaller states, especially small, unproven ones as Scotland would be, don't have that luxury and probably wouldn't get away with carrying it for years. To eliminate it, however, would take almost another decade, with growth of spending held at 0.5 per cent – another long bout of austerity.

The other assumption, however, is that Scots GDP growth will be about 1.5 per cent – double the UK's figure for 2017–2018. If Scotland leaves the UK and joins (or re-joins) the EU, it will, says the report, avoid the hit the UK will receive when it leaves. But the report doesn't discuss the much larger loss of a considerable proportion of the more than 60 per cent of its present trade with the rest of the UK, four times more than EU trade. Trade, of course, wouldn't cease with England, Wales and Northern Ireland but the loss would be substantial, likely to be more than any quick, or even longer-term, gain from increased Scotland–EU trade.

Putting sugar on the pill, the IFS commends an emphasis on improving productivity, boosting immigration in a country ageing faster than the rest of the UK and making a 'sober assessment of the weak fiscal position'. The central issue, however, remains: while the summary of the difficulties facing an independent Scots state are franker, the prose less urgently persuasive and there is an unapologetic reliance on British government publications and analysis, the moves and measures outlined for Scotland to gain independence with relatively little pain are seen as shaky structures to which to entrust the launch of a new nation state.

This isn't only the response of died-in-the-wool unionists. The prominent (Scots-born) economist and *Financial Times* columnist, John Kay, a former member of the SNP's board of economic advisers, wrote that the SGC report was 'like watching a teenager grow up', leaving behind its fantasies of success and glory – in this case, the 2013 'Scotland's Future' – and beginning to confront life as it is and will be. Yet, even so, the SGC 'falls short of presenting an economic case for independence'; Kay notes that 'Scotland needs a single market with England more (than with the EU).'

Kay's gentler critique finds a match in a longer and more detailed analysis by John McLaren, an economist and former adviser to Scottish Labour: McLaren's periodic 'Scottish Trends' reports provide a sharp and informed commentary on the Scots economy. He has worked with Andrew Wilson, and even provided a paper for the Commission's deliberations, on Scottish balance of payments, although had no hand, he writes, in the final report.

He thinks the SGC report is right to say little on oil, since future revenues will be limited (even an oil price of $100 a barrel would yield a revenue to government at most £3bn) and probably significantly less. He sees the fiscal projections as appropriately modest, and the pro-migration policies liberal and sensible. But he thinks that the costs of health, social care and education will rise more quickly than foreseen, that the SGC underestimates future debt and that there is 'a lack of analysis of the negative implications of breaking up the UK free trade area'.

In an interview with me, McLaren was highly critical of the account-ability of Scots politics and society: he doesn't think there's the close attention and a resulting critical commentary essential to a developed democracy. 'There's far too little holding to account. The parliamen-tary committees worked ok before the SNP took over. The opposition parties are branch parties with little money or expertise. The press had been tough on us when I was a special adviser but now they, too, have no money. Newsnight Scotland had been quite good, but now they fill it with celebs and sports stars. The think tanks are few, small and only one, the Fraser of Allander Institute, has the resources and expertise to do well on the economy.'

McLaren said that 'everyone accepts that the Growth Commission report was a lot better than Scotland's Future. It accepted the chal-lenge: said there would be a decade of austerity. The biggest criticism came from the SNP left – they had been deprived of the promised land. The focus of the report and the very fact that it is more realistic means that the Party is worried about losing part of its support. Will it lose the harder left, who think it's all about austerity? Or the hard-line nationalists, who just want to get out and think it's too cautious? The squeeze might come on them from Corbyn's Labour Party and the people returning to it now that it's more radical. [John] McDonnell [the Shadow Chancellor] made a speech in July 2018, saying the SNP is now the austerity party.

'The detail is where the Report came unstuck. The small country stuff was fluff – meaningless. And, an example, health spending in a country like Scotland will have to rise by three to four per cent a year

– and GDP growth will be far below that. People don't know about debt but they do know about health and, if they demand more, what gets less?

'Productivity is crucial: it's what determines the standard of living. It's lower in Scotland than in the UK; we don't understand, when it's gone down, why there hasn't been a bounce back. There isn't a solution, except to do what governments can do, which is to make education better – though it's getting worse.

'Scotland is more statist and the view there is that it isn't a bad thing. Politics of any side doesn't go there. In power, the Tories were patrician: they left the running of Scotland to the senior civil servants. Certainly there has been the growth of a dependency culture. And there is good reason for it. No other country I know suffered the same boom – at the end of the nineteenth and beginning of the twentieth centuries – and then bust in the 1920s, then relief during the war, then bust again, affecting Glasgow, and textiles in the Borders, and Dundee.'

McLaren, like much of Scots academia, is centre left: so is another close observer, Brian Ashcroft, an Emeritus Professor of Economics at Strathclyde University: his wife, Wendy Alexander, was leader of the Scots Labour Party (2007–2008). Ashcroft, who began his working life as a guitarist in a rock band successful enough to survive for a few years, gave his inaugural lecture to Strathclyde in 1996 on the theme of entrepreneurialism,[17] a subject not popular in today's far-left Labour party, with which both he and Alexander are out of sympathy. In the lecture, Ashcroft, quoting the Austrian economist Joseph Schumpeter, said in the lecture that though the Scots had been great inventors, they had been poor entrepreneurs for new ideas or projects: 'a task entirely different from the inventing of it'.

Calling up the golden age of Scots engineering and shipbuilding, he wrote that 'my reading of the works of the historians and economists who have looked at this period leads me to conclude that there was a general failure to realize new productive opportunities by introducing new products, processes and organizational arrangements in the declining heavy industries'. Scots, he was saying, had garnered many laurels in the nineteenth century, and then the beneficiaries of the great boom rested on them for the twentieth. Would they be won again in the twenty-first, with independence?

In a long talk with me in Glasgow, Ashcroft stressed that the owners, especially when enriched, had 'a number of interlocked directorates and were very conservative, all protecting their own in a society of powerful families, who didn't, in the main, take on professional management . . . though they were good at lobbying the Scottish Secretary – but it was bad for the Scots economy, because they got money to keep the enterprises going rather than modernizing and changing'.

This conservatism, Ashcroft believes, has had a long tail through the twentieth into the twenty-first century. 'Foreign investment saved Scotland to an extent in the 1960s and 1970s, but there were negatives – it may have dampened springs of native entrepreneurialism. Business enterprise research and development is still very low – about 0.7 per cent of GDP. In Sweden it's 2.5 per cent.'

Ashcroft doesn't share the popular view in Scotland, especially among the nationalists, but also on the left, that the concentration of financial power in the City of London is, as the nineteenth-century radical Richard Cobbett liked to call it, a 'Great Wen', a tumour on the national body, draining it of energy. He sees it as a neglected resource: 'I've argued for years that people in Scotland shouldn't criticize London and the City. We should use the growth hub of London as part of an integrated economy, to make the whole economy larger. We should remember that Scots resources, including Scots' brains, flow into London and the south east.'

The need for entrepreneurs is mentioned in the SGC, but not much stressed. Ashcroft is part of the consensus that it's more realistic than Scotland's Future – but not realistic enough. 'Scotland's trend rate of growth has tended to be lower than the UK since the 1960s – two per cent as against 2.3 to 2.5 per cent for the UK. Now it's clear that the trend rates have dropped. The Office of Budget Responsibility is forecasting weak growth. Brexit will make it worse. The Growth Commission doesn't take that into account. It's better, but it's very heavily politically structured. The whole report is contingent on growth forecasts, which are certainly over-optimistic. The export base is very small.

'Would independence make any difference to our low productivity? I'm doubtful. And I believe that if you have an economy as integrated as that of the UK, politics must follow.'

A guiding light on the global centre left, the Nobel Memorial prize-winning economic commentator for the *New York Times* Paul Krugman is more frankly discouraging. Professing himself sympathetic to a nation wishing to leave 'David Cameron's England' (he was writing in September 2014, just before the independence referendum), he says he is 'worried that the Scots government's view on independence seems deeply muddle headed'. To continue to use the pound will be possible, but 'the lesson of the Euro crisis, surely, is that sharing a common currency without having a shared federal government is very dangerous'. If there were a slump, then 'as part of the United Kingdom, Scotland would receive large de facto aid, just like a US state (or Wales); if it were on its own, it would be on its own'.[18]

From the centre-right Policy Exchange think tank, a note by its head of economics and social policy Warwick Lightfoot, a former Royal Bank of Scotland economist and Conservative government adviser, points out that, in confronting the 'awkward challenge that comes from the combination of developed and expensive welfare states bearing the costs of aging populations and increasingly competitive markets', Scotland outside of the UK will find life more, not less, hard, 'since the fiscal challenge on being deprived of the Barnett subsidy will involve difficult financial choices: either significantly lower spending or significantly higher taxes'.

Spreading his scepticism beyond the nationalist camp, he notes that: 'Since 1998, Scottish ministers in the Labour, Liberal Democrat, and SNP parties have used their discretion to undo partially public-service reforms made in the 1980s and 1990s, and to avoid the public reform agenda since 2000. Scottish ministers have accommodated public-sector producer interests, rather than challenged them. The conduct of the Scottish executive since 1997 does not suggest that an independent Scotland would be a model of efficiency, economy, and effectiveness, in which the public sector would adjust to changing and difficult circumstances.'[19]

The harshest response to the SGC report came from an English-born, Scots-based entrepreneur, Kevin Hague, founder and executive director of the M8 retail and Endura cycling accessories companies and chairman of the pro-Union group, These Islands, which published his critique.[20] Hague thus comes from an angle disposed to be hostile, with a reputation for hard talk: but the blitz of sharp disagreement with the Commission's views often shares the more gently expressed reservations of others, and probes painfully into the weaker areas.

Hague has invested some money and a great deal of time opposing Scots nationalism, mainly through critiques of its economic policies and claims. In a talk he gave at the University of St Andrews in February 2019, he laid out his view that 'the European Union has been built around a single market, which allows for freedom of movement of goods, services, capital and people. This, of course, requires common market regulation which, by covering areas like environmental protection, workers' rights, policies on immigration and much more, requires a degree of moral solidarity, an acceptance of shared values and a shared sense of responsibility. The Union that is the UK shares these characteristics, but goes further – it is a much deeper union. This is most obviously illustrated by the fact that the UK, in contrast with the EU, does not require its constituent nations to be fully fiscally autonomous; within the UK there are fiscal transfers which mean that for citizens of the UK's constituent nations, access to education, healthcare and social welfare are not constrained by their nation's economic performance. Any economic union requires a degree of moral solidarity: with its fiscal transfers, single currency and shared defence budget, the UK is demonstrably a far deeper union than the EU, and that has been built on a much deeper, although rarely articulated, sense of moral solidarity.'

Hague is not an economist by training: but his response to the Sustainable Growth Commission has been reviewed and endorsed by several senior economists.[21] He has taken it upon himself to try to educate the Scots electorate on the fragility of the SNP's promises: 'On the EU – the biggest single question is the currency. If independent, Scotland's currency would not be its own, nor stable; so the EU would likely insist it joined the Euro. It would have to make cuts in public spending of about 20 per cent, and that would hurt a lot.

'The Nats are always keen to show that the process of becoming independent would be short and cheap. In fact, it would be prolonged, and cost billions. But, of course, if you're a nationalist and want independence, *any* price is worth paying!'

As he pulled apart the Growth Commission report, his main criticisms include:

- the report's selective choice of high performing small countries from which to draw a conclusion about the performance of small countries in general, and the fact that while explicitly rejecting the low tax, high income inequality models of countries like Singapore and Hong Kong, the report still includes them in their 'small advanced economy' comparison cohort;
- his observation that the countries whose policies the report most aspires to emulate – New Zealand, Denmark and Finland – do not in fact out-perform larger economies at all, using the Commission's own chosen comparison metrics;
- that, therefore, when the Commission asserts an independent Scotland pursuing the report's recommendations could achieve the economic performance defined by their 'small advanced economy' cohort, this contradicts the empirical evidence the report itself provides;
- that far from being more realistic than the White Paper it purports to replace, the Commission is in fact even more optimistic about the cost savings that an independent Scotland would be able to realize painlessly;
- that the report underplays to the point of disguising the fact that a decade of austerity is being recommended, far harsher than that historically imposed by the UK government;
- underplaying the adverse effects of 'sterlingization' and of losing access to the UK single market, including the significant job losses implied by the latter.

Hague's shrewdest blow is to argue that the SGC report, 'by implication, makes a strong case for Scotland staying in the UK'. He supports this by pointing out that:

- The Report itself admits the volatility of small countries' economies, and that large advanced economies have the advantage of being able both to smooth out regional economic problems and sustain relatively large deficits;
- The Report's assertion that Scotland underperforms is undercut by a separate statement that 'economic output per head is the best of the regions outside of London and the south east';

- That the 'underperformance' the report observes is based on Scotland's notional GERS deficit, which in turn is almost entirely explained by Scotland's higher per capita spending, something that is enabled by 'an effective fiscal transfer from the rest of the UK of £9bn to 10bn per annum';
- That the economies of scale available in a large UK market will disappear in a small Scots one.

What this means, he writes, is that the report helps us understand how being in the UK allows Scotland to enjoy the benefits of a shared currency and large domestic market; how it allows Scotland to avoid the fiscal constraints that would inevitably apply were Scotland a stand-alone economy and how Scotland within the UK benefits from levels of public spending that would otherwise be unsustainable.

In conversation, the SGC report's author, Andrew Wilson, is agreeable, low key, fluent. He does see independence as 'a great liberation' but defines it as an opportunity, 'to be allowed to grapple with reality'. He readily acknowledges that a hard border with England would be 'very bad' and hopes for 'a thoughtful and orderly transition'. He believes that a realistic goal would be to raise exports from 20 per cent of GDP to 40 per cent. He believes strongly in branding and says that Scotland must work much harder on its brand: 'New Zealand spends ten times more on its brand than Scotland.'

He sums up the challenge as 'going for three 'ps' – productivity, participation and population'. Productivity comes from better education, better infrastructure, higher skills. Participation, 'a situation where people feel involved and participate in a common project', instancing a project, the Big Noise Programme, started by the retired Episcopalian Bishop of Edinburgh, Richard Holloway, where children from poor areas are taught to play musical instruments – a programme which reports a high degree of success and growth. Population 'is the biggest thing we have to do – we have few people foreign born compared to England. Of the migrants, the Poles are the largest, then . . . guess . . . Americans! Then Germans, Irish and Indians. We must encourage more people to come. We must make Scotland a beacon for people.'

I asked if he thought it might spark an anti-immigrant backlash. 'The issue needs firm leadership on this. In creating the strategy we should try for cross-party agreement. When a national debate is had, people can become convinced it is in the public interest.'

He again stressed the need for realism in attaining independence: 'the core of the debate is this – that we face up to a transition that will be difficult, but we succeed in making the country ready to forge ahead and to emulate the records of the small countries that are successful. It will be hard work but it will be worth it. We tell people it's hard but that we can get through it.'

In fact, Wilson aside, the leaders of Scots nationalism *don't* tell their followers it will be hard: perhaps one reason why he wasn't invited to present the Growth Commission Report at the 2019 Edinburgh conference. They do say it will be a liberation. Wilson's comment that independence would allow Scotland to 'grapple with reality' is in contradiction to the still-dominant rhetoric in his party: he points to a time when Scotland is on its own, no longer protected by the rest of the UK, testing its mettle in a rapidly changing, bitterly competitive world. It has a noble ring to it, perhaps more noble in its implications than he meant. It suggests an impatience with the English subsidies, even with the long-term argument made by the nationalists that these are an inadequate attempt to substitute a handout for uniquely Scots access to the riches of the North Sea.

Instead of this demeaning relationship, it would be better, even with a dwindling patrimony of oil, to face the world with ardour and courage, cast aside the English dole and its leaders' sentimentalism, such as that voiced by then Prime Minister David Cameron, speaking in September 2014, just before the referendum vote, who said that he spoke for the millions of the British 'who would be utterly heart-broken by the break-up of the United Kingdom'.[22] Enough of all that guff! Grasp instead a non-violent, Scots version of the Irish republican motto (and organization) *Sinn Fein*, ourselves alone, with and against the world as it is. This would not be the world filtered through the sophistications and compromises of the Foreign and Commonwealth office and the Treasury, but revealed in all its fears and promises. If that is the purer vision suggested by 'grappling with reality', and it must be that in some measure, then it assumes a much greater gathering of the national will and perseverance than anything so far promised to their members and followers by the nationalists.

The efforts to convince Scots of future wealth when made independent by the SNP, and the government it has occupied since 2007, have been unseemly. The re-creation of Scotland as an independent nation state after more than three centuries of Union, the largest part of that beneficial to its economy, is owed more than hyped-up economic forecasting, deliberate ignoring or minimizing of evident problems and the promise of becoming Denmark in a decade. Though Wilson has, with some resistance in the party, moved the official position to one which recognizes some hard facts and grounds economic strategy in the market within an open economy, the Growth Commission could not escape the need to grossly over-sweeten the pill of independence.

It cannot escape that imperative, because with the great gains made by the nationalists in the first two decades of the 2000s came a dilemma familiar to any successful grouping that comes in from the margins to the centre of politics – in the SNP's case, to dominate the centre. When marginal, protests and propaganda against the powers that be are the sharpest, often the only weapons in the rhetorical armoury. When central, the public begins to insist on plans that make sense.

The SGC's commitment to a market economy also roused protests from Common Weal, a nationalist grouping with a news website, CommonSpace, situated to the SNP's left, seeking to harden the Party's considerable left against the Commission's conclusions.

Arguably, the left and other nationalists demanding more say on the party's direction should be careful what they wish for, since more open debate would reveal the fragility of the Party's position. No frank assessment of the process of achieving independence and maintaining support for it through the early years could be other than a warning of years of spending cuts and economic shocks, reducing the economic level of the new state below that which it enjoyed as one of the UK nations. That would need to be coupled with a list of essential and hard reforms to again raise the economic level, and to maintain it among or close to the ranks of the successful small economies which the SGC report sees as Scotland's proper place.

But if such a frank assessment were produced, the project of independence would need to fall back on the bedrock of a strong, popular momentum for independence at any cost: a minority sentiment in Scotland. The nationalists are stuck with proving that a Scottish state could break out of slow British and European growth – the experts' forecasts for both decline as this is written – and demonstrate a capacity for innovation, entrepreneurialism (whether private or state-led), successful export performance, high educational and training standards and governance at national and local levels, which supported economic expansion as their prime mission. None of these necessary elements have been demonstrated, except fitfully, by the Scottish governments since devolution and, in some cases, the reverse has been the case.

Were 'grappling with reality' to be the motto of an independence movement, it would be at once stirring and daunting: stirring, because it presupposed a nation united in its determination to be a small but exemplary force in the world; daunting, because it presupposes decades of hard work and belt-tightening to produce an economy and society akin to that developed by Japan from the 1960s onward (and now threatened by demographic decline, as is Scotland, if less dramatically), followed by its maintenance through self discipline and focused governance at every level, public and private.

There is no a priori reason why Scots could not attempt such a national project. But the nationalist movement has not prepared them for it, nor is likely to. It has instead insisted that independence is a deliverance from all British evil, and especially that independence is a route to prosperity. It may be, ultimately: but cutting away the rest of the UK cannot but mean years of a lower GDP than would have been all but certain, were it to remain in the Union.

The sector that most reveals the failure of the nationalists to prepare Scotland for a great, independent, leap forward is education. The failure is the most damaging, because Scots believed that their schooling, and their universities were among the best in the world: indeed, were a model for the world.

That Scots were among the best-educated people in the Western world over the past three centuries or more, was no myth. Presbyterianism, the exacting, Calvin-derived, religion that, under the leadership of John Knox, captured much of the Scottish imagination from the sixteenth century till the twentieth and demanded unmediated reverence for the word of God as transmitted in the bible. This, and a system of teaching in schools which were, by legislation, attached to the kirks (with, to be sure, uneven teaching by poorly paid dominies), ensured that many in the peasant and working class could read.

The *Calvinist Book of Discipline*, which laid down proper behaviour for the faithful, prescribed literacy as being 'at the very heart of the programme for religious revolution. It was the means by which the essential precepts of religious belief were to be instilled in the young' . . . to 'foster the virtuous education and godly upbringing of the youth of this realm'.[23] It meant that Robert Burns could write, in his sentimentally evocative 'Cotter's Saturday Night', that the head of the family, the cotter (tenant farmer) could after supper take the family bible, 'ance his Father's pride' and 'priest-like . . . read the sacred page'. That, in most of Europe, and even in England of the late eighteenth century, would be the exception. In Scotland, Burns was, probably unthinkingly, using the example of his own pious father.

That father, William Burnes (so spelled) was himself a cotter, and both devout and literate, fluent in Scots and English, so ambitious for his sons' education that he went private, convincing several of his neighbours with children to hire a young (still a teenager) teacher, John Murdoch, to teach reading, writing, mathematics and, of course, the scriptures, since 'he saw education and morality as bound together'.[24] That binding of a Protestant religion which rejected, as he put it in the 'Cotter's Saturday Night', '[Catholicism's] pomp of method and of art . . . devotion's every grace, except the heart!' was designed to remove intercession by priest and pope, to empower the faithful Christian to understand the word of God as transmitted by the bible, and to enjoin him to a fervid obeisance (Burns stayed with the words, and mainly skipped the obeisance).

The claim of a democratic national system was always open to qualification: as ever, the better off came off better in the matter of education. But it could be fairly said, in the eighteenth and nineteenth centuries and into the twentieth, to be usually more democratic, in the sense of being more open to students of varying social status than in England, the comparison which always matters most, in everything. By the sixteenth century, Scotland had five universities: St Andrews, founded

1413; Glasgow, 1451; two in Aberdeen: King's, 1495 and Marischal, 1593, merged in 1858; and Edinburgh, 1582. England had but two, if considerably older: Oxford, c.1096 and Cambridge, 1209.

The cold northern universities were serious centres of study, and became more so: in the eighteenth century, they were among the best in Europe. Adam Smith, who studied (from the age of fourteen), and later taught, at Glasgow, had a spell in Oxford's Balliol College in the 1740s, and wrote, in *The Wealth of Nations*, that most of the professors had given up teaching: Smith had a miserable time, though he read a great deal from the stacks of the Bodleian library.

The Scots' were cheaper than the two English universities: they gave a wide general education, but also trained young men in the law, in medicine and in theology: 'they certainly appealed to those seeking to make a career in the world on the basis of ability and training rather than of inherited position'.[25] Since there were many fewer good careers open to educated young men in Scotland than in England, they tended to look abroad: the expansion of empire, and England, gave them place.

The country's universities have retained many of their high standards, though they are now eclipsed, in the *Times Educational Supplement*'s rankings of world universities, by several in England. Oxford and Cambridge are first and second in the *TES* 2019 rankings, with London's Imperial College at ninth and University College London fourteenth. The top twenty are, England's star performers apart, mainly American. Edinburgh, the first Scot in the rankings, comes in at twenty-ninth. The Complete University Guide 2020, for the UK only, has Cambridge and Oxford first and second, with St Andrews third: Edinburgh is sixteenth, Glasgow eighteenth and Aberdeen twenty-ninth. Apart from the consensus on Oxford and Cambridge, guides vary considerably, including on the rankings of the Scots: but all the old Scots universities usually feature in the top one to 30 of the 130 in Britain.

Large debates swirl about Scots universities, as about universities everywhere: yet there are no serious, long-term concerns about the overall quality of the ancient centres, nor of the newcomers, such as Dundee University, formerly a college of nearby St Andrews, which achieved independent status in the 1960s following the Robbins Report on Higher Education in 1963. Robbins also prompted the creation de novo of the University of Stirling, as well as university status for

Strathclyde, in Glasgow (formerly the Andersonian Institute) and Heriot Watt, with a distinguished history, from the 1820s, as a school of arts, science and technology 'for the working man' (women came, earlier than in other colleges, in 1869), in 1966.

The largest charge against the Scots universities in the twentieth century was less on quality, and more on culture, and on loss of individuality to waves of Anglicization. It came in George Davie's *The Democratic Intellect*,[26] much admired by nationalists for its uncompromising championing of a Scots educational system which it sees as rich in teaching the useful arts but committed, still, to 'general studies of a non-utilitarian kind', along French rather than English lines. The latter was seen as ignoring the search for an equalization of the understanding of students from quite different social backgrounds, and shrinking from the inculcation of a respect for the moral virtues. Davie lamented the movement in the twentieth century towards English-style specialization: though in fact, both English and Scots educators sought inspiration on the continent, especially in Germany and France.

Scots schools are, and are especially in the twenty-first century, a different matter: and are, in the 2020s, one of the most contested areas of the nationalists' policies.

The Presbyterian concern for children's souls and their need to be literate enough to read scriptures was, at least formally, blind as to class: all were equal in the sight of the Lord. This was an evangelical religion: and, as today, in Africa, South America and parts of the United States, it appealed as much if not more to the lower classes as to the elite; hence the more numerous lower classes were sought out as vessels to be filled with the Lord's words. Yet, as the cities and trades developed, and as agriculture, much improved through emulation of the more advanced English systems, and pulled by increased trade in the decades after the Union, produced a larger surplus, so both a middle and an artisanal class grew, and the now starkly familiar inequalities of a class-divided society took hold.

Their children, pushed by their tiger mothers, or tiger fathers like William Burnes, to get on, were the beneficiaries of the improving standards of primary, then secondary education: their instruction in the basics of arithmetic, reading, writing and other skills was a spur to the wealth of the nation of Scotland, and a large part of the backbone of empire, especially India. These boys were the basis of the Scots claim for national primacy in teaching the people: it was justified as far as it went, and in contrast with other nations. But the children of the poor, especially the poor Irish families who flooded in their thousands into Glasgow and the west coast conurbations as they grew in the mid to late nineteenth century, often couldn't or wouldn't put their boys through an education in schools often hostile to their religion, and whose cost, though modest, was too exorbitant for their earnings.

In the twentieth century, those who could afford it sent their sons, and increasingly their daughters, to fee-paying schools. Edinburgh has the highest percentage of private school pupils of any city in the UK, with a quarter of Edinburgh children attending one. The lower classes, whose education had been in a sometimes rich, sometimes skeletal mixture of religious, parish and private schools were increasingly mar-shalled into state provision, which, under the guidance of the Scottish Education Department, divided the school population into two. This was defined by the secretary of the Department, George MacDonald, as 'the majority of distinctly limited intelligence, and an extremely important minority drawn from all ranks and classes who are capable of responding to a much more severe call'.[27]

The explicit discrimination between the 'distinctly limited' and the 'extremely important', codified in SED circular 44 in 1923, was highly controversial and in places ignored: but it did set a limit of twelve years of age on the education of the 'limited' while giving the 'important' another five years, and a path to university. It was modified by stages and the general spread of comprehensive schools with common teaching gave the 'limiteds' paths to 'importance', which many took.

Its effects lingered long, however. The school I went to was comprehensive in the sense that everyone but the sons and daughters of some of the professional and relatively wealthy families in the East Fife catchment area, mainly fishing and farming villages, went to the same school: but in the 1950s and 1960s, it strove hard to make the small academic stream in the 'A' class feel special. We were assigned which streams to join according to the results of the '11+' exams, taken in primary school. The 'A' boys played rugby while the rest played football: a games teacher liked to quote, after Oscar Wilde, that 'rugby is a game for barbarians played by gentlemen, football a game for gentlemen played by barbarians'. The 'A' students came to the school, in the largest of the fishing villages, Anstruther, by train if they lived in other villages: the rest by bus – an extraordinary division. We in the 'A' stream, of course, got nearly all the prizes, such as the medals for science, mathematics, languages, English. The head boy and head girl, and the prefects, were always from the 'A' stream. My tiger mother, a beautician, who would have sent me to Eton had she had the money, liked the system, as I think did most of the other parents with 'A' stream pupils. One or two didn't. A boy in my stream, his father a skipper, demanded to play football and, with a cloud of disapproval over his head, was permitted to do so.

That's gone: comprehensive schools avoid such distinctions like the plague, though the bullying of the academically inclined by the non-academically inclined, marked in my school, continues everywhere. The decades'-long division of schools into 'junior' and 'senior' second-ary schools was ended, with an immediate sharp rise in pupils staying on till around age eighteen, taking 'O' and 'A' level exams.

The new battleground on education puts the nationalist government in its centre. In large measure, the party which has done most to claim Scotland's special virtue stands indicted for ruining Scotland's once most prized virtuous boast. The boast wasn't empty, even recently: in the OECD's annual PISA rankings (nothing to do with the leaning tower: it's the Programme for International Student Assessment) showed, in 2000, Scotland's students near the top, as, many Scots thought, was only natural, given the country's traditions. Six years later, the fairest-of-them-all looking glass was shattered: a score for science had fallen from 513 in 2012 to 497 in 2016 – below the international average, and below England's score of 512: the UK score was 509. Reading and mathematics also declined, but were at average rather than below it. Sir Michael Wilshaw, the former head of the education regulator Ofsted, complained that Scotland and Wales (the latter had a science score of 485) were damaging the UK's standing in the rankings.[28]

This wasn't all. The bi-annual Scottish Survey of Literacy and Numeracy, a Scottish government data set, showed a decline from 2012 to 2014, and a further decline from 2014 to 2016. In response, the gov-ernment ended the survey. This meant, a cross-party report published in April 2019 claimed, that John Swinney, the Education Secretary and deputy SNP leader, could not tell if literacy and numeracy were improving, or not. Nor did parents, which would seem to have been the reason for ending the survey.

Ruth Davidson, the then Scottish Conservatives' leader, told her conference in March 2017 that she would launch a 'back to basics review' of the system used in schools, a system known as the 'Curriculum for Excellence'. Her choice of words was pointed at a growing target: the Curriculum for Excellence is now thought, by many critics, to be the culprit in the decline of Scots education: and by many of these, including the most influential, to run counter to Scots tradition, which they believe was the true carrier of Scots excellence.

The Curriculum for Excellence is not, however, an SNP invention. It came out of a consultation exercise early in the life of the Scottish government, in 2002, when Labour was in power in Scotland, and in the UK. A nineteen-member Curriculum Review Group, all Scots education professionals, was put together to produce the model for a new style of teaching, and to lay out the purposes for education in the twenty-first century: in 2004, it produced a report, which proposed that the purpose of teaching, from the ages of three to eighteen, was to 'enable all children to develop their capacities as successful learners, confident individuals, responsible citizens and effective contributors to society'. All the political parties, including the Conservatives, endorsed it. There was a relatively lengthy period of preparation, and then the new system was introduced into schools in 2010–2011.

An early review of the new Curriculum's progress by Mark Priestley and Sarah Minty of the University of Stirling in 2014 was titled: 'Curriculum for Excellence: a brilliant idea, but . . .'[29] In fact, the title should have read 'a brilliant *ideal*', and could then have lost the 'but'. Successfully teaching pupils to learn, to acquire or increase confidence, to become responsible citizens and make an effective contribution to society are all fine goals. They are, however, hardly novel ('while the language is idiosyncratic to Scotland, the basic concept is more widespread'): and they better describe what the end result of teaching should be, not the context within which the four capacities are presented to pupils, nor the content of the teaching.

When the ideas are translated into policies and activity, as they must be if they are to be acted upon, they find, in the schools, large and apparently unforeseen problems. Teachers like the ideal and many, in interviews for the Priestly–Minty research, said they had long hoped for an approach that allowed more flexibility, more independent initiative on the part of the teachers and more freedom for the children to explore. Priestly and Minty noted, however, that to their surprise they saw these 'same teachers launching trenchant criticisms at the CfE'.

Many said they didn't know what was expected of them; several felt they were 'floundering in the dark'; that injunction to collaborate with each other in lessons raised issues of specialism and different approaches, which weren't easy to overcome; only a few discussed collaboration with other colleagues and undertook inter-disciplinary learning (IDL) with them; that the pupils, encouraged to be more creative, sometimes took this as an opportunity to be more noisy; that some felt they could no longer control the class as they had been used to do, though some, mainly primary school teachers, did enjoy the greater freedom both for themselves and their pupils.

In a finding that seems to be among the most important, the authors reported that in spite of the CfE's insistence that children learn best through active engagement and experience as well as dialogue with other learners, many teachers 'harbour implicitly transmissionist views of knowledge and learning, viewing it as the delivery of content' ('transmissionism' does not seem, to one long out of school, to be in itself bad). One teacher said that 'at the end of the day you're going to be looking at kids trying to get these qualifications to get a job or further study. And you have to make sure they get there.'

It's clear from the research that many teachers, on balance, liked the new approach and many, on balance, didn't: it's hard to tell which side wins out. The Priestly–Minty research was done only two or three years after the CfE was introduced, and some of the findings point to the problems of a system, any system, still bedding down. Yet in a blog in February 2019, Priestley, Scotland's foremost specialist on educational curricula, found that inter-disciplinary learning, strongly recommended in the CfE, had not been widely or systematically adopted, and his language was harsher than in the earlier research report in saying so: 'Early experimentation with CfE saw some innovation, much of it fairly dubious, and often driven by a fallacious assumption that the new curriculum was replacing a focus on knowledge with an emphasis on skills acquisition, leading in many cases to (inter-disciplinary learning) that ignored a key component – disciplinary knowledge.'

'Disciplinary knowledge' has become the central element in the critique of the new curriculum. There are wisps of myth around it: a virtual nostalgia for the days when 'lads o' pairts', clever young men from all levels of society, would read philosophy in their mid-teens under the guidance of strict but clever dominies. Still there were substantial issues to answer, which the nationalists have not.

The most persistent and distinguished critic of the CfE is Lindsay Paterson, Professor of Education Policy at Edinburgh University. He's been unremitting in reminding Scotland's political parties that they all agreed to introduce the system: 'the SNP, Conservatives, Labour, Liberal Democrats and Greens may now argue vociferously over whether the curriculum is a beacon of progressive ideas or an underfunded shambles, but they are all responsible for its existing at all'.[30]

Paterson does not believe it is progressive, and regards the shambles as an expression, not the root, of its basic flaw. That flaw is a replacement of knowledge by process, children being encouraged to lead discovery by saying what they want to know, not being told what they should know: 'there is no recognition in the curriculum of a canon of necessary ideas or practices, no acknowledgement of any kind of theoretical framework that might give coherence to each curricular subject'.

He gives an example: if a teacher encouraged twelve-year-olds to investigate a local canal, they would find that 'there are potential themes relating to ecology, economic history, gender relations in the past, sport and exercise today, and much else. Fine, but none of this makes proper sense without some systematic knowledge of each of these specific contexts. The ecology of a particular place can be understood only in an overarching framework of how plants and animals co-exist. Interpreting the history of a two-century-old mode of transport requires a wider understanding of the industrial revolution. And so on: new knowledge requires old knowledge.'

Most damagingly: the CfE discriminates against those from poorer homes, an outcome that Scots education, with various degrees of sincerity and effectiveness, has long striven to avoid. 'Knowledge can . . . be emancipating, and knowledge acquired through schools provides that opportunity to people who would not get it from home. If schools stop teaching structured knowledge, then inequality of access to knowledge will widen, because the children of the well-educated and the wealthy will get it in other ways.'

Paterson, in interview, says that major changes began once the comprehensive system had become universal in Scotland, save for a few private schools. 'For example in mathematics: you no longer had to give a proof. Until the 1980s, you did. And there was always Shakespeare, but in one case the question was prompted by a quote from an essay by Orwell, and I think now teachers would assume that most kids didn't know who Orwell was. Until then, any seventeen-year-old at any level *would* be assumed to know. And thus literature doesn't get the background to anchor it to a time and place; see Alan Bloom and the closing of the American mind.

'The Curriculum for excellence is a symptom of this approach. See Eric Hirsch – he was horrified when he learned that many of the black pupils in school had no idea about literature and current events – many didn't know who Martin Luther King was. He argued for much more foundational knowledge, and he was called conservative.

'The new arguments say that subjects must be free of artificial constraints, but all learning is "artificial", and has constraints. If you don't take the core approach you write off centuries of knowledge.'

Eric D. Hirsch, ninety-two in March 2020, is Emeritus Professor of Education at the University of Virginia, and writes books arguing for a core curriculum and strong basis of knowledge. Hirsch says he is of the left – 'old left'. The old left, and right, agreed on the need for core teaching: and the old left also wanted it to be open to all. His determination that children from poorer backgrounds not be disadvantaged led him to found and direct the Core Knowledge Foundation, which supplies curricula and assistance to those schools teaching a core agenda. According to Hirsch and Paterson, the new left want to make it fairer by taking away, or diluting the core.

It can't be said that the nationalist government ignores children: it has gone out of its way to care for and protect them. Since 2017, it has given every family with a new-born baby a 'Baby Box' containing baby clothes, a blanket, a bath towel, a baby wrap, toys, bibs, an ear thermometer and nursing pads: a substantial gift for a poor family. The government went too far, in claiming that the box itself, if used as a crib, reduced infant mortality: the Finnish welfare agency Kela, which pioneered the baby box, objected, saying no such evidence existed and that the low infant mortality in the country was attributable to the healthcare system, not the box.

In fact, Scotland's infant mortality level is lower than in England and Wales, and was before the box was introduced: indeed, in 2017, it was the lowest in Europe, so the claim was pointless. The baby box's real merit lies in giving children in poor families something of a better start in life than they might otherwise have had. Where it may make a difference is not the babies' health, but to Scotland's birth rate – still in decline among Scots-born families, growing only thanks to the births in recently immigrant families.

However, a more ambitious project has focused active opposition. The 'Named Person Scheme' would give every child, at birth, a 'named person', who might be a midwife, a health visitor or a head teacher, who would be a point of contact for both parents and children if they wished advice or had concerns. The project was seen as intrusive from its inception, especially by the churches: and was strongly opposed by the Scottish Conservatives. A claim that the proposed law breaches human rights legislation was thrown out by the Court of Session in Edinburgh: but an appeal to the UK Supreme Court produced a judgement that parts of the legislation breached rights to privacy and family life, while stating that the aims of the measure were both 'legitimate and benign'. Some of the fears about the project's introduction were that children could use the named person to attack parents in a domestic battle: more solidly, the named person could have access to the children's and the parents' data.[31] As popular resistance grew, the project was dropped in September 2019.

The commentator and former teacher Elga Graves believes the SNP's approach to children and families to be both patronizing and misdirected, especially in the case of women: 'almost everything the SNP government touches or says in relation to children and families fails to resonate with women', she wrote in the *Scottish Review*:[32] and echoes Paterson in arguing that the CfE 'demands a certain standard of literacy as a prerequisite, a standard that Scotland did not and does not have'. In an interview, she said that 'teachers are swamped: they don't know which way to turn. It is right that children should have more experiential learning but it's the way it's done that's wrong. For example, the weight of evidence suggests that the child who comes from a poorer background requires radically different teaching.'

Radically different teaching was what the Glasgow businessman Jim McColl planned through his creation of Newlands College, a small school, opened in 2014, for children between fourteen and sixteen from very poor families, aimed at giving them both vocational training, and teaching in mathematics, literacy and English. The children were chosen by the heads of the schools in which they attended, or had ceased to attend.

In an interview, McColl said that he had, in the early 2000s, chaired a welfare working group and had spoken to head teachers on the state of education in Glasgow. 'I learned that 20 per cent of the kids just disappear – they don't engage at all with the system – go into poverty, into crime, they go to jail, they're often in poor health.'

McColl said that 90 per cent of the children who came to Newlands College stayed on. 'They often come from a family that's broken and we give them a family: we expose them to the world of work; some are taken on, others stay on and go to college – they had thought this was out of reach. We see them growing up into adults, with manners, smartly dressed.'

Newlands, opened in 2014, operated for five years and then was closed. It depended on public money, from the Scottish government and Glasgow Council: the Council said that it had gone through a 'demonstration phase', but that no more public money could be available. It blamed the Newlands management team for 'the appalling way' they handled the announcement of the closure, which would seem to be a minor criticism.[33]

Reports spoke of suspicions by teachers and officials that Newlands would be an example for English-style academies and free schools: a direction the Scots government has always refused to take, seeing English education as productive of inequalities. An advisory group set up to monitor progress in education contains some Scots experts: the rest are mainly from the US and Canada, with no English representative.

The former Director of Education in Clackmannanshire, now an education consultant, Keir Bloomer, deplored the Newlands closure, asking rhetorically if Scotland could ever entertain any experimentation in schools outside of the standard comprehensive. In an interview, Bloomer also lamented the drop in Scots educational standards: 'in 2000 Scotland was in the top quartile of the PISA results in all three subjects – English, mathematics and literacy. Now it's in the second quartile. If you take away the poor and developing countries, we would be very low down.

'Yet improvement can come. In 1988, under the Blair government, the London Challenge came in. It greatly improved teaching in London, which was something of a disaster zone. An average London family's kids will be better educated than rich kids elsewhere in the country.

'I think most failures (in Scotland) have been policy failures, not implementation failures. It's a consequence of the government being a campaigning group. Pleasing as many constituencies as possible is most important.' Bloomer's strictures appear to have some basis. A new Education Bill which promised 'radical change' and prescribed standardized tests beginning at age five, was scrapped by Education Minister John Swinney after strong opposition from the teaching union, the Education Institute of Scotland, and the local authorities. In the two occasions I have heard Swinney speak outside of parliament, he has spoken under the aegis of the EIS and in the company of Larry Flanagan, the general secretary. On both occasions, he strongly attacked critics of his policy on the grounds that they were insulting Scots teachers, a way of closing down debate. He was, however, constrained to back down on two of the party's central programmes: in June 2019, an education bill described as the centrepiece of a revived schools curriculum was abandoned as unworkable.

Education policy is a war zone among experts: but the experience of London has been that strongly directed learning of the basic subjects, improved discipline and inspired teaching produces results, often, but not universally, in academies and free schools. The aversion to English examples may be damaging Scotland's children, as, according to Paterson, the Curriculum for Excellence will ensure that, 'since children only get one chance to learn, a whole generation will have been betrayed'.

5

TO BE YERSEL'

The supposed dreariness of domination by the English was not, in the post-war period, reflected in Scotland's creativity. Indeed, since the 1960s, Scots writing has been described as undergoing a renaissance. This has mainly been centred on fiction: but in a culture which produced little in the way of drama, with the major (and usually ignored, except by the public) exceptions of James Bridie and J. M. Barrie, Scotland has seen a flourishing of drama for both stage and TV, by those including David Greig, David Harrower, Gregory Burke, Armando Iannucci, Alistair Beaton, John Byrne, Sharman MacDonald, Simon Farquhar and Catherine Grosvenor, among others.

In the academy and out of it, there has been strong growth of a large scholarly community writing on Scots literature (Scottish studies, once a Cinderella, has surely taken off). Hundreds, if not thousands, of essays and books, often stimulating, from a large variety of authors, not all Scots, on Scots writing and art, from the first Irish–Scots fragments in pre- and early medieval times to the art of the twenty-first century – some of it brilliant and some of it disputatious, like their subjects, if usually less violently so. Never have those who wish to understand Scots culture of the past and present had so much material to assist them: and much of it of high quality.

This isn't an attempt to join the critical community, to pursue an

assessment of the output of contemporary Scots writers. It is to note
that leading Scots writers in the twentieth and twenty-first centuries
have, in many cases, been remarkable, not so much for putting Scots
identity, politics, character and relationship with England at the centre
of their creative work (Scott, above all others, did that) as for seeing
Scotland caught in a cultural crisis caused, in the main, by the loss of its
political centre since the Union of 1707. The poets Hugh MacDiarmid
and Edwin Muir; the novelists Alasdair Gray, James Kelman and
William McIlvanney and many others played and some still play a very
large part in setting the political scene for the Scots and some of the
English and foreign intelligentsia, especially that (by far the largest)
part of it on the left.

Many others played or play a more modest part: even a poet of
private life and closely observed quotidian society as Douglas Dunn
feels occasionally impelled to enter the political lists, if moderately.
And nearly all would claim that Scots are more caring, more inclined
to social democracy: Sir Tom Devine, the country's leading historian,
came out for independence a little before the 2014 referendum, saying
to *The Observer* that 'Scottish people . . . are wedded to a social democratic agenda and the kind of political values which sustained and were
embedded in the welfare state of the late 1940s and 1950s.'[1]

The SNP describes itself as a social democratic party, which has not
always been the case: others within its ranks, and outside of them, call
for full-blooded socialism. The journalist Neal Ascherson, among the
foremost commentators from the nationalist side, suggests that 'the
Scots are communitarian rather than individualist, democratic in their
obsession with equality . . . spartan in their insistence that solidarity
means more than free self-expression'.[2] This was a common view, one
of the many points of contact between nationalist politicians and writers and commentators, in a society notable, on the nationalist camp,
for the closeness of the artist–politician relationship which, in others, is
usually more fraught, or at least distant.

More than any other literature on these islands and more than many
in the world – France and Russia are prominent exceptions, both much
admired by many Scots writers, in some cases because they are not
English – does Scots literature attempt to define the character, what a
Russian of the nineteenth century and even now might call the *soul* of

the country. The most visible literary and critical writers of the past century or more are confident that it has one, but that an all-too visible worm, England, has sickened it, and is destroying its life.

That has meant that, increasingly, artists in Scotland tended in the twentieth century to the socialist and nationalist side of the spectrum. Eric Linklater's *Magnus Merriman* (1934) was written after he stood, dramatically unsuccessfully, as a nationalist parliamentary candidate in East Fife in 1933: but the comically satirical portraits of leading nationalists marked it as the writing of one coolly detached from politics, devoted to his art, more concerned with authoritarianism abroad than nationalism in his own country, where his attachment to it seemed pretty much a dilettante one.

Nothing dilettante about Scots literature's largest twentieth-century figure: he was its opposite. He was also opposite to Linklater in another way: he was more attracted to authoritarianism abroad than to democracy in Scotland. Hugh MacDiarmid, like Walt Whitman was in life and remains in legacy, large, contradicts himself, contained multitudes, drove himself through these multitudes of contradictions within himself to try to get at an art, often an explicitly political art, which veered this way and that but was always seen, in his eyes and in that of his disciples, as necessary for Scots poetry but, much more, necessary for Scotland and the Scots.

One of these disciples, among the most loyal, was Alan Bold, himself a poet, who wrote a fine and very admiring biography,[3] describing him as one who saw no intrinsic value in consistency: he was at different times and sometimes at the same time a mystic, a Marxist, an atheist and an Advaitin (a branch of Hinduism which seeks self knowledge): 'a nationalist with a poor opinion of the nation he lived in; a communist who scorned the low level of the proletariat; an advocate of social credit who had little interest in economics'.

Bold believes that his most famous poem, 'A Drunk Man looks at the Thistle' 'contains the complexity of the man': and indeed, both the poem and MacDiarmid's career can seem like the interior monologues of one who is animatedly drunk, the mind skittering this way and that, seeing all thoughts and projects as possible.

Much of his legacy and many of his beliefs were terrible: he really did hate, not just Englishness but the English, shunning them when serving with them during the First World War, in Salonika, where he was a sergeant in the medical corps. Recalling the period in an interview a year before his death in 1978, he said that 'I was never, to say the least, an anglophile . . . when comrades were Scots or Irish or Welsh we got on all right, but we always had a difference from the English, we didn't get on with the English at all and I became more and more anti-English as time went on.'

The enthusiasm for hating the English, which MacDiarmid encouraged through his long life, was in the days before the SNP had to mind its public image, marked. In his *Battle for Scotland*, Andrew Marr, the BBC's foremost intellectual, wrote that an SNP group issued a pamphlet in the 1950s called 'The English: Are They Human?', and found that it 'apparently concluded they were not', being 'rotten with class privilege and class war, putrid with sexual perverts and shameless adulterers in high places'.

He was inspired by Benito Mussolini in the early 1920s, when the Italian dictator came to power and began a series of large public works and called for a Scots version of fascism, dropping it when Mussolini's imperialism became more apparent. He joined the National Party of Scotland in 1928 (in 1934, merged with the Scottish Party to create the Scottish National Party, which it has remained): expelled for his leftism, he joined the Communist Party in 1934 and, though expelled (for being nationalist) he remained more or less faithful to the Communist ideal, re-joining the party in 1956 to show his support for the Soviet invasion of Hungary.

He had, in 1931 in the 'First Hymn to Lenin', written: 'As necessary and insignificant as death / Wi' a' its agonies in the cosmos still / The Cheka's horrors are in their degree / And'll end suner! What matters't wha we kill / To lessen that foulest murder that deprives / Maist men o' real lives' – a rationale for the millions rounded up and killed or sent to the Gulag by the Soviet secret police, one based on the promise of a higher state of consciousness in humanity once the necessary clearing of the bourgeoisie and 'traitors' had been accomplished. It's a rare glimpse into the particular idealism of totalitarian rulers and thinkers: the sense that 'real lives' can be given space, once the clearances of the unnecessary people were accomplished.

Yet in 1932, he also seemed taken with emerging Nazism, enthusiastically hailing a friendly, 1931, biography of Hitler by Wyndham Lewis, seeing what Lewis described as the Nazi leaders' 'admirable tenacity, hardihood and intellectual acumen' as 'the model of what ought to be the spirit of the Scottish Movement'. He takes from Lewis' biography the concept of 'blutsgefuhl' (blood feeling), seeing it as a way in which people of the same culture and race would draw more and more closely together.

To put these into a box labelled 'eccentricities' is to miss the significance of MacDiarmid's shifting political allegiances – shifting, but with the steady consistency of support for anything anti-English/-British, and preference for the authoritarian superman over the workings of a democratic system whose base was the Scots population. For fellow Scots, he had mainly contempt, sneering at 'the moronic character of most of our people', one of a number of such dismissals. Friedrich Nietzsche's similar contempt for the masses aroused MacDiarmid's enthusiasm for the German philosopher. He approved Nietzsche's straining to surpass the constraints and moralities of good and evil: in 'Drunk Man', 'Guid and Ill that are the same / Save as the chance licht (light) fa's'. Even more importantly, he embraced the philosopher's injunction to his followers to 'be what you are': it appears in the 'Drunk Man' in several passages, as 'To be yersel's – and to mak that worth bein' / Nae harder job to mortals has been gi'en'. For MacDiarmid, and for those who aspired and still aspire to follow him, being yourself was to discover one's inner, true Scot and the mission of such a character: to 'mak' a unity' of Scotland's 'contrair (contrary) qualities', and thus make it a fit nation to live in once again.

This wasn't something he grew out of, or which fell from him during the shock of the Second World War. In 2003, the researcher John Manson discovered, among MacDiarmid's papers in the National Library of Scotland, poems and notes, some of which, written during the early years of the war, express a continuing hatred of the English, especially Londoners, who were then bearing the brunt of the blitz. One, untitled, reads 'The leprous swine in London town / And their Anglo-Scots accomplices / Are, as they have always been / Scotland's only enemies.' Another, written in June 1940, claimed he would 'hardly care' if London were destroyed … 'It may as well be London … Nay, London far better than most … earth's greatest stumbling block and rock of offence.' Again, 'Is a Mussolini or a Hitler / Worse than a Bevin or a Morrison [both Labour ministers in the war coalition government]?'

In the preface to the book which contains the discovered poems, the editors, Manson, with Dorian Grieve (MacDiarmid's grandson) and the Glasgow Professor of Literature Alan Riach, one of the foremost of MacDiarmid's interpreters, are evasive on the import of these comments, stressing that the poems were not published and might never have been, while the comments were notes in a private notebook (and thus, one would think, the more likely to be MacDiarmid's real beliefs).[4] The consistency of his thought speaks for these being his settled opinion: that the English and unionist Scots were 'Scotland's only enemies'; he pushes that thought further than usual, however, in wishing London and its 'leprous' citizens to be destroyed. The editors comment that 'there is ample literary precedent for denouncing London as the centre of an evil empire' – an extraordinarily foolish rationale for wishing the death of millions. These thoughts were evidence that his poetry existed, as he put it, 'whaur extremes meet' and is justified, by him and by some of the commentators on him, as one who could boldly defy conventions and limits, as if frank bigotry were praiseworthy for being frank.

He's also consistent in the stress he places on his own extraordinary self-discipline, dedication and genius: his struggle, that of the solitary seer, who points the way to a society which transcends the commonplace and the bourgeois. In his 'On a Raised Beach', Bold commends it as 'arguably his greatest poem in English'; the inspiration he takes from the stones on the beach prompts the thought that 'These bare stones bring me back to reality / I grasp one of them and I have in my grip / The beginning and the end of the world / My own self, and as before I never saw / The empty hand of my brother man / The humanity no culture has reached, the mob/Intelligentsia, our impossible and imperative job!' In the same vein, he writes that 'It will be increasingly necessary to find / In the interests of all mankind / Man capable of rejecting all that all other men / Think, as a stone remains / Essential to the world, inseparable from it / And rejects all other life yet.'

'On a Raised Beach's' first twenty-four lines are unintelligible to one without wide historical reading and a knowledge of several specialist vocabularies, including geology. MacDiarmid consistently put himself in the position of one hard to understand, even with a knowledge of Scots (since his synthetic version of the dialect, taking words from all areas, is one that no one person spoke); and this is further rendered obscure by a deliberate choice of words little used, such as in 'On a Raised Beach', 'optik' and 'haptik', the first, relatively common, the second, of specialist use, pertaining to data gathered through touch. 'By eye and hand' would be a reasonable, intelligible substitute. The first lines of the poem would defy any reading without constant recourse to the dictionary: 'All is lithogenesis – or lochia / Carpolite fruit of the forbidden tree / Stories blacker than any in the Cabaa / Cream-coloured Caen stone, chatoyant pieces / Celadon and corbeau, bistre and beige / Glaucous, hoar, enfouldered, cyathiform / Making mere faculae of the sun and moon.'

In his memoir on his friend Muriel Spark (1918–2006), Scotland's outstanding twentieth-century novelist, the literary journalist Alan Taylor recognizes MacDiarmid as 'the most influential and visible figure' in Scotland of the first half of the twentieth century; but quotes Spark writing that 'I see no point in a dialect that the average intelligent reader in Essex or Worcestershire cannot understand. I see no point in offering Scots dialects (which in any case are not regionally consistent) to the intelligent readers in the United States or Australia. The object of art is to diffuse intellectual pleasure.'

Other Scots writers of MacDiarmid's time and a little after used dialect, and their poems do need the aid of some translation, as Robert Garioch's verse does, if for a Scots speaker, relatively little. See, for example, this verse, from his moving short poem by the grave of Robert Fergusson, a brilliant Edinburgh poet of the mid eighteenth century, who died at the age of twenty-four: 'Canongait kirkyaird in the failing year / is auld and grey, the wee roseirs are bare/five gulls leam (gleam) white agen the dirty air / why are they here? There's naethin for them here.' Contemporary Scots poets use little if any Scots: one of the best, Andrew Greig, in a poem, 'Wynd', about the small town in which we both grew up (at different times) uses Scots sparingly – 'wynd' itself (narrow lane: also used in Northern England), 'roan' (a gutter), 'the day' instead of today.

Scots-born Carol Ann Duffy, the best known of the contemporaries and British poet laureate (appointed 2009), writes entirely in English, specializes in anti-war poems (as of the Iraq invasion in 2002); has writ-ten a poem, 'Rings', to celebrate the wedding of Prince William and Kate Middleton, and another to commemorate the 60th anniversary of the Queen's coronation in 1953. In a sprightly poem, 'The Scottish Prince', she imagines herself coming to the Highlands of Scotland, every year to dance with a prince and then go back to England: 'At the end of summer, I say goodbye to the Scottish Prince / and catch a train to the South, over the border, the other side / of the purple hills, far from the blue and white flag, waving farewell / from the castle roof. The Prince will expect me back again / next year – here's a sprig of heather pressed in my hand as proof.'

It's a light piece, her leaving of Scotland (her family moved to Stafford, in the West Midlands, when she was six) transmuted into the dream of joyous return, a little regretful ('Ask me, ask me, to dance to the skirl o' the pipes.') Her political engagement – considerable – picks up on a major theme of the British left: a poem on the Iraq war is an exercise in revealing the lies and evasiveness over torture and cover-ups.

'Guantanamo Bay – how many detained? *How many grains in a sack?* Extraordinary Rendition – give me some names. *How many cards in a pack?* Sexing the Dossier – name of the game? *Poker. Gin Rummy. Blackjack.*'

It's an effective idea, with real resonance: the cover-ups over water-boarding and rendition were legion. As is usually the case in such work, there is no mention of the vast horror which was Saddam's rule. A British poet laureate should have had some thought of the nobility, as well as the degradation, of ending the rule of such a man.

Literary poetry, especially of the twentieth and twenty-first centu-ries, is often hard to understand, and sometimes escapes literal meaning entirely. MacDiarmid is unusual among poets in that his obscurities are often in the service of deliberate linguistic intent: most of all, an intent to produce a body of work in his 'purified' Scots. Yet in his more didactic and in shorter poems, he is often lucidly lyrical. The poem, 'At my father's grave', pictures the poet conjuring up in his mind 'the great darkness o' your death', so that 'A livin' man upon a deid man thinks / And ony sma'er thocht's (smaller thought's) impossible'. Or in another moving poem, where he compares the 'stillness of foetal death' of a dead, unborn child in the mother's womb to the 'foetal death in this great cleared glen . . . The tragedy of an unevolved people', a meditation on a site of the clearances from the Highlands in the eighteenth and nineteenth centuries. His support for tyranny is also usually made clear: in the First Hymn to Lenin, he makes his hero-worship of the first Soviet leader and his (both Lenin's and MacDiarmid's) contempt for democracy clear, seeing Lenin's power '"No" in the majority will that accepts the result / But in the real will that bides its time.'

All Scots writers, especially literary writers, scholars and critics have had to come to terms with Hugh MacDiarmid (who at times bewailed his lack of wide acceptance). In a remarkable PhD thesis for Glasgow University,[5] the literary scholar Gerard Carruthers, now a professor at that university, began the work by throwing down a challenge to the dominant strain in Scots literature in the twentieth century. He cites an incident at the 1962 Writers' Conference at the Edinburgh Festival, where MacDiarmid called Alexander Trocchi, a Glaswegian who lived then in Paris, wrote pornographic novels (among others), published an avant-garde magazine and experimented with drugs, 'cosmopolitan scum'. He says that 'the most important thing it reveals about MacDiarmid's mindset is its long-standing cultural essentialism: what he was attacking was impurity' (reportedly, the two men later had a friendly conversation). 'MacDiarmid, along with Edwin Muir, led Scotland from the 1920s and 1930s in . . . the belief that Scottish culture is to be seen in relation to a state of idealized entity. In construction of this 'essentialist Scottish literary canon-mould', wrote Carruthers, 'MacDiarmid was pivotal.'

In this, the poet owed much to a turn-of-the-century Scots literary critic, George Gregory Smith, who in his *Scottish Literature: Character and Influence* (1919) coined the concept of the 'Scots antisyzygy': a particularly Scottish phenomenon, in part derived from Matthew Arnold's view that Welsh and Scots culture was 'Celtic' as against the English 'Saxon', which in practice came to mean that in the Scots mind, contradictory ideas and ideologies are yoked and fight it out. MacDiarmid bought into it enthusiastically, adapting it to his need to see the Scots mindset as quite separate from the 'Saxon', or English, leading him both to adopt the 'Celtic' name of Hugh MacDiarmid in preference to his birth name of Christopher Murray Grieve, and to construct a synthetic Scots, though he still, especially in later life, wrote in English as well.

The determination to create what Carruthers calls a holistic, even if internally contradictory, and unique culture met opposition from one of the early twentieth-century's finest poets, and once friend of MacDiarmid's, Edwin Muir: but it was an opposition that rested on a belief more radical than MacDiarmid's eclectic and militant restorationism ('All dreams of imperialism', he once wrote, 'must be exorcised, including linguistic imperialism.') Muir, in a short book *Scott and Scotland* (1936), vitiated much of post-medieval Scots writing entirely: Allan Massie, in a preface to the book, writes that 'Muir doubted if there was such a thing as Scots literature', that there was 'a constant whine of incompleteness in Scots literary writing, as if we were tied to a people so much less worthy, or at least so much less romantically tormented, than we are'. Muir himself wrote that the Scots writer had to face up to the fact that he or she 'works in a country that has become a sham: (the problem) is how to work in an intensely philistine nation', a view of the Scots which he shared with MacDiarmid.

Language is the central issue, and the cause of the central emptiness: 'the curse of the Scottish literature is lack of a whole language which finally means the lack of a whole mind'. Muir's main villain was Scots Calvinism: after the sixteenth century, when 'a quality which might be called wholeness' was 'lost to Scottish poetry' as the Presbyterian religion drove out Catholicism, so the 'concord' which had existed, of a 'high culture of the feelings as well as of the mind (was) . . . destroyed by the rigours of Calvinism, so that hardly a trace of it is left'. Muir's last true Scots poets are the medieval 'makars', led by William Dunbar and Robert Henryson: 'Burns' 'Tam O' Shanter', though great, is still a lesser poem than Henryson's 'Testament of Cresseid' (a horrifyingly powerful narrative poem).

Scott was, Muir writes, the greatest Scotsman but 'his picture of life had no centre because the environment in which he lived had no centre': had he been working in a 'whole' country, he would have been 'incalculably greater'. He stresses the obvious fact: 'to most of us who were born and brought up in Scotland, dialect Scots is associated with childhood and English with maturity'. Only by embracing English can a national literature be developed, as the Irish had already learned. Curiously, Muir wrote some of the loveliest poems of the pre-war period: and he also wrote, in 'Scotland 1941', a poem of absolute loss: 'We were a tribe, a family, a people / Wallace and Bruce guard now a painted field.' Calvinism enrolled Scots courage and intelligence – in the service of religious suppression – 'We with such courage and the bitter wit / To fell the ancient oak of loyalty / And strip the peopled hill and altar bare / And crush the poet with an iron text.'

Of the Scots literary world, Muir made a desert of emptiness and 'sham bards'; MacDiarmid made of the Scots people a wilderness of moronic halflings, filled with entertaining rubbish, which he centred on the figure of the hugely popular (in all the Anglophone countries) of Harry Lauder (1870–1950), a singer and comedian whose global popularity made him for a time the highest paid performer in the world, and whose records, of sentimental songs like 'The End of the Road' and 'I Love a Lassie', sold over two million copies. Lauder, in the mind of MacDiarmid and of the cultural critics who followed him, was of a piece with the popular 'kailyard' (cabbage patch) writing and public speaking, which sentimentalized Scotland and the Scots and which, in MacDiarmid's view, conveyed an image of Scottishness composed of 'qualities of canniness, pawkiness (sly humorousness) and religiosity which have been foisted on the Scottish people by insidious propaganda as a means of destroying Scottish national pride', a ludicrous estimation of Anglophone evil, even by MacDiarmid's standards. As David Goldie observes, 'like many leftist intellectuals of the time, he took few if any of the values from this mass [of the Scots working class], but demanded rather that they adapt their tastes and judgements to those he had acquired through his professedly superior reading and culture'.[6]

MacDiarmid is ritually described as Scotland's greatest twentieth-century poet: to be sure, he dedicated himself for much of his life to his art, with little reward until nearing the end of his life, and often in real poverty; and his embrace of his art and determination to have space for thought commands respect. Though prescriptive as to politics and poetry, he still had followers among the outstanding poets of the post-war decades, as Norman McCaig and Sidney Goodsir Smith: and left space for those who didn't follow him, such as Robert Garioch. But he was most influential in his stony insistence that Scotland was a quite different place – culturally, politically, morally – from a despised England. Part of his legacy must be the application of his immensely powerful personality to deepening the antagonism between the English and the 'Celtic' people of the British Isles, above all the Scots, and giving that antagonism a cultural rationale.

More, his insistence that a Scot should 'be yersel' meant that he or she should be a particular kind of Scot, and that he, as Alan Bold writes,[7] was the prophet, the 'supreme Scottish hero' who showed his fellow Scots how Scotland was to be reborn. MacDiarmid's reading of Friedrich Nietzsche, Martin Heidegger and Jean Paul Sartre and their (differing) accents on authenticity predisposed him to embrace the need to choose, freely, what one should be. With Sartre, he believed that the highest form of morality was the assertion, and acceptance, of the fact that the individual was free. Heidegger, in his freedom, chose Nazism as his political home: Sartre, with Simone de Beauvoir, chose Maoism in its most murderous period. MacDiarmid was, by contrast, relatively moderate, but still clear in his preference for the authoritarian over the democratic. He flirted with fascism, and as his unpublished wartime poem on London shows, he saw England as a greater foe than Nazi Germany. With hindsight, it's hard to understand how men so intent on seeking the truth of the human, or the national condition should be so determinedly purblind, in maturity and into old age, to the consequences of movements they joined, or promoted.

In a time, in the 1960s, when battles between and among factions of the Marxist left were better attended to than they have been since, the historian E. P. Thompson wrote a lengthy response ('The Peculiarities of the English') to the theses put forward by the Marxist intellectuals Perry Anderson and Tom Nairn in the *New Left Review* on the nature of the (then) current crisis in the British left. Towards the end of it, Thompson, a Marxist himself but with a less scornful view of his country, chided them severely, especially Nairn, for his habit of comparing 'history to a tunnel through which an express races until it brings its freight of passengers out into the sunlit plains'. Such a history, he claimed, had no place for light and dark events in the passengers' real lives, when, even if they lived in capitalist times, they had good moments and episodes of happiness. 'An historian', Thompson wrote, 'must surely be more interested than the teleologists allow him to be in the quality of life, the sufferings and satisfactions of those who live in unredeemed time.' It had something of the approach of Muriel Spark to MacDiarmid's language: come off your high horse, observe how people live, think, speak and take pleasure, even in conditions you regard as degraded, make your writing, even when demanding, intelligible.

This joust took place in the mid 1960s: by the 1980s and 1990s, when Nairn's most important work on Scots nationalism appeared, his habit for painting only in the darkest colours had not changed. For him, in *The Break-Up of Britain* (1981) and *After Britain* (2000), the time Scots spent and still spend under the jackboot of Britain/England is 'to live and die in unredeemed time'. Son of a Fife schoolmaster, Nairn studied philosophy at Edinburgh, taught in England and elsewhere, lived in various places in Europe, then for nearly a decade in Australia, to come in 2010, in his late seventies, to Durham University's Institute for Advanced Study.

Since his collaboration with Anderson, Nairn has developed what is a necessary posture for Scots secessionists to take: that Scotland's present state cannot be borne. Why call for the exhausting and risky renunciation of a settled statehood, in a relatively wealthy, multinational country in which the dominant nation begs you to stay and uses its tax income to give you more public spending per head than it does to its majority population, for anything which is not intolerable? Nairn's uncompromising disgust at England is of a piece with that of MacDiarmid, and has been more directly influential on the mindset of nationalists: it has, after all, accompanied the rise of the SNP. It set the tone: and the brilliance and savagery of his prose commended it to a relatively wide audience. After him, nationalists who had imbibed, first or tenth hand, his philippics against their neighbour could only experience, or anyway represent, their continued imprisonment in Britain as agony: if not physical, then psychic.

This one Scots writer has been more influential in the nationalist cause than any other: one who has achieved what many intellectuals desire; that is, to have a marked influence on a movement or a period. Of the contemporary intellectuals, academics and commentators of widely diverse views and specialisms who have put the British Union, and Scots independence, at some times near the heart of their work – Neal

Ascherson, Arthur Aughey, Anthony Barnett, Gerard Carruthers, Linda Colley, Carol Craig, Tom Devine, Michael Fry, Jim Gallagher, Brian Girvin, Chris Harvie, Gerry Hassan, Pat Kane, Colin Kidd, Michael Keating, David McCrone, Iain McLean, Ian Macwhirter, Andrew Marr, Allan Massie, Alex Massie, Robert Tombs, David Torrance, Christopher Whatley (there are many others, including many foreign academics who have taken an interest in the subject) – Tom Nairn is the one who can be most counted on to be a reference. He is the one who has laid down the battle lines of attack on the Union and on England; and who is seen as best at articulating the imperative that Scotland, to be itself, to express its autochthonous character, should be free of England.

In 2007, Arthur Aughey wrote that Nairn approached the decline of England and its immuring in the protocols, hidden and overt, of class and privilege, in order to 'explore it politically in the way in which John Le Carré's novels explored it artistically';[8] a good simile, if something of an overestimation of Le Carré's hostility, understating both the novelist's mournful attachment to English verities, and Nairn's detestation of just these verities. Invoking the latter's work in concert with Perry Anderson, the long-time editor of the *New Left Review*, Aughey wrote that 'what was most distinctive about their critique was its hostility to any flow of sympathy with English culture, and its erection of an index that measured only exceptional national inadequacies against a European, specifically a French, (exemplary) model'. The result was a template for a narrative of decline which saw England/Britain as an unfinished country, its development arrested, a critical intelligentsia absent, the 'Glorious Revolution' of 1688 (when a Protestant king was placed on the throne to deny it to a Catholic) represented as a failed bourgeois revolution, which blighted the following decades.

This is a trope extended into the economic state of the UK up to the present and one that suffers from an overdose of ideology, a lack of fact and example. From the original failure of the bourgeois revolution came a crippling history of further failure, with a ruling class indifferent to, or at best inefficient at, developing the British productive economy: an absurdly sweeping critique. In his *The Rise and Fall of the British Nation* David Edgerton writes that Britain had 'come in for a lot of ill-informed criticism, much of which suggests that it was, by implicit comparisons with other ruling classes, backward. Its many supposed failures, to be tough or business-like enough, have sometimes produced a fantastical picture of stupidity, decay and ineptitude . . . any realistic assessment needs, however, to note the strength and accomplishments of the haute bourgeoisie and aristocracy'.[9]

Nairn's style is to accentuate every trace of failure and to dam up any 'flow of sympathy' to anything or anyone he dislikes. No other motive for action is permitted, except the malign construction he puts upon it. In a remarkable paragraph early in his *After Britain* he manages to suggest that then Prime Minister Tony Blair's 'impressive personal commitment' to securing the Belfast Agreement was void because it could not turn itself into 'a polity redefined by other and more modest aspirations . . . at some distance from the historic centre stage', which meant to make '*real* (Nairn's italics) changes to the central state', as if the achievement of a ceasefire with the main terrorist grouping and their acquiescence in confining the struggle to parliamentary politics were a small matter.[10] Having established that Britain's polity, under New Labour, was no different to what went before in its desire to grandstand internationally, he dismisses an effort by then Foreign Secretary Robin Cook to develop an ethical base to British foreign policy, as well as the efforts Blair was making in the late 1990s to wind down the conflict in the Balkans, as no more than seeking 'the glamour of appearing to bestride the world once more'.

He is a man for monocausal analyses: a ruthless way with events and motives, which reduce the complex of reasons for any major project or policy into the one which fits with the given meta-analysis of Britain as a fading actor on a stage it once commanded and thinks it still can. It's imagined as a poor player, an Archie Rice (in John Osborne's 1957 play 'The Entertainer') strutting across a diminished stage, desperate for attention, while the audience leaves the crumbling theatre.

In his *Break-Up of Britain*, Nairn can scarcely contain his fury and scorn. The British world is a 'sinking paddle wheel state' an 'indefensible and inadaptable relic, neither properly archaic nor properly modern' . . . needing a 'motorized wheelchair and a decent burial' while 'Great British chauvinism dragged the state from imperialism into a dead end . . . (a) paralytic decline of the old state'. 'England . . . has fallen into ever more evident and irredeemable decline.' 'England lurched downward on the road to relative under-development . . . (a) long-term irreversible degeneration . . . (within) the hopelessly decaying institutions of a lost imperial state.' The Labour Party's so-called 'social revolution' of the post-war years led 'not to national revival but to . . . rapidly accelerating backwardness, economic stagnation, social decay and cultural despair'. This is 'the last era of thickening twilight' in which can be discerned 'the dwindling pace of the City in the fabric of international capitalism'. Showing his hand, he writes that the 'neo nationalist renaissances' (in Wales and Scotland) are due to 'the slow foundering of the British state, not in the Celtic bloodstream . . . (Scotland) incontestably leads the way, and currently dominates the devolutionary attack on the British system'.

Guilt, implicitly or explicitly, plays a large part in Nairn's analyses, a guilt he heaps upon the English (too often too ready to accept it) both for historic active imperialism and for an inability to rid itself of present passive imperialism. In alliance with English liberals who are disposed to feel guilty about Englishness: 'in leftwing circles it is always felt that there is something disgraceful about being an Englishman': Orwell's remark, in *England Your England*, remained true, or truer, for successive generations – Nairn has placed himself in a unique position, which has been of huge use to Scots nationalists. He has picked up on what Eric Kauffman has referred to as 'the Western tradition of opposing one's own culture',[11] developing in leftist cultural communities in the late nineteenth century in opposition to bourgeois values – and uses it to oppose *English* culture, but from the outside. He gives Scots nationalist culture both a free pass and a mission: to rid Scotland of the troublesome state in which it is unworthily encased. It should, he strongly believes, be encased in Europe.

Europe is the solution, England the problem. Unlike the surrounding states, it has stubbornly refused to realize its own nationality, sullenly hiding it under a melange of royalty, Britishness, imperial pretension and/or nostalgia, much of that under the loyal attention of the Labour Party, itself determined to keep the old show on the road with only the façade of modernization and egalitarianism. The literary example on which he draws deeply is Robert Musil's *A Man Without Qualities*, written in Vienna in the 1930s, a rich novel set in the decline of the Austrian empire at the turn of the nineteenth/twentieth centuries: plans for a grand but empty ceremony to celebrate the pacific and civilized qualities of the empire merely confirm its decadence. Nairn saw in it a parallel with the position of England within the UK, burdened with the UK empire which it can no longer properly control nor let go, but addicted to monarchy and empire.

The novel, to which a reading of Nairn introduced me, as it must have others, is an intricate piece of work: the parallel gave him the word Kakania, used by Musil, deriving from the commonly used abbreviation by the Viennese *K und K* to signify *kaiserlich und königlich*, or imperial and royal. Nairn then transmuted that into UKania: like Austria, the UK's 'domestic 'empire' was at the end of its rope. Musil writes (a passage Nairn must have read, though as far as I know he has not quoted it) that 'However well founded an order may be, it always rests in part on a voluntary faith in it, a faith that, in fact, always marks the spot where the new growth begins, as in a plant; once this unaccountable and uninsurable faith is used up, the collapse soon follows; epochs and empires crumble no differently from business concerns when they lose their credit.' For anyone who seeks the end of the UK, that is a deeply comforting paragraph.

In a similar metaphor to Musil's use of a bankrupt business, the British-Iranian scholar Ali Ansari, has a metaphor for the British, or any, state: that is, as he told me, that a just and well-functioning political system puts out large quantities of its efficiency and equity day by day, to function well. It must also take in sustenance, in the form of civic behaviour on the part of its citizens, who reaffirm their loyalty, can give voice to their criticisms and objections but do not exit, or seek to exit, from the political entity which encompasses them. That implicit democratic and civic deal is failing and too little is being returned, Ansari fears.

Nairn, in common with all Scots nationalists, hopes this is the case: his use of Musil's novel as scaffolding isn't illuminating unless you too think the UK is 'kakania'. It does show how he, and many, many others of the declinist tendency like to look at Britain's largest nation, especially as it struggled, from 2016 on, to shake itself free of the EU. The historian J. G. A. Pocock writes of the extended parallel that 'all Nairn wants to say by these means is that it is absurd for the English to think they can bring about a multinational politics. In fact, he is more afraid that they will do so than that they won't. The aim of his satire is to lessen their political will, not to transform it.' It is, however, now evident that those who wish to see a multinational politics retained in the UK have work to do: in part because of the challenge of Scots nationalism, in larger part because the centuries' old assumptions and practices of Britishness are decaying. See the next chapter.

Perhaps to protect himself from charges of anti-Englishness, Nairn has a chapter in *After Britain* on 'Not Hating England'. It's a reasonable question to ask of it – is the chapter's name an ironic joke? For a large part of it are reasons why Scots *should* hate England, or rationalisms on why they do. Writing that 'There is *of course* (his italics) antagonism towards 'England' among Scots', he ascribes that to the assimilationist bargain of the Union agreement of 1707 – Scots 'found they had signed up to an intensifying unitarism, to an historical over-centralism, in fact, which would meet its unsurpassable climax only in the Thatcher years'. He does not mention that the most enthusiastic for a Union in the seventeenth and early eighteenth centuries were Scots; nor that, after a period of active unpopularity, the Union began to be accepted for the greater wealth it brought, the wider horizons it opened and the substitution of an at least potential enemy by an ally, including one, for Presbyterian, lowland Scots, an ally against the Jacobites, powerful in Scotland and (until the early years of the 1700s), in England and dedicated to the restoration of the Catholic Stuart dynasty.

It is true that everyone who accepts the Union, even passively, must accept the sovereignty of the Westminster parliament. It remains in theory absolute: but with the devolution of powers to the three small nations which are practically impossible to be taken back without the consent of the national assembly to which they have been devolved, that sovereignty has been greatly diluted. Before devolution, Scots had accepted the incorporating Union with little protest for three centuries: and even after the SNP became the dominant, and most popular party in the 2010s, commanding the devolved parliament, 55 per cent voted in the 2014 referendum to remain under Westminster's jackboot.

Nairn writes that any antagonism is mainly aimed at the 'upper class' and those designated as 'snooty'. The anti-English sentiment is the expression of a political wound, nursed for three centuries, now allowed release as nationalist feeling rises and becomes socially legitimized, the more because it is aimed only at upper-class snobs, ever fair game. Yet how many Scots cared about the terms of the 1707 settlement? Viewed their Scottishness as choked off by 'an historical over-centralism'? That there is class resentment at upper-class snobs is evident: and it would apply as pointedly to the Scots upper class as to the English, in both cases depending more, for its fervour, on how they behaved than on their accent.

The English attitude to prejudice, he writes, means the belief on their part that 'peripheral tribes are bringing trouble upon themselves, through unreasonable hatred of *us* (English): the childish dreads and charms of ethnicity lie within their nature, but never in *ours*. Such a form of self-exorcism requires the evidence of (anti-English) "incidents", or even their invention ... the aim is reassurance: that is, peaceful certitude that the country of Stephen Lawrence and of so much malign Euro-scepticism is *not* succumbing to its own brutish prejudice or post-imperial exclusiveness.'

That casual slur needs parsing. Stephen Lawrence was a black British teenager from Plumstead, in south London, who was murdered in 1993 by a gang of white youths while waiting for a bus. The murder was logged by police as racially motivated, and after several false starts over several years, two of the white youths were found guilty of the murder and given long sentences. Their initial acquittal raised a storm of protest, led by *The Daily Mail*, the most 'pro-English' of daily papers, whose then editor, Paul Dacre, proclaimed his outrage, defying the law to name the youths and pronounce them guilty.

A series of enquiries led to the description of the Metropolitan Police as 'institutionally racist' for which apologies were made to the Lawrence family, while subsequent enquiries revealed corruption within the Met, and further apologies to the Lawrence family were made. Stephen's mother, Doreen Lawrence, who campaigned for justice for her murdered son, was appointed to the peerage; the *Mail* journalist Stephen Wright, who wrote much of the paper's coverage, was given a Special Campaign Award. A memorial plaque was placed at the spot of the murder; a Stephen Lawrence Centre was opened and a Stephen Lawrence Trust, focused on the achievement of social justice, set up.

Nairn's raising of the Stephen Lawrence murder as the main exhibit in his demonstration of 'brutish prejudice or post-imperial exclusive-ness', makes an implicit point which is the near opposite of the facts of the case. 'Nearly', because it was clear from the enquiries that racism *was* the impulse for the murder, and that racism *did* exist in the police force. Yet Nairn's effort to turn the blame back over the border wholly ignores the fact that English society was convulsed over the murder; and while much of the apologizing and the efforts to tackle racist behaviour both in society and in the police happened at an elite level, the polling and media evidence at the time was that there was widespread disgust over the crime, and still more over the years in which the youths identi-fied as murderers remained free.

Racism continues, in police forces and in the public at large: it suf-fered a reverse because of the Stephen Lawrence murder, because it forced reflection on its consequences. A YouGov poll in 2012 showed that 66 per cent of the British believed that the sentences passed on the only two white gang members to be convicted, Gary Dobson and Stephen Norris, fourteen or fifteen years before consideration of parole, were not harsh enough, compared to two per cent who said they were too harsh. They also showed that 67 per cent of the British thought that extreme racist views were still common: in Scotland, this was 70 per cent, with 56 per cent in London and 58 per cent in the south of England.

A kind of anti-Englishness *was* built into Scots society My grand-father who, with a partner, made a living in later life fixing the diesel engines of the East Fife fishing fleet, exulted in the theft of the Stone of Scone from under the coronation seat in Westminster Abbey in 1950: but he was a strong unionist conservative, as were most of the working and lower-middle-class people who made up the majority of the town. He wasn't keen on Catholics, but he went to my mother's second mar-riage, with a Polish Catholic, when I was about nine: though thereafter the house – his – was tense with largely unspoken dislike and occasional eruptions.

Anti-Englishness was much less virulent than anti-Irishness, and (linked) anti-Catholicism had been, in the early part of last century – with still some remnants of that left, especially in Glasgow and the surrounding conurbation, and in Dundee. It was dramatized by the Scots composer James MacMillan, a Catholic, in 1999, in a speech at the Edinburgh Festival ('If this ingrained, unconscious hostility to that which is regarded as different from the supposed norm remains, the implications for multicultural progress are huge. The sense of threat and hostility is there and has huge implications for Scotland's potential'): at the time, there were few charges of anti-English incidents. Dharmendra Kanani, head of the Commission for Racial Equality in Scotland at the time, agreed with MacMillan about the Catholics and added that 'anti-Englishness is not the problem. It's racism against Asians and blacks, just as it is elsewhere in Europe'. He said that of the eighty to ninety complaints received by the CRE each year, three or four concern anti-Englishness while the rest are cases of whites' attacks on Asians. Interviewed by the *Guardian*, a shopkeeper, Mohammed Aszal, described as 'living in fear in an Edinburgh housing estate', said that 'It's every day. The police do nothing either, no matter how many times I have complained: every day it's "black bastard" this and "Paki" that. They threaten you with violence. And it is getting worse. I don't know why, but it is getting worse.'[12] Scots violence against the English isn't absent – there was a slight increase in reported incidents during and after the 2014 referendum: but it was and is very minor.

Nairn does seem to hate the English, if not with MacDiarmid's virulence, then enough to believe English society to be much more riven with prejudice, empire-derived racism and mendacity than Scotland. The idea that Scots are 'a more moral people' lives on, in diverse forms, including in Nairn's work.

Thus, unsurprisingly, he was testy with the English when they refused to understand that their duty is to fall in line with continental European states, and embrace their nationalism for what it is – English, not British. Until it does that, the Britishness which is a mere extension of Englishness constantly drags the Scots backwards, through 'some fatality like Blair's war, some set of traditional wreckage, or set of blindly sentimental habits'.

The reference above to 'Blair's war' is not that of Iraq: written at the end of the 1990s, *After Britain* was too soon for that. Instead, the book defaults back to the active involvement of British forces in Kosovo under sustained attack from the Serbian army. The need for an intervention was laid out by Blair in a 1999 speech in Chicago, in which he argued that armed intervention in other states was permissible on certain conditions: 'acts of genocide can never be a purely internal matter. When oppression produces massive flows of refugees which unsettle neighbouring countries, then they can properly be described as "threats to international peace and security". When regimes are based on minority rule they lose legitimacy – look at South Africa.' He linked Slobodan Milosevic, president of Serbia, with the President of Iraq, Saddam Hussein, and when, in 2003, Britain joined the US in the invasion of Iraq, he deployed the same arguments.

For Nairn, the eagerness Blair demonstrated to take seriously the much debated 'responsibility to protect' – that is, to protect peoples repressed and murdered by their own leaders – is merely a means of 'driving the emerging concerns of Scotland off the air' because of 'an engrained longing for another fine hour upon the world stage'. With his customary ruthlessness, Nairn scrubs out any consideration of the possible merits of Blair's case. Yet, even if one were to conclude that intervention was a cure worse than the disease, as some (most vigorously Alex Salmond) did over Kosovo and many more did over Iraq, still there would seem to be a responsibility on an intellectual to credit the commitment of military force in a war against a state which was mass-murdering its own and neighbouring peoples with *some* purpose other than driving Scotland off the news, and finding a stage on which to pose as a third-rate Churchill.

Nairn's view of Blair as a posturing warmonger became popular in national circles: Salmond pressed, after Iraq, for Blair to be tried as a war criminal. When Salmond joined the Russian propaganda channel RT, it was around the time when Russia had seized the Ukrainian province of Crimea and had sponsored the rebellion of ethnic Russians in the Donbass region of eastern Ukraine and assisted the Syrian dictator Bashar al-Assad to suppress all opposition to his rule. The Western states, with minor exceptions, stayed out of it: the death toll, still rising as this is written, is something like twice that of Iraq.

Ruthlessness is necessary to bolster further the central purpose of Nairn's work: to represent England as a dangerous imperial predator, half dead but still dangerous; one still able to drag Scotland off the front pages into some egotistical post-imperial nightmare. England must decide! – for the Scots 'have not come this far, through so much defeat and disappointment, in order to curl up inside an uppity hive of blethering British whingers, curmudgeonly husks who can go on surviving in defeat only because the English have not spoken yet'. But when they are speaking, as they are, about nationalism and the need for voice, they don't want to speak Nairn's script: nor, for that matter, do the Scots, at least not so far.

Nairn's writing remains highly influential: though by the 2020s, he was writing much less. The last piece I could find – there will likely be others – was a 2014 essay published on the Open Democracy website, urging Scots to vote for independence in the referendum of that year: 'the Scots will have some chance of getting through (or at least moving towards) the Exit later this year. Let's do it, rather than hang around for more decades of brooding about it, and trying to sum up enough self-confidence to take on the new age. The confidence will come from doing it, and helping to foster the incoming tide of real inter-nationalism in our own way: new colours in the rising house, new tunes that Robert Burns might recognize as he sees the parcel o' rogues in the removal van at last.' It was a way of saying '*On engage et puis on voit*' (you make your move, and then you see the result: more pithily – Let's Just Do It), as Napoleon may have said, and Lenin adapted to his own revolutionary ends. MacDiarmid would have approved of that.

In 2012, a collection of short essays by twenty-seven Scots writers, addressing the issues of Scotland's politics, devolution and independence, was published under the title of *Unstated*. It appeared as the country and the politician class were limbering up for the referendum of 2014, when all living in Scotland of the age of sixteen or over were asked if they did, or did not, wish Scotland to become an independent nation state. Had it succeeded, Scotland would secede from the UK, breaking the (then) 307-year-old Union with England and Wales (and later Ireland, later still Northern Ireland). Before a vote that fateful, the writers of Scotland should have their political say.

Scott Hames, editor of the collection, a lecturer in the University of Stirling's English Studies department and an expert on the writing of the Glasgow novelist James Kelman, wrote in the introduction that its purpose was to contrast the politicians' and journalists' 'facile arguments and factoids . . . reduc(ing) the discussion to slogans, fantasies and nightmares' for a 'bogus debate', with 'more radical, more honest and more nuanced thinking' applied to 'the truly thorny, exciting and difficult questions about self-determination'.

Hames wanted the collection to 'document the true relationship between the official discourse of Scots nationalism and the ethical concerns of the some of the writers presented as its guiding lights and cultural guarantors'. He quoted the Glucksman Professor of Irish and Scottish Studies at Aberdeen University, Cairns Craig, as saying that 'cultural devolution' had happened some years before the 1997 vote for political devolution, with the 'radical voices' of (among others) Matthew Fitt, Janice Galloway, James Kelman and Ali Smith.

The 'dissenting energies' of Scots writing after the 1997 devolution decision should be preserved, Hames believed, from being channelled into 'debates which exclude in advance any alternative to neoliberal capitalism and parliamentary democracy'. He wrote that 'the politics of Scottish devolution, and the contemporary debate over political independence, are self-evidently far less radical, passionate and imaginative than the politics of the writers most often invoked as symbols of their "cultural" rootedness and legitimacy'.

These are high claims for the class of '97 writers. The advantage politicians possess is that, in government, they have the power to make large changes to the lives of the citizens they govern, although within legal, economic and political constraints. The advantage that writers possess is that in having no such power, they also have no such constraints: they are thus free to be as radical, passionate and imaginative as they wish, though with varying degrees of effect. Political power and imaginative power move in different spheres, though the latter frequently excoriates the former: Hames' claim is that the latter are closer to the promotion of real change, which he defines only vaguely, than politicians, including nationalists. The Scots unacknowledged legislators of the world are, as both Hames and Craig agree, novelists, superior in the presentation of a radical interrogation of politics, including parliamentary democracy itself.

If they are granted the capacity to point up the future, they are also often charged with an innate, structural pessimism. Their writing, claims David Goldie, 'posit(s) the impossibility of a satisfactory Scottish narrative practice under prevailing conditions. The stories that many Scottish writers told themselves in the mid century were of failure, decline, and paralysis: of a people who had become separated from their history, had lost confidence in their language, had been denatured and class-riven by a now failing industrialization, and who stood islanded from the currents of global culture.'[13] In 2014, David Manderson writes that Scottish 'miserabilism', especially strong in the arts, is 'like a bad teacher (who) prevents us from believing in ourselves and from celebrating our existence. It's also the bit of us where we're never to blame.'[14]

James Kelman stands out in Hames' *Unstated* collection. He does so in part because he is among the most lauded and (literally) prized of the generation of writers who, in Cairns Craig's view, devolved the Scots imagination some years before the politicians got round to their own version; and because he is more strongly and clearly opposed to 'Englishness' than most well-known writers, with the possible exception of Alasdair Gray, also represented in *Unstated*. (Alasdair Gray died in December 2019, the day after his 85th birthday.)

Kelman's essay makes clear his belief that Englishness is 'the controlling interest . . . perceived as Anglo Saxon . . . more clearly an assertion of the values of upper-class England and their validity despite all and in defiance of all . . . to be properly "British" is to submit to the English hierarchy and to recognize, affirm and assert the glory of its value system . . . those who oppose this supremacist ideology are criticized for not being properly British, condemned as unpatriotic'. He writes that writers like him are found guilty of being 'too Scottish', both outside of Scotland and by 'Anglocentric Scottish critics (who) condemn Scottish writers for their "lack of diversity".' He argues that both class and racist categories are used in this: being 'too Scottish' is to assert a Celtic rather than an Anglo-Saxon heritage: while 'Scottishness equates to class and class equals conflict'. Writers with a working-class background, as his, are condemned 'for confining our fiction to the world of the urban working class . . . none can step beyond the limits of this world . . . barren of the finer things in life . . . working-class people cannot engage with art and philosophy'.

He writes that 'the bourgeoisie tend to go with the colonizers and the imperialists as a means of personal and group survival and advancement'. 'Colonizers' is likely to be used in the same sense as it is by

Alasdair Gray: in *his* essay in *Unstated*, he divides the English who live in Scotland as 'settlers', who have the same status as Asian restaurateurs or 'the Italians who brought us fish and chips', making it clear that he regards the English as being as foreign as Asians or Italians, even if possibly useful: the other category is 'colonists' who 'look forward to a future back in England through promotion or by retirement'. Thus the 'colonists' are similar to the British imperialist officials in India, who could be promoted, or retired, back to, as Kelman puts it, 'England': though a disproportionate number of the colonists, including one third of the governor generals, were Scots, who may have wanted to return to Scotland, as might the Irish colonists to Ireland and the Welsh colonists to Wales.

Kelman's detestation of the English is so great that he claims to read fiction from all other countries – the US, France, Russia – except England. 'I wouldn't have been reading English literature, because of the class barrier. Why would you want to read things that were treating you as an animal? The Scottish voice was equated with being working class. If you weren't working class, you would have lost it and assimilated to the bourgeois, as people still do whether it's Morningside or Kelvinside [upmarket areas of Edinburgh and Glasgow], an approximation of Hampstead Heath is what they attempt.' It's a feature of Kelman's essay, and his interviews, that statements like this aren't accompanied with examples.

In fact there are very few major pieces of literature written by English writers about Scotland and Scots, and none I know of which treat them as animals. Scholar and poet Robert Crawford highlights only three English authors between the seventeenth and twentieth centuries with a major work on the Scots: Shakespeare's *Macbeth* (1606), Samuel Johnson's *Journey to the Western Isles of Scotland* (1775) and Virginia Wolf's *To the Lighthouse* (1927). In *Macbeth*, the eponymous central character and Lady Macbeth are treacherous regicides, though possessing considerable courage: all other Scots characters, as Macduff, Macduff's wife, Banquo, King Duncan and his son Malcolm are both brave and noble: none, good and bad, could be said to be portrayed as animals.

Johnson's approach to the Scots was always rebarbative, and his judgement in the *Journey* was, as Crawford writes, 'that Scotland still required English assimilation if it were to develop from ruin to civilized prosperity', a statement with which many Scots of the time would agree. It is, however, also some way from animality, a likeness England's most famous critic never came near to using. *To the Lighthouse* is set in Scotland, but hardly explores Scots themes, or the landscape, though the novel's action, such as it is, takes place in one of the most beautiful of the western isles, Skye.

Crawford's main point is that all of these are 'very much England's Scotland': in *Macbeth*, it is wild, lawless, desolate, and the despotism Macbeth forced upon it when king, needed 'gracious England's' military intervention to restore divinely ordained regal order. In Johnson, the country needs a good dose of English moderation and sense to sort itself out; in Wolf, it is hardly imagined for itself, only as a site for her 'preoccupation with English behaviour'.

No major nineteenth-century English literary novels are written about Scotland: nor were any in the twentieth, or so far in the twenty-first, century. Ian McEwan, brought up in England whose Scots father attained the rank of Major in his army career, says he is not a British, but an English writer, and that the Act of Union has 'not been an act of union of literary cultures . . . imagination has a specific quality tied to landscape and locale, to community, to neighbourhoods. Even the rise of the modernist novel with its certain internationalist flavour . . . well, look at *Ulysses* [by James Joyce]: what could be more local and provincial as it were and specific to a place and time than that, but it's the modernist bible, the central text.'

Literary fiction has eschewed what popular fiction explores: Ian Fleming, grandson of the Scots banker Robert Fleming, had James Bond born to a Scots highland laird in Glencoe: little is made of it in the novels, though the last scenes of the film *Skyfall* (2012) take place in the semi-deserted family mansion in a desolate part of the Highlands. Two political figures: Michael Shea, Scots born, a diplomat and press secretary to the Queen (1978–1987), wrote two novels dealing with Scots independence;[15] Douglas Hurd, Home Secretary (1985–1989) and Foreign Secretary (1989–1995), also put Scots independence at the heart of the action, inventing the Scottish Liberation Army, an armed terrorist group impatient with the moderation of the SNP as a major piece of the narrative machinery.[16] Neither man regarded writing as their main activity, and must have written quickly: the characterization is shallow and undeveloped. But both were shrewd, and illuminated controversies and tensions latent in the system, which became larger after the publication of their novels.

In Hurd's *Image in the Water*, an ambitious and ruthless Tory politician plays the English card against the Scots, laying bare the extra funding for Scotland and Scots over-representation in some professions, as the media and trade union leadership. Having founded a New England Movement with a scarcely disguised intent to provoke Scots independence and thus make England more likely to vote Conservative, he stirs up both English resentment and Scots national feeling. In a speech he gives at Leith town hall, he thunders against 'the twisted statistics' which every year 'justify the extraction of extravagant subsidy for Scotland from the British exchequer . . . either the Scots must accept fair play within the United Kingdom . . . or, sadly indeed but firmly, we should say that if the Scots wish to run their own affairs they should do so plainly and openly, bearing the cost of separation, shouldering their own burden without the English subsidy or special benevolence, competing with other foreigners for English investment'.

None of the above, including the Shea and Hurd thrillers, is animality: without guidance from Kelman, it's hard to know where to find it. Nor is it easy to know what the 'class barrier' between the two states is, since their social structures are roughly similar. The venom of his view of the English, which he has retained into his early seventies, is not softened by his many awards: especially not for his winning the Booker prize in 1994. The prize was for his novel, *How Late It Was, How Late*, a journey through drinking and criminal Glasgow of Sammy, an ex-convict in his late thirties back from England to his native city, beaten up by police so badly he has lost his sight, who at the end of the novel decides to get back to England. The narrative, with no chapter breaks for 350 pages, veers between a third person keeping Sammy going and Sammy's own language, thick with 'fucks' and 'cunts'.

It seems to me a fine if sometimes monotonous novel, which built up the character of a man containing within himself spurts of rage, of longing, of resignation, of greed, while round him the figures who engage with him, sometimes brutally, sometimes with concern, sometimes cruelly bureaucratically, emerge from, then sink back into the phantasmagorical spaces through which he, unseeing, shuffles. Layer after layer, his desperation is revealed, a despair countered by the constant unillusioned injunctions to himself to keep on, since keeping on is all he, or anyone, can do, meaningless as it may be. 'It's a game but, so it is man, life, fucking life I'm talking about, that's all ye can do man start again, turn ower a new leaf, a fresh start, another yin, ye just plough on, ye plough on, ye just fucking plough on, that's what ye do, that's what Sammy did, what else was there, I mean fuck all ... know what I'm saying, fuck all.' As this excerpt shows, it's quite comprehensible to an English speaker: the few Scots/Glaswegian elements, as the use of 'but' at the end rather than the beginning or a phrase, or 'ower' for over, are small obstacles. A greater obstacle is the tendency to over-extend scenes for no narrative purpose: but these can be skipped. A reader who objects to obscene language should be warned away, but.

Its choice by a majority of the Booker jury for the most coveted literary award in the UK that year prompted a literary scandal. The jury voted against the strongest of protests from one of their number, the Liberal Rabbi Julia Neuberger, who said it was 'unreadably bad' and the prize's awarding 'a disgrace'. The columnist and former *Times* editor Simon Jenkins (not on the panel) called it 'cultural vandalism'. These are abrasive comments for an author to read: yet the book was given the prize by a jury composed of three Englishmen: the chairman, literary critic John Bailey (Eton and Oxford), the literary critic James Wood (Eton and Cambridge) and the literary scholar Alastair Niven, a former director of Literature at the Arts Council of Great Britain; one Englishwoman, Rabbi Julia Neuberger (South Hampstead Girls School and Cambridge) and one Scotsman, Alan Taylor, founder and editor of the *Scottish Review of Books* and a former managing editor of *The Scotsman*.

The brief biographies of the jury do underscore Kelman's point – that it was drawn, with the exception of Taylor, from an upper-class English intellectual–literary elite: Taylor is one of Scotland's foremost literary journalists, and must be counted among the Scots artistic bourgeoisie. In an article written after the prize, to criticize the 'political' horse-trading that went on to get to the winning book, Wood wrote that he 'liked *How Late* ... a great deal'. It should have been hard, in the face of such a judgement by such figures, to cleave to the view that

England is hopelessly mired in bigotry against him in particular and Scots in general, on both class and identity lines. But he does.

His other large complaint is that the Scots language, and especially the working-class Scots accents, are marginalized and discriminated against 'in pursuit of "total assimilation to Britishness where Englishness is the controlling interest" of the "Scottish bourgeoisie and ruling elite"'. It's true that from the eighteenth century those Scots who wished to improve themselves in society sought to speak English rather than broad Scots, and to soften their accents: in his *Journey*, Samuel Johnson condescends to praise 'the great, the learned, the ambitious and the vain' among Scots for losing the use of the language, 'which is likely in half a century to become rustic and provincial, even to themselves'. It's also true that, at least until the 1970s and even now, teachers in Scots schools, Scots themselves, insisted that pupils would, at least in the classroom, 'speak properly': that is, in English.

In my primary school in East Fife, it was strictly observed, to the point of punishment if not. The dialect in the fishing and farming villages in the area was strong, especially among the fishermen and the farm-workers, mostly incomprehensible to an English-only speaker. But my generation lived in a period where radio and then television, with the London broadcasts always in 'posh' English tones (like the accent the Queen still retains) and the Scots announcers and presenters speak-ing with their accent sometimes all but inaudible, were cutting into the conversations. My mother, would speak Scots to most of her customers in her beautician's parlour in the front room of our house, especially to the young women from the oilskin factory nearby, who would seek her expertise to look bonny for a night out, or when their men were home. But she spoke non-Scots English too, if heavily accented. She had been based in England for much of her wartime service in the navy, and my father, whom she left when pregnant, was English: her second husband was Polish, who spoke good English but not Scots.

Those of us in the upper streams of the local comprehensive who were upwardly mobile, were in a linguistic and emotional no-man's-land. Speaking *properly* when you didn't have to invited mocking or a thumping from the majority in the school who would leave at fifteen, many of the boys going to the tough jobs on the fishing boats, or on farms while we, like Sammy, fucking ploughed on, in our case through trigonometry and Shakespeare's tragedies. Scots was for us more mixed with English, or Americanisms from rock songs: we would say disnae (doesn't) and wunnay (won't) and cannae (can't), but also, for some of us, climbing up the vocabulary steps in English was more rewarding. Three of us boys would address each other in cod Shakespearian: 'Good even to you, my gracious lord, how does your lordship?' One, Robert Fyall, unable by the laws of the Brethern sect to which his family belonged, to watch or listen to the drama he loved, learned great swathes by heart. He's now a popular evangelical preacher. Another was Christopher Rush, a teacher and a successful writer, who wrote among other works *Will* (2014), a brilliant fictional biography of Shakespeare.

We were taught by 'the two Alastairs', men from working-class Aberdonian families with first-class degrees from the city's university, come separately to our school to teach the natives English. The older, Alastair Leslie, was a model teacher, both patient and inspiring, rendering books, which for most of us were foreign to our homes and families' conversation or knowledge, open to us, little by little, so that we began to grasp something out of their daunting pages, relate their images to ours, help us climb a little. I went for the Americans – Steinbeck, Hemingway then Mailer, Baldwin – some of it showing off, understanding at first only part of what I read.

Alastair Mackie was a disciple of MacDiarmid's: yet one whose poetry I would say (a biased view) is among the best written in Scots, but who remains in relative obscurity. Mackie taught well, even passionately, when engaged: he was frustrated because, in a comprehensive school, he had to teach boys and girls who didn't understand, or try to understand, what he was struggling to tell them. In one of his English poems, 'Schoolboy', he had a kind of poetic revenge on the hard-to-teach pupils who were the school's majority: 'His squat, aberrant body, face of lard / his finger's podgy delta, was the field / morbid forces won and made him yield / so that he was made fist and struck out hard.'

For the few of us in his class who did try to respond to his passion, it was a delight to see him come fully alive, to teach, for example, 'On the Resurrection of Christ' by the medieval poet (1460–1465? to 1513–1530?), William Dunbar, with the incantatory Latin end line to every verse, 'Surrexit Dominus de sepulcro' (the Lord rises from the tomb), he reading it in a shout. And his cackling at Dunbar's 'Flyting of Dumbar and Kennedie', a literary jousting, in this case between Dunbar, or Dumbar, and another poet, Walter Kennedy, especially at the lines (in translation), 'Since thou with worship would so fain be styled / Hail, sovereign senior, thy balls hang through thy breeks [breeches].'

Mackie was a poet, chained to his art. When he went home to his wife and two daughters, he would eat, then sit alone in the small sitting room of the house, tearing through the essays and exercises he had to mark to get to his own verses, which included translations from the Russian: Akhmatova, Mandelstam, Yesenin, Pasternak: the Italians, as Quasimodo and Leopardi: the French, as Mallarmé, Rimbaud, Verlaine. (I'm not sure if he worked from originals, or from existing English translation. I had to learn Russian in later life, and can barely imagine how he would have been able to grasp such a hard tongue while teaching, marking and writing.) One of his poems, 'Bigamist', imagined his withdrawal into his words-world as going to a second wife, while his first would 'sit knittin' mebbe / finger nebs (ends) like fechting (fighting) spiders / you and your sprauchle o twa quines (two sprawling girls) / glowerin at the TV / My exilt family in the livin' room'.

There's much more to be said about Mackie's work, which was vast: my schoolmate Christopher, whose career as teacher and writer partly mirrored Mackie's but with much more public success, became very close to him ('the son I never had', Mackie told him a little before his death in 1995). He undertook the very large labour of sorting through paper piles in the chaotic work room and shaping them into a volume of *Collected Poems, 1954–1994*, which he and I and others paid for to be published in 2012, in a handsome book by Three Rivers Press. Bias no doubt informs this, but the more I re-read them, the better they seem, as good as anything written in Scots since the war.

Here, I wanted to note a particular thing: his dislike of England, something that we never fully discussed. He was, perhaps the last or among the last of Scots poets who consciously followed MacDiarmid: that is not to say that he took his politics from him, but that MacDiarmid's constant and consistent efforts to keep as much of England out of Scotland as possible struck a chord, as it did with many. Though MacDiarmid excoriated most of Scots society, high and low, for its philistinism and apathy, he must have been conscious of working to an extent, with an anti-English grain, even if a passive one. Many Scots in the later twentieth and the twenty-first century could always be persuaded a certain way down the anti-English road, whether by a joke, or an accusation of bias, or the belief in a real or imagined slight.

Like Kelman's, this was partly class-based in Mackie, whose father had been a labourer in a granite quarry. In one poem, 'Wimbledon', he opens with 'Wimbledon, your genteel fechts scunner me (genteel struggles annoy me) / The guff (whiff) o' Eton in the commentator's braith', then, imitating the upper-class drawl, 'thet was a maavellous beck-hend by Baawg (Borg).' The game is saved for him only when Ilie Nastase, number one in the tennis world in the early 1970s, 'ettles (has a mind to) argie bargie wi' the linesman / that I like to see decorum pish itsel'.

His poem, 'Princes Street' (Edinburgh's main street) begins in the same, squaring-for-a-fight style, 'Street chained like a convict tae your English stores.' He views, in 'Braemar', the tartanry, which forms a large part of Scots tourism, 'trokked (sold) in ony shape/your siller (money) can afford . . . the foreign tourist / buys Scotland at ony price'. This is MacDiarmid lite, but it is also a homage. On MacDiarmid's death, in 1978, he wrote that the occasion was 'as if a mountain / that held up the lyft (sky) had sunk into the mools (graveyard)'.

Still, he fucking ploughed on, turning a little to collages, two of which he gave me, but mainly poem after poem, too little recognized, including by MacDiarmid, to whom he sent poems and letters, without so much as an acknowledgement: 'He did nothing for me personally', he told Christopher. Later, he wrote, 'He has a totalitarian cast of mind for which I feel an increasing revulsion.' His official life was teaching; his life of the mind and heart was the struggle to express himself, night after night; he was a little like the dissident Soviet writers, he told me once when I came to see him in a break from an assignment in Moscow. Much of what he wrote was 'for the drawer': the Soviet dissidents put them there because they would never be allowed to publish them; he because he had few openings for doing so. Scots, for him, was a verbal jewel which had to shine not just in its own nation, shrunken as it was and is, but in contact with the languages of the world, able to reach out and give meaning to them in the near-discarded words of a once-virile European tongue.

Kelman's complaint of 'total assimilation' was also Mackie's fear, which he kept at bay a little by shouting out Dunbar in the classroom: but the Glasgow writer's claim is over-polemicized. Scots may still be receding, much more slowly than Dr Johnson predicted and wished in the 1770s: but that isn't the fault of a number of contemporary efforts, public and private, to revive it. The Scots nationalist government created the position of Scots Makar, or poet; that has been occupied since 2007 by Edwin Morgan, Liz Lochhead and Jackie Kay, all of whom, however, prefer English to Scots. Kay, who succeeded Lochhead in 2016, now lives in England and is a professor of creative writing at Newcastle University, did use a slew of Scots words in a poem called 'Old Tongue', but only to mourn that, having been 'forced south' at the age of eight, she had 'lost my Scottish accent / Words fell off my tongue'.

Perhaps because the Makars were giving no leadership in this, Creative Scotland (formerly the Scottish Arts Council) and the National Library of Scotland combined, in 2015, to create the position of the Scots Scriever (writer). The first holder of the two-year long post was Hamish MacDonald, a freelance writer in Scots and English and a former director of Moniack Mhor, the country's creative writing centre: in 2018, the scholar and writer Dr Michael Dempster was appointed, who has written plays and graphic novels in Scots, as well as working to remove the stigma of speaking Scots in communities and schools.

Teaching Scots isn't compulsory in Scots schools, but it is given the status of a separate language, which pupils can choose to study as a second foreign language. A survey by Mercator's European Research Centre on Multilingualism and Language Learning in 2017 found that it is taught in some schools, where teachers are interested in doing so, but there is no standard approach. The survey comments 'some teachers whose natural voice is Scots will deliver lessons in this, although there are no written textbooks in which the medium of instruction is Scots. It is compulsory at Higher National level that pupils study a Scottish text although, in practice, this might be written in English rather than in Scots language. It is therefore possible for some pupils to receive no introduction to Scots literature or language throughout the duration of their school life.'

The Mercator survey notes that 'a large majority of the Scottish people, including good Scots speakers, see it as an inferior version of English, despite its vibrant existence in family life, literature and society'. Efforts to combat this pejorative view of a widely spoken dialect now take the form of several official projects to re-popularize the use of Scots, these co-existing with private initiatives, of which the most prominent is Itchy Coo, founded in 2002 by James Robertson and Matthew Fitt to publish books in Scots for children and encourage teachers to work in Scots. It is, probably inevitably, top down, where, as Kelman makes clear, the use of the Scots was and largely remains a working or lower-middle-class practice. Decades, even centuries, of the official, educated and public voice being largely in English has made Scots instinctively put the demotic use and the official use into separate mental boxes, even as the number of Scots words used declines.

In East Fife, still a place where Scots is relatively widely spoken, my mother's generation, and even more mine, was at the beginning of this linguistic distancing: they and we would put some Scots words and phrases between virtual inverted commas – as intoning, with appropriate signs of irony, the much used, resigned remark, 'Whit's fur ye'll nae gan past ye', a way of saying 'what will be, will be'.

To turn round this cast of mind will take a big shove over years: but it may be possible. In Ireland, use of Irish as a first language declined steadily, until it is now the first language of only two per cent in the Republic, 0.02 per cent in Northern Ireland. Yet the teaching of a language which is compulsory in school has produced (as well as exasperation on the part of many children obliged to learn it) a rising number of 'Gaeilgeoirí', usually highly educated men and women who have chosen to become fluent in their country's first official language, even as those in the western parts of Ireland speaking Irish, the Gaeltacht, decline. That seems to speak to the official route being modestly effective: though the Irish have the advantage of learning a language quite different from English, thus suffering no unconscious stigma as an inferior form.

Kelman's brusque assumption that the English speaking, Scots bourgeois world conspires to run Scots out of town doesn't accord with the facts: though writers, including the officially appointed Makars, use only occasional Scots in their writing and their speeches, the great and the good of the Scots cultural world have put time and public money into preserving Scots: it may work, at least to some extent. There is a possibility that it may return to the status which it had in Enlightenment Edinburgh and Glasgow, where the leading lights of the movement, as David Hume, spoke broad Scots (for which he sometimes reproached himself) but wrote in sonorous, perfect English, as in his *History of England*, completed in 1761. It would be a fine thing if many people of all walks of life had Scots as a language used for other Scots, English with those who don't speak it, as Sicilians switch between Sicilian (far enough away from standard Italian to be classed as a separate language) and Italian. So that instead of, or as well as saying: What are you up to these days? we might say, unselfconsciously: Whit'r ye dae'in noo? Even as I write this, it seems strange, even silly: but many new things do, yet catch on, and often enrich.

In his contribution to the *Unstated* collection, the poet Douglas Dunn chided obscenity speech, perhaps a tilt at Kelman's writing, in a stern little verse towards the end of a longer poem 'English: a Scottish essay', a testimony to his use of English. He wrote: 'Who legislates when Jock does something foul / To rolling consonantal R, or vowel / Or lards his speech with epithets of F? / *Well we should.* So clean up your act. Turn down / The dreary, forthright volume, before we're deaf / From all that cursing from the angry town / And its intensifying Fs and Cs / Indignant, crude monstrosities!' He makes a few passes at posh English: 'That patronizing sound of patronage': but mostly he wants to defend his own, limpid, phrasing of his poems, in English: 'Who cares whose fingers run across the keyboard? / "A note don't care who plays it", a wise man said' (it was the Jazz trumpeter Clark Terry, 1920–2015: the full remark was 'A note doesnt care who plays, black, white, green,brown.')

Between Dunn's gentle chiding and dignified defence of his poetry and Kelman's 'cursing from the angry town', Scotland's literary figures tend to range themselves behind the nationalist flag, mainly stoutly, but sometimes with ambivalence. In an interview with me, David Greig, best known and most prolific of a new generation of Scots playwrights, a man who has said Yes to independence and toured Scotland rousing support for it before the 2014 referendum, showed this ambivalence. He sees himself and his generation of writers as no longer shackled to

MacDiarmid's nineteenth-century nationalism: he speaks of 'layers of sovereignty. The point is to renegotiate the Union . . . the organization of sovereignty needs to be shoogled [shaken] about. People are going through a transformation process and are seeing the world differently. Devolution has already changed everything. I'm not happy to see all power centralized in London, an imperial capital with no empire.' He's a post-nationalist nationalist, with no SNP card

Almost all of the writers in *Unstated* proclaimed their working-class roots, or spoke to working-class interests. For Scots literary folk, a working-class background is almost essential, a sign that, though 'creative', they are of or from the people.

One strand of contemporary Scots writing, highly regarded and in some cases globally successful, is crime writing. Its origin is held to be a novel called *Laidlaw* by William McIlvaney:[17] the eponymous detective, unillusioned but dedicated, operates in a grim, oppressive world of bile and racial and religious prejudice. What has been dubbed 'tartan noir', from a conversation between the best known of writers working in this vein, Ian Rankin and the Californian crime writer James Ellroy, has among its outstanding practitioners Iain Banks (d. 2013), Christopher Brookmyre, Val McDermid, Josephine Tey (d. 1952) and many others. Irvine Welsh, best known for his very successful *Trainspotting*,[18] has worked a little in this genre, his approach brutal, unsentimental.

By contrast, Alexander McCall Smith, with Banks the most popular author in this group, has with his series of novels featuring Mma Precious Ramotswe of the No. 1 Ladies Detective Agency set in Gabarone, Botswana, worked a vein of characterful, humorous and intriguing detective fiction. Where Ramotswe uses shrewd insight to solve crimes that are rarely bloody, a vast way from, for example, Brookmyre's opening of his first novel, with a disfigured corpse covered with faeces and vomit.[19]

What a difference a century has made! In the early 1900s, the foremost Scots man of letters was John Buchan, son of a Free Kirk Manse. He produced a dozen or more adventure novels – 'shockers', he called them – together with a number of fine biographies of Walter Scott, Oliver Cromwell and the less well-known James Graham, First Marquess of Montrose, who had sided with the Scots covenanters then switched to take command of the army of Charles I. He produced numbers of short stories, newspaper and magazine articles and histories, such as a multi-volume history of the First World War, in which a younger brother was killed. He lived in or near London for most of his life, and married into the English upper class : his final and crowning post was as Governor General of Canada.

That which he never doubted, his Scots nationality and culture, is in complete opposition to the ideal Scot implicit in contemporary Scots nationalism. Buchan saw no conflict between his imperialist, Anglified, elitist, Conservative unionist self and the Scots identity he always proudly espoused and about which he was immensely knowledgeable, and about which he was, at times, apt to become sentimental.

He was British first, at least in politics. He gave, in December 1912, a speech opposing the Liberal government's Home Rule Bill because 'he thought that union was strength, and a more progressive force than narrow nationalism'. Yet, loving his native land in his fashion meant that he took for granted that while his state was Britain and much of the world was in the British Empire, his nation was Scotland.

In his adventure books his most vivid characters include the Glasgow grocer Dickson McCunn, the band of Glasgow street kids, the Gorbals Diehards and Sandy Arbuthnot, a 'scion of a noble Scottish house but a wild dreamer, master of disguise.' His most famous hero, Richard Hannay, a Scots-born mining engineer, established, in *The Thirty Nine Steps*, the template for his major Scots characters: bold enough to pre-vail over the invariably foreign evil forces who threaten the existence of an Anglocentric world. Even the minor ones have nerves of steel and hearts of gold, dedicated defenders of king, country and empire, while remaining wholly Scots in speech, culture and sentiment.

Hannay foils a foreign plot in Buchan's best-known shocker, *The Thirty-Nine Steps* (1915). In *Greenmantle* (1916), Hannay again, together with the Scots aristocrat 'Sandy' Arbuthnot, foils a German–Turkish plot to rouse the Muslim masses against the British empire in the Middle East and India. In *The House of the Four Winds* (1935), the former Glasgow slum boy turned Cambridge scholar 'Jaikie' Galt defeats a foreign plot against the rightful rulers of the Central European state of Evallonia.

In these figures, Buchan created the SuperScot, modest, even shy, but in the end, the Winner, the Hero. Scotland, for Buchan, produced men of martial valour, dedicated to the United Kingdom and to Empire, with their hearts still in the Highlands, or on the shores of Fife (where Buchan was born, in his father's manse near Kirkcaldy), or in the Borders, where Buchan's farming relatives lived, and where he loved to walk and fish. It's a world largely gone, since its lynchpin, the Empire, has gone: there are echoes, though, in the 2020s, in one like the International Development Secretary Rory Stewart, raised in a Scots mansion, Etonian, soldier, Iraqi region governor, liberal Conservative, with a father who was nearly head of MI6, who in 2019 ran for leadership of the Tory party and later in the same year, out of sympathy with his party's leader, Boris Johnson, resigned from the party to announce his intention to run for the post of Mayor of London as an independent.

Buchan wrote nearly all of his colossal output in England, or abroad, in South Africa, where he was a young administrator for two years from 1901; and in Canada, where he was Governor General from 1935 until his death in 1940. He conforms to Scots literary practice in one thing at least: in the twentieth and twenty-first centuries, many of the popular authors were or are more likely to write in England, or abroad. Many does not mean all: Allan Massie, essayist and historian as well as novelist, William McIlvanney, Alexander McCall Smith, and Ian Rankin write in Scotland. There are others: and some might put J. K. Rowling, the world's biggest fiction seller, on the list: she lives in Scotland, has married a Scots doctor and enters into the Scots political debate on the centre-left-unionist side. She was, however, born and raised in Gloucestershire, coming to Scotland with her child when she was twenty-two.

Scotland's most popular writers in modern times have tended to be cosmopolitans, Dying just before the twentieth century at the young age of forty-four in Samoa in 1894, Robert Louis Stevenson travelled in and attempted to settle in Europe from his twenties: his *Treasure Island* (1882), *Kidnapped* (1886), and *The Strange Case of Dr Jekyll and Mr Hyde* (1886) became and remain popular, the last sometimes seen as a dramatic satire of Scots schizophrenia, or late Victorian hypocrisy. James Bridie (1888–1951) is, according to Gerald Carruthers, 'one of Scotland's most successful cultural activists and her greatest dramatist of the twentieth century',[20] though one rarely celebrated now: Carruthers added that 'Bridie's is a drama that does not work in today's contemporary culture, which often has such shallow certitude about what is sociologically right and wrong. Bridie's frequent dramatic meditations on the difficulty of both goodness and evil have become sadly unusable and this, it might be argued, is a sign of our own contemporary existential impoverishment.'

James (J. M.) Barrie, the creator of *Peter Pan* (staged 1904) and writer of *The Admirable Crichton* (1892), *Quality Street* (1901) and other plays popular in the early part of the century, lived, and was lionized in London for most of his life. Archibald (A. J.) Cronin (1896–1981), a Scots doctor, wrote a series of novels, including *The Citadel* (1937), *The Stars Look Down* (1935) and *The Keys of the Kingdom* (1941), drawing on his work among mineworkers in the Welsh valleys before: his less successful novel *Country Doctor* (1935) was the basis for a long running BBC serial, 'Doctor Finlay's Casebook'. Giving up medicine for a highly successful writing career, he lived in London, in the USA, while a number of his novels were made into successful films; he died in Montreux, Switzerland.

Of the outstanding contemporary Scots novelists, James Meek was born in England, raised, educated and began in journalism in Scotland, writing his first fiction there. A *Guardian* journalist in Russia, his breakthrough novel was *The Peoples' Act of Love*, drawing on his time in and reading about Russia, a vividly described story set just before and after the 1917 revolution which 'above all . . . reminds us that true believers, in anything, nearly always end up sacrificing their humanity for abstractions'.[21]

William Boyd, born in Ghana to Scots parents, came to wide attention with his 1981 novel, *A Good Man in Africa*: in 2013, after three decades of successful writing, he published the James Bond continuation novel, *Solo*, set in the fictional country Zanzarin (perhaps derived from the Italian word *zanzara*, a mosquito), a thinly disguised version of Biafra during the civil war of 1967–1970. It was a war which had added to the fame of another author, Frederick Forsyth, with his *Dogs of War* (1974), who had covered the Biafran–Nigerian conflict mainly as a freelance reporter. Boyd, who lives in London or in Paris, said in an interview for *The Times*: 'I'm not perceived by the Scottish literary culture as an insider.[22] I don't lie awake at night fretting about it, but these ripples are interesting': at the time, his most recent novel, *Love is Blind* (2018) was partly set in Scotland at the turn of the nineteenth/twentieth centuries, with a Scots hero, Brodie Moncur, who makes a living as a piano tuner. Boyd calls it his 'most Scottish novel ever', and picked out parts of Stevenson's biography with which to clothe Moncur. The hero's father is a portrait of a massively hypocritical, public-pleasing Presbyterian minister, a tyrant to his cowering, trapped daughters and a hater of Brodie, the one child who got away.

Andrew O'Hagan's first novel, *Our Fathers* (1991) was what reviewers call 'assured': and so it was. It was built around a family whose patriarch, Hugh, is dying, with both the socialism to which he had adhered and the flat block in which he lived crumbling. The death scene is done with great emotional strength: the life and work of the dying man, being, as he died, investigated for corruption because he cut corners and bought cheaper materials to build more flats for families desperate for modern homes is similarly well handled. A later novel, *Be Near Me* (2006) is of an English Catholic priest come to Scotland and shows the same, deepened skill: his journalism, including an attempt to tell the story of Julian Assange, is lucid, sharp and illuminating.

In 2002, O'Hagan wrote, in the *London Review of Books*, with which he has long been connected, a review of Neal Ascherson's meditation on Scotland, *Stone Voices* (Granta, 2003). It was a sharply critical review of a writer whom he saw as ignoring Scotland's grim truth, that it 'play(s) the part of the good father, coddling Scotland into a state of temporary sleep with the singing of old lullabies'. For O'Hagan, then, Scotland was cemented with resentments, 'from ruined monastery to erupting tower block: blame, fear, bigotry and delusion, their fragments powder the common air and always the fault is seen to lie elsewhere, with other nations, other lives. Scotland is a place where cultural artefacts and past battles – the Stone of Destiny, Robert Burns, *Braveheart*, Bannockburn – have more impact on people's sense of moral action than politics does. The people have no real commitment to the public sphere, and are not helped towards any such commitment by the dead rhetoric of the young parliament.'

There is much more like it: a list of Scotland's self-serving, self-pitying, self-obsessed keening about others, mainly the English, stealing their birthright and smashing their culture. He ends with an unambiguous endorsement of the Union: 'there can be no argument, now . . . about how well Scotland did from the Union. All considered, it did better than England . . . Scotland must go on now to establish its role in bringing about a new United Kingdom within a new Europe.'

I read and re-read that piece, for the verve of its indignation at what O'Hagan considered was Ascherson's misreading of our nation, though I thought then, as now, that he overdid the revulsion. Most Scots with whom I grew up, and have known since, spend little time on keening, unless they are nationalists. I liked it because the last sentiment was a rare sentence to come from a Scots writer and intellectual or, indeed, an English intellectual.

So O'Hagan's conversion to nationalism, unveiled at the 2017 Edinburgh Book Festival, was a surprise. Like the Ascherson review, it was uncompromising: he gave a brief nod to his earlier view: 'Scotland used to feel too sorry for itself . . . but that notion is now as old as the people who said it, and I should know because I'm one' but went on to rejoice that Scots were now in the 'garden of the imagination, digging for fresh truth amid too many old prejudices'.

He had watched a count of the 2014 referendum and, musing on it, wrote that 'though the case for nationalism had not been fully made, it began to seem to me that the ground was shifting nonetheless, regardless of opinion, and that a re-constituted Scotland was already in process. Despite the seeming defeat and the constant punditry and a comic debility of Westminster power, what if we were already in the early days of a better nation, with the idea carefully minted and the coin merely to follow?' Scots still raged, not now against false betrayals, but 'for fairness and equality'. Scotland could put aside the imperialism, and of course 'neoliberalism', forced upon it by England.

The conversion takes nothing away from O'Hagan's skill as a writer, both of fiction and of journalism. It does show, though, the power of the myths he once denounced: that the country is the moral superior of its larger neighbour, and that thus an escape from the British embrace was necessary to realize its true essence, its identity, its authenticity.

CONCLUSION: THE RE-IMAGINING OF THE UNION

The Union of 1707 still serves Scotland best. Brexit strains it: Prime Minister Boris Johnson may do so too (though with this politician-chameleon, nothing can be certain). Even with both of these, Brexit does not come down so heavily on the side of secession to make it a good idea.

First, if a second referendum on Scots independence takes place, the issues that were ignored, or seen as minor in the 2014 exercise will impose themselves. Scotland's secession will have a profound effect on all other British citizens, who have no voice in the referendum: this includes Scots living elsewhere in the UK, many of whom often intend to return to Scotland, either for retirement or to seek a new job or because they found they preferred to live there. They objected then, and would object more loudly in the future, if they continued to be excluded from voting for a matter about which many feel deeply.

Could a second referendum work on the basis that 50 per cent plus one ushers in a new nation? It would be dangerous to assume that the minority would tamely accept the result: a new nation state would be launched on a deeply divided country. More, since what had been a common market would become two sovereign countries, with one (England, Wales and Northern Ireland) out of the EU and Scotland seeking to join the EU, and a hard border would thus be likely in the future. Many companies and financial institutions would see the major market recede behind future tariff walls and re-locate to England. A new nation state would be launched into deepening unemployment and falling living standards.

There is an example that the UK should follow, or adapt. It comes from Canada, which an imperial Britain created as a state in the eighteenth century and which, in facing its own secessionist challenge at the end of the twentieth century, learned lessons that it can now teach the UK, whose own engagement with Scots secession has so far been less considered than was Canada's.

In 1995, a referendum on independence in the French-speaking province of Quebec scraped a victory for the NO side of the argument with 50.58 per cent of a vote of over 90 per cent of the population. In the aftermath of the vote, the leaders of the Parti Quebecois, buoyed by their near victory, continued to press for another referendum to get over the 50 per cent line, including a claim that a vote for independence in the National Assembly, Quebec's parliament, would suffice to secede.

In 1996, the Liberal government under Jean Chrétien appointed Stéphane Dion Minister for Intergovernmental Affairs, a post which gave him responsibility for the relationships between Canada's provinces, and especially Quebec. Dion was born and raised in Quebec City, with a secular, academic father, himself pursuing an academic career, with the governance of Quebec as his main interest. A Quebec nationalist when in his teens and early twenties, Dion had turned into a strong federalist, and was publishing books and articles arguing the federalist case. Chrétien, in need of one, preferably a French speaker, who could argue the case for federalism, found a safe seat for Dion and quickly gave him the hot potato of Quebec to hold, and cool, as Minister for Intergovernmental Affairs.

Dion's approach, at once cerebral and determined, is a model for British unionists. In the year of his appointment, he posed three questions to the country's supreme court: could the Quebec National Assembly legally declare and pursue independence? Does international law allow a unilateral declaration of independence by Quebec? Which assembly takes precedence in the result of a clash – the Quebecois or the Canadian governments? The court ruled that while Quebec had the right to secede, it did not have the right to do so unilaterally; this even though Canada, unlike most other democracies, does not outlaw secessionist movements or votes.

Dion then engaged in an open and detailed argument with the PQ leadership. Most significantly, he wrote three letters in 1997 and 1998: two to Lucien Bouchard, the PQ leader (1997–2001); and one to Jacques Brassard, the Quebecois Minister for Canadian Affairs.[1] These were not couched in bureaucratic or ministerially proper language: though never insulting, they were strongly argumentative and at times chiding. Their theme was the need to respect Canadian and international law, coupled with a warm endorsement of a Canada in which Quebec and the Quebecers had thrived, and contributed largely to the country's success as one of the most multicultural states in the world.

His main point to both ministers was the need for clarity. Canada, and its supreme court, accepted the right of secession – 'highly unusual' as he wrote in his first letter to Bouchard, 'in the international community': but the court specified that the question put in a referendum had to be unambiguously clear; that a unilateral declaration of independence had no legal force; and that a narrow vote taken as a basis for independence would open up endless conflict .'It is customary for a democracy to require a consensus for serious, virtually irreversible changes that deeply affect not only our lives but those of future generations . . . it would be too dangerous to attempt such an operation (as secession) on the basis of a narrow, "soft" majority, as it is commonly called, which could evaporate in the face of difficulties'.

In his letter to Brassard, Dion's questions were more urgent and pointed: 'what does your talk of "effective control" mean? How would you exercise such control following a unilateral declaration of independence that was not accepted by the government of Canada? What would you do faced with the many citizens who would claim their right not to lose Canada on the basis of such a procedure? . . . a break-up of the country could only occur after Quebecers had very clearly expressed their desire to renounce Canada and after the conditions of secession had been established.'

In his last letter, the second to Bouchard, he was at his most categorical. In the ('unfortunate') case that Quebecers had voted in large numbers for secession, the vote would not automatically be followed by acceptance on the part of the federal government but by negotiations, which would include judgements on whether or not the question asked was clear: 'You will appreciate that the federal government, among others, cannot surrender its responsibility to evaluate the clarity of a question which could result in the break-up of the country ... [the obligation to negotiate secession] itself depends on clear support for secession, respect for the constitutional framework and a good deal of mutual good faith ... the time for stratagems and "winning tricks" is over. Instead of concocting the question that will snatch a few thousand more votes, do your job. Explain to Quebecers why we would be happier if we were no longer Canadians *as well*' [my italics].

Dion's insistence on clarity was reflected in law: the Canadian Clarity Act,[2] passed in 2000. It had been preceded, in October 1999, by a conference on federalism, where, on the first day, speakers including Bouchard excoriated the federal government's interference in what, they believed, should be a Quebec-only affair. They were supported by a representative of the SNP, George, later Sir George Reid, an MSP who in 2003 became presiding officer of the Scots parliament. Reid, repeating his party's orthodoxy, told the conference that 50 per cent +1 should be enough for secession: he was feted by the PQ ministers present. The star turn, however, was US President, Bill Clinton, who spoke strongly against secession, emphasizing, in Dion's vein, the seriousness of the decision and the myriad of questions a successful separation from the larger state would pose.

The Clarity Act reserves for the federal government the decision on the clarity or otherwise of a question put to citizens in a referendum, and to cancel the result of the referendum if it was decided that its conduct breached any part of the Act; it lays down that the question must only be one for or against secession, with no attempt to weight the question either way; that a consensus, not closely defined, must be achieved before negotiations on secession begin; and that all other provinces, and representatives of the 'First Nations' (the descendants of the indigenous inhabitants) should be involved in negotiations. This does two main things: it avoids the would-be independent state starting life with a deeply split population: and it recognizes that the nation state as a whole has a right to take part in the decision. The law is vague in some respects: but, since the pressure for secession in Quebec has greatly diminished and was dropping soon after the referendum failed, it's unlikely to be tested soon.

An Act of that kind is needed in the UK. It is arguable that, where a vote for the non-status quo is a momentous one, the majority should be at least 60 per cent. That, or even something higher, would speak, if attained, to a public serious about, even passionate for change. That would be combined with a commitment to consult and debate, in parliament and nationwide, on the issue where the majority for change is over 50 per cent: but 60 per cent, at least, would remain the necessary threshold for transition to a radically different state of affairs. Even then, a period should elapse before an agreement is made between representatives of the two sides of the referendum.

A Scots-only referendum is presented by the SNP as the country's absolute right: yet while Scotland, like Quebec, has the right to secede, there is no implied right that the referendum should be confined to Scotland only. An act of the kind the Canadians have adopted would offset the manifest unfairness of the exclusion of all but those living in Scotland from the decision. Emile Simpson, a Scot and former army officer, now a fellow at Harvard University, wrote that 'Scotland is free to leave the union if it wants to. However, to recognize the justice of Scotland's right to choose its own future is simultaneously to recognize the injustice that all other British citizens have no democratic voice in the future of their own state . . . to have no voice feels culturally unjust. Not just for many of those among the 830,000 people born in Scotland who now live elsewhere in the United Kingdom (and thus can't vote), but for many British citizens who feel that Scotland is inseparably intertwined with their broader cultural identity.'[3]

The experience of preparing for Brexit, and the fraught negotiations with an unyielding European Union, teaches a lesson to both sides in any future division of the UK. Whether leaving the EU is as momentous as the break-up of the United Kingdom after more than three centuries of the Union can be debated: I would argue that the latter is more damaging. But both were conceded unwisely, with apparently little thought by the Cameron government. The EU Leave/Remain vote has grievously divided the UK population: the Scots independence debate would have had the same effect, had the nationalists won. Where a referendum is thought to be necessary, the representative democracy on which the UK's politics and government depends cannot be narcotized, and transformed into a mere instrument of popular will which could, as George Reid assured the Canadians, come down to 50 per cent +1. Both popular demand and parliamentary democracy need to have a say.

The referendum vote for leaving the EU must, however, be respected: it was advertised as binding, and both the ruling Conservatives and the opposition Labour Party committed themselves to carrying the decision of the people through. To argue, as *The Economist* did a few days after Boris Johnson entered No.10, that 'there is no mandate for no-deal, which was not in the Leave prospectus nor advocated by any party in the last election',[4] and thus a new referendum must be mounted, is bad faith. The referendum question was 'Should the United Kingdom remain a member of the European Union or leave the European Union?': the manner of leaving was not specified. No democracy can remain undamaged if it cancels out such commitments on such a frail reasoning. But the damage which a hastily conceded, thoughtlessly overseen referendum can do, or would do, is now clear. Parliamentary democracy must have more faith in its own rights and duties, to good governance. It must make clear that it opposes a secession which will, probably irreversibly, change radically the British state: it must be militant in the defence of the Union. Dion showed that sharp, informed argument can undermine the rhetorical tropes of the nationalists: too little of that happened in the UK, in either referendum.

Something else is also clear. To unpick legislation and commercial links made over nearly half a century of EU membership is a gargantuan task for a relatively large and efficient British civil service. To do so over more than three centuries would leave a much smaller Scots bureaucracy with a near impossible demand.

On the rest of the UK side, the lesson that would be taken from the EU negotiations for a future independence deal would be to adopt clear red lines – clearer and more durable than those the former Prime Minister, Theresa May, struggled unsuccessfully to maintain – and give way as little as possible. Negotiations over the remaining oil would be particularly tough, the more since third parties would be part of the negotiation, including the major companies extracting the oil, none of which is Scots-owned.

The constant efforts of the SNP to secede, their hostility to England and to Westminster government as well as the abuse put out by many in the cultural sphere has encouraged a move towards English nationalism; not, as is frequently asserted, an expression of far-right politics, but a recognition that devolution, and Scotland's pressure for independence, requires a new ordering of the United Kingdom. For the nationalists, this is used as another reason for leaving the Union.

As this book has argued, the economic prospect set out by the nationalists is hugely over-optimistic: the more, since a period of minimal growth, perhaps a recession, will make all reasonable forecasts turn down. The nationalists have not prepared the Scots people for an event as immense as secession, and have based much of their politics on an assurance that independence will solve all problems and raise all boats.

The British Union is being put aside in favour of the European Union at a time when the latter is undergoing a deepening crisis. The Central European states – Czech Republic, Hungary, Poland and Slovakia – are large receivers of European funds, and disagree with the Union on fundamental issues. For some, membership has done nothing to make their governments less corrupt: rather, it seems, the opposite. As this is written, the Prime Minister of the Czech Republic, Andrej Babis, is fighting for his political life against serious charges of fraudulent use of EU subsidies. In Romania, Liviu Dragnea, head of the ruling Social Democratic Party, was jailed on corruption charges, with more pending: the head of the anti-corruption office which had pursued Dragnea, Laura Codruta Kovesi, was arrested in March 2019 on a series of charges, barred from leaving the country and forbidden to speak to the news media (she was later released). Kovesi was later head of the European Public prosecutors' Office, a new institution set up to investigate crimes committed in relation to EU budget funds. Romania, at the time holding the presidency of the EU, strongly opposed the appointment.

In Italy, two populist–nationalist parties, the Lega and the Five Stars Movement, formed a rackety coalition in which the two party leaders constantly warred with each other, while a powerless Prime Minister threatened to resign. The most powerful politician, head of the Lega Mateo Salvini, said he will break EU constraints on the Italian budget in order to fulfil campaign promises. The coalition collapsed in August

2019: a new coalition, between the Five Stars and the centre-left Partito Democratico was formed, without an election to give it a popular mandate. The German coalition between the Christian Democrats, Christian Social Union and the Social Democrats is extremely fragile, as the country faces reduced growth. Marie le Pen's Rassemblement National narrowly beat President Emmanuel Macron's En Marche party in the May 2019 Euro elections, though other far-right parties in Europe did less well. For the SNP, the EU is a safe harbour for a small country that had left its habitual anchorage: the chaos of Brexit obscured the large problems facing Europe. There is also no clarity as to how the EU would treat an application to join from Scotland and whether or not it would demand that it adopt the Euro, as new members are obliged to do.

The creation of a new state will always create disruption, and typically cause a drop in GDP. For citizens of the seceding state, that can be worthwhile if its position within a larger state is felt by a majority to be oppressive, as a majority of Irish citizens did in the early 1920s.

Scotland is in no such position. After years of nationalist hegemony (from 2007), it remains split nearly equally over secession: only an irresponsible government would seek a referendum in these circumstances. The reason for the reluctance of the (so far) majority against secession is one that nationalists cannot recognize: that is, that most Scots have felt comfortable enough in their joint nationality – Scottish and British – even if they prefer to define themselves as Scots. The ties of family and friendship, of work and financial commitments, of shared cultures and histories, make Union a more deeply civic experience than a nervy nationalism. Three centuries of Union have not wiped out Scots national feeling, or cultural distinctiveness: it was not the intention of the 1707 Union that it should.

For those who wish to deepen their experience of being Scots, now is a time of greater possibility than ever. There is provision, usually free, to learn, or re-learn, Scots and Gaelic. There are thousands of books, programmes and websites on aspects of Scots history, culture and the different regions. The devolution of powers has been extensive: the possibilities of greater involvement in civic life wide. Scotland, in the twenty-first century, is both as free and secure a nation as the world of the early twenty-first century allows. It would be worse than a mistake, a crime, to hazard that for an independence which can bring nothing better.

There's a further question to be asked of Scotland's nationalists, who may well be on the way to winning their secessionist aim or even, by the time this book is published, have won it. That is: is the SNP a liberal party?

Any democratic party will carry the seeds of authoritarianism and, especially if successful in election, it will be tempted to sow them. The SNP has been hugely successful: indeed in 2015, one year after losing the independence referendum, it won 56 of the 59 Westminster parliament seats, courteously leaving one each for the Conservatives, Labour and the Liberal Democrats. It was the third largest party in the House of Commons. In the 2016 election for the Scottish parliament, the Party took 63 seats – two short of the majority in an election where the Conservatives surged to take 31 seats, sixteen more than before. But with the support of the Greens' six seats, a comfortable enough ruling majority.

There were and are disturbing signs. In that referendum campaign, Ed Miliband, then Labour leader, was so badly heckled when on a pre-election walkabout he gave up his efforts to talk to people, and later said he had seen 'an ugly side' of the pro independence side. The following May, the comedian Eddie Izzard and the then leader of Scottish Labour, Jim Murphy, were jostled and shouted down when they attempted to address a crowd: two SNP members, identified as leading the fracas, were later placed under 'administrative suspension' by the SNP. There were many reports of intimidation of known unionists: several said they were afraid to display stickers of placards saying 'NO' to independence.

The Party has a strong cult of leadership, which surrounded both Alex Salmond and since 2014, Nicola Sturgeon. Their appearances at conferences and meetings were choreographed to concentrate applause and attention upon them when they appeared: delegates, when speaking, usually praise them; challenges to their leadership style and policies, and those of the leadership, are, in public, rare. Much of that is no different, except in degree, from other parties' gatherings, the major exception being that in the SNP conferences there is little time given for real, especially critical, debate. A huge part of the business of the conferences is dominated by appearances of members who, for various reasons, praise the Party.

After he resigned as leader, Salmond took a post as a chat show host on the Russian international channel, RT (Russia Today). RT does do incisive reports on some aspects of Western lives; in the main, those that reflect badly on the Western democracies. In July 2019, RT was fined £200,000 by the media regulator Ofcom for breaking the regulator's code on objectivity. On several occasions, interviewers had failed to challenge, or agreed with, interviewees who, for example, supported the Russian support of the government of Syria's president in his scorched earth campaign to root out his opponents, or who agreed with the Russian government line that the attempts to murder the former double agent Sergei Skripal, a military intelligence officer, in Salisbury in 2018, were 'fake news'.

The concentrated hatred of England, the English and Westminster by supporters of independence has been and still is especially strong among supporters in the cultural sphere but comes out, too, in the politicians. The leader of the SNP in parliament in the 1970s and 1980s was Donald Stewart, who wanted to separate from an England 'eaten by the maggots of permissiveness and decay'. To produce and encourage rhetoric of that kind of a neighbouring democracy with which Scotland has been in amicable and profitable union for so long betrays, indeed, an ugly side to nationalism, and shows the Party's need for a detested enemy. It's a common contemporary complaint that the parliamentary committees, especially in the period when the SNP's dominance was near-absolute, are feeble at holding the ministers to account, chaired as they are by SNP parliamentarians. Criticism for other parties is often condemned as 'running down Scotland', a line often taken by John Swinney, when facing opposition from MSPs of other parties on his handling of the education brief, characterizing the criticism as disrespectful to Scots teachers.

The Party tends to represent all Scots as desperate for independence, when the most evident test of feeling on the issue, the 2014 referendum, showed a 55 per cent majority against it. This, at a time when the SNP was at its most dominant and popular.

These signs are not trivial. But the Party's conduct is, if not impeccably, mostly convincingly democratic. The Scots nationalists don't concern themselves much with political philosophy: and the intellectuals who support it haven't produced much in the way of a description and programme for the civic, social democratic nationalism it proclaims. This is not surprising, since it was right of centre until the 1980s: it has no roots in a political tradition on which it can draw: everything is suborned to a fevered charge for independence.

Yet it broadly respects, or at least does not attack, the verities of a democratic movement: periodic election, the results of which are respected; observance of the rule of law; freedom of speech, division of powers. It adheres to the general rules, both written and unwritten, of parliamentary democracy and civil society. Nicola Sturgeon is clearly uneasy with the name of her party, saying, during an Edinburgh Book Festival conversation with the Turkish author Elif Shafak, that it was 'hugely problematic' and had a 'negative meaning' for her. 'Those of us', she said, 'who do support Scottish independence ... could not be further removed from some of what you would recognize as nationalism in other parts of the world.' If pious, it's a recognition of a wish to mark a deep trench between the SNP and, for example, the German Alternativ für Deutschland or the French Rassemblement National. Still, the party is stuck with it: as it is with the aim of finding an independence which would, described as 'nationalist' or not, will damage the nation.

The nationalists, with the exception of some of the most ardent spirits, remain within the constraints of British liberal politics. The Scots had, with most other peoples who had undergone the twentieth century's 'experience of infamy', understood that the rules of civilized existence had been smashed: as the political philosopher Isaiah Berlin remarked, 'because these rules were flouted, we have been forced to become conscious of them'.[5] So far, that understanding has held (though in the twenty-first century, it looks shakier than in the latter half of the twentieth). The SNP is not in the business, as are the other European nationalists from whom Sturgeon wishes to distinguish her party, of testing the limits of a revived respect for a post-war, post-communist moderation in politics, sustained, as Michael Ignatieff writes, 'this time not by faith in, but fear of, mankind'.[6]

Devolution of powers from Westminster has tended, in the first two decades of this century, to benefit the nationalists. But it must now be grasped as an opportunity for the Union. The emergence of an English national movement opens the possibility of a re-working of the three centuries' old institution in which the people of England have begun to speak, and where the complex, but refreshing effort of crafting a new relationship must now be faced.

Objections to a 'solution', which simply treats each of the four nations in the UK as states in a federation – essentially, the proposal of the Salisbury-sponsored Bill presented to the House of Lords – are well founded. England would dominate everything: yet there is a clearly growing movement for greater devolution of powers to regions and cities, a movement which would reduce the weight of England in the 'state of nations' which is the UK.

Every one of the nations and nation states so involved would have skin in the game to improve the way in which they relate: necessary for the British Union, it's also needed by the European Union, badly needing to clarify to itself and to the world whether it is a federal state in the making, or a single market of closely aligned states who recognize and work with each other's separate statehood.

The European Union was created to end centuries of intra-European wars, especially between Germany and France, through the creation of a federal state called Europe. That's presently unattainable: the straining for statehood was an ideal too far. The scholar and politician Ralph (Lord) Dahrendorf, himself a young EU Commissioner (1970–1977) came to believe that the EU could not become a fully democratic institution but that it was vital that the nation states continue to be democratic. Noting that the EU has disregarded Dahrendorf's advice and seeks to create some sort of democratic system at the European level, Jan Zielonka, Professor of European Politics at Oxford, observes that 'If the EU had listened to Dahrendorf, we would probably have been able to avoid the present disordered politics, with all the negative implications both at the European level and in the member states.'

What is attainable may be a community that recognizes that states still command loyalty and provide rights and will do for the foreseeable future but which has created a framework of cooperation and a fund of amity that can be used to foster close cooperation, common projects, defence of the environment and the promotion of peace. The Union of the United Kingdom was a move to come together to defend against threats that no longer exist and to protect a religion which, in Europe, no longer requires it. It remained after the threats receded because it had proven its use, with the large exception of what is now the Republic of Ireland. It created a comity of nations whose peoples have mingled and merged, from nations which have remained culturally distinct.

Reality will not be what the nationalists' policy and economic papers predict: the less so, as the economic skies darken over Europe (and the world). Scotland's leaders, in the nation's more than two decades of devolved government, have ducked, ignored or mishandled many of the challenges the country faces, or will face. The reality that will await them on independence, losing the support on which it has counted from the Westminster parliament, will be an exceptionally tough one, more likely to lead to a series of political and economic crises than the brave new morning of the rebirth of a nation state.

What could lead to a better Scotland would be engagement in the forming of a British Union with clarity both in the division of national powers and of the assignment of responsibilities. Then, the nations which have come together in union could enter a period both of grappling with their separate realities and cooperating, in mutual support, in the fashioning of a globally active, progressive state, capable of putting some weight into the very large tasks that need to be accomplished if the world is to survive in greater equality and remain at peace. Our state of nations would do that better if together, than apart.

NOTES

Introduction: Breaking Britain

1 Michael Keating, *Small Nations in a Big World: What Scotland Can Learn* (Viewpoints), Luath Press Ltd, Kindle edition

2 https://www.scotsman.com/news/politics/scottish-independence-most-scots-would-back-independence-under-pm-boris-johnson-1-4952657

3 Arthur Herman, *The Scottish Enlightenment: The Scots' Invention of the Modern World*, pub. Fourth Estate, 2002, p. viii

4 Gerrard Carruthers and Colin Kidd, *Literature and Union*, Oxford University Press, 2018, p. 27

5 Alice Brown, David McCrone and Lindsay Paterson, *Politics and Society in Scotland*, Macmillan Press, 1996, p. 205

6 https://standpointmag.co.uk/features-may-14-independence-nothing-for-scots-nigel-biggar-referendum /

7 https://www.thetimes.co.uk/article/we-are-failing-to-make-the-grade-in-education-q3vg8gjv6

8 https://www.opendemocracy.net/en/opendemocracyuk/eight-reasons-scotland-is-more-remain-and-what-will-happen-if-its-dragged-out/

9 http://downloads.bbc.co.uk/radio4/reith2019/Reith_2019_Sumption_lecture_2.pdf

10 Michael Fry, *A New Race of Men*, Birlinn, 2013, p. 395
11 Gordon Brown, *My Scotland, Our Britain*, Simon and Schuster, 2014, p. 239

1 The Other Union

1 https://www.embl.de/aboutus/science_society/discussion/discuss ion_2006/refl-22june06.pdf
2 https://www.ft.com/content/d739d2e4-cb17-48c8-9010-b03d5402 38bd
3 https://www.foreignaffairs.com/articles/1997-01-01/power-shift
4 https://www.foreignaffairs.com/articles/united-states/2019-06-11/- globalizations-wrong-turn?
5 https://www.spiegel.de/international/germany/surprise-european- commission-nomination-for-von-der-leyen-a-1275984.html
6 Mehreen Khan, 'New Hanseatic states stick together in EU big league', *Financial Times*, 27 November 2018. https://www.ft.com/- content/f0ee3348-f187-11e8-9623-d7f9881e729 f
7 https://www.foreignaffairs.com/articles/europe/2018-12-10/brok en-europe
8 https://www.foreignaffairs.com/articles/world/2019-02-12/brok en-bargain
9 David Goodhart, *The Road to Somewhere*, Hurst, 2017, p. 21
10 https://www.foreign affairs.com/articles/2001-01-01/will-nation-st ate-survive-globalization
11 https://www.ft.com/content/ade39e66-a6dc-11e9-b6ee-3cdf3174 eb89
12 Gerry Hassan and Russell Gunson, eds., 'Brexit, the SNP and Independence', in *Scotland, the UK and Brexit*, Luath Press, 2017
13 https://quarterly.demos.co.uk/article/issue-1/sovereignty-and-the- crisis-of-democratic-politics-2/
14 http://ucparis.fr/files/9313/6549/9943/What_is_a_Nation.pdf
15 Benedict Anderson, *Imagined Communities: Reflections on the Origins and Spread of Nationalism*, Verso, 2016
16 https://www.elijahwald.com/borderblog/frederick-douglass-on- immigration/
17 https://www.nytimes.com/2018/08/27/books/review/francis-fuku yama-identity-kwame-anthony-appiah-the-lies-that-bind.html

18 Miguel Beltran de Felipe, *Myths and Realities of Secessionisms*, Palgrave, 2019
19 https://www.theguardian.com/world/2018/jul/12/catalan-presid ent-cites-scottish-model-in-call-for-independence-poll
20 James Mitchell and Gerry Hassan, eds., *Scottish National Party Leaders*, Biteback, 2016, p. 281
21 David Torrance, *Salmond: Against the Odds*, Birlinn, 2010, p. 256
22 https://www.heraldscotland.com/news/12336000.winning-praises-nationalist-rebirth-cardinal-sees-future-in-europe/
23 https://www.thetimes.co.uk/article/letters-reveal-snp-crisis-over-presidents-anti-catholic-diatribes-jsl7b3xbb0m
24 Interview with Alex Salmond, *The Tablet*, 25 July 2009

2 The English Speak
 1 Vernon Bogdanor, 'The Future of the Union', Legatum Institute, November 2014
 2 Martin Laughlin, *The British Constitution: A Very Short Introduction*, Oxford University Press, 2013
 3 https://www.theguardian.com/politics/2007/feb/27/immigration policy.race
 4 Dominic Lieven, *Empire*, John Murray, 2000, p. 414
 5 *Independent*, 18 February 2019
 6 https://www.theguardian.com/news/2017/nov/09/brexiters-put-money-offshore-tax-haven
 7 Christopher Coker, *The Rise of the Civilizational States*, Polity, 2019
 8 https://www.theguardian.com/world/2016/sep/13/michael-goves-claims-about-history-teaching-are-false-says-research
 9 Magne Flemmen and Mike Savage, *British Journal of Sociology*, 68, S1, p. 252
10 Fintan O'Toole, *Heroic Failure*, Apollo, 2018. The section on O'Toole adapts articles I wrote in *The Irish Times* (23 January 2019) and the Washington Post (27 March 2019) criticizing his book.
11 Roger Scruton, *New Statesman*, 2000
12 Michael Kenny, *Politics of English Nationhood*, 2014, p. 69
13 Ibid., p. 68
14 Ibid., p. 70

15 Carruthers and Kidd, *Literature and Union*, op cit., p. 332
16 https://www.newstatesman.com/politics/2014/05/whatever-happe
ned-english-democrats
17 Vernon Bogdanor, *The New British Constitution*, Hart Publishing,
2009, p. 271
18 https://newleftreview.org/issues/II5/articles/j-g-a-pocock-gaberlu
nzie-s-return

3 The Cash Nexus

1 *New Statesman*, 21 September 2019
 2 Robert Tombs, *The English and their History*, Penguin, 2015,
p. 329
 3 Ian MacLean and James Gallagher, *Scotland's Choices*, Edinburgh
University Press, p. 66
 4 House of Lords: Select Committee on the Barnett Formula; 1st
Report of Session 2008–2009, HL Paper 139
 5 'Berwick residents vote for move to Scotland', *The Scotsman*, 16
February 2008
 6 https://studylib.net/doc/8699659/1-the-moral-economy of deind
ustrialization-in-post
 7 https://www.tandfonline.com/doi/full/10.1080/09692290.2011.
561124 (with Ben Clift)
 8 http://eprints.gla.ac.uk/90818/1/90818.pdf
 9 J. Phillips (2015), 'The closure of Michael Colliery in 1967 and the
politics of deindustrialization in Scotland', *Twentieth Century British
History*, 26(4): 551–72
10 Martin Adeney and John Lloyd, *Loss without Limit*, Routledge,
1986, p. 299
11 Michael Russell, *Grasping the Thistle*, Argyll Publishing, 2006
12 https://www.marxists.org/reference/archive/smith-adam/works/-
wealth-of-nations/book05/ch03-3.htm
13 Iain McLean, *Adam Smith, Radical and Egalitarian*, Edinburgh
University Press, 2006
14 Alex Salmond, 'Scotland "didn't mind" Thatcher Economics', *The
Scotsman*, 20 August, 2008
15 Ruth Davidson, Former journalist, on politics, family and what
makes her angry, BBC, 23 April 2014

16 George Kerevan, ed., *Tackling Timorous Economics*, Luath Press, 2017, p. 668
17 Ibid., pp. 85–125

4 The Crumbling Pillars

1 Ray Perman, *Hubris*, Birlinn, 2012, loc. 591 Kindle edition
2 Ibid., loc. 924
3 Paul Moore, *Crash Bang Wallop*, New Wilberforce Media
4 Ian Fraser, *Shredded*, Birlinn, 2014
5 John Lanchester, 'It's Finished', *London Review of Books*, 28 May 2009
6 Gillian Tett, *Fools' Gold*, Abacus, p. 109
7 James Buchan, *John Law, a Scottish Adventurer of the 18th Century*, McLehose Press, 2018
8 Arthur Herman, *The Scottish Enlightenment: The Scots Invention of the Modern World*, pub. Fourth Estate, 2002, p. 27
9 Christopher Whatley, *The Scots and the Union*, Edinburgh University Press, p. 167
10 James Buchan, op.cit.
11 B. A. Farbey, C. R. Mitchell and K. Webb, 'Change and Stability in the Ideology of Scottish Nationalism', *International Political Science Review*, 1(3) quoted in Sabrina Elena Sotiriu, '"It's Scotland's Oil!": The use of nationalist rhetoric in SNP propaganda', University of Ottawa, 2011
12 Peter Lynch (2009), 'From Social Democracy back to No Ideology? The Scottish National Party and Ideological Change in a Multi-level Electoral Setting', *Regional and Federal Studies*, 19(4): 619–37. Sotiriu, op. cit. p. 15
13 Alexander Kemp, *Official History of North Sea Oil*, 2 vols., Routledge, 2011
14 http://www.oilofscotland.org/mccronereportscottishoffice.pdf
15 Geoffrey W. Lee (1976), 'North Sea Oil and Scottish Nationalism', *Political Quarterly*, 47, July–September: 307–17
16 https://www.ifs.org.uk/publications/13072
17 Brian Ashcroft, 'Scotland's economic problem: too few entrepreneurs, too little enterprise', Dept. of Economics, University of Strathclyde, 10 December 1996

18 https://krugman.blogs.nytimes.com/2014/02/24/scots-wha-hae/
19 https://policyexchange.org.uk/scottish-independence-a-political-
question/
20 Kevin Hague, These Islands: Response to the Sustainable Growth
Commission, July 2018
21 https://www.these-islands.co.uk/publications/i313/gc_endorsem
ents.aspx
22 https://www.independent.co.uk/news/uk/scottish-independence/-
scottish-independence-full-text-of-david-camerons-no-going-ba
ck-speech-9735902.html
23 Tom Devine, *The Scottish Nation, 1700–2000*, Penguin, p. 91
24 Robert Crawford, *The Bard*, Jonathan Cape, 2009, p. 19.
25 Devine, ibid., p. 98
26 George Davie, *The Democratic Intellect*, Edinburgh University Press,
1961
27 Quoted in T. C. Smout, *A Century of the Scottish People*, Fontana,
1997, p. 227
28 https://www.theguardian.com/education/2017/mar/21/may-sturg
eon-scottish-education-neglect-science
29 https://dspace.stir.ac.uk/bitstream/1893/11356/1/Curriculum   for
Excellence_SER_FINAL.pdf
30 https://blogs.lse.ac.uk/politicsandpolicy/curriculum-for-excelle
nce/
31 https://www.bbc.co.uk/news/uk-scotland-scotland-politics-3575
2756
32 http://www.scottishreview.net/ElgaGraves453a.html
33 https://www.bbc.co.uk/news/uk-scotland-glasgow-west-47094231

5 *To Be Yersel'*

1 https://www.theguardian.com/politics/2014/aug/17/scottish-indep
endence-tom-devine-yes-vote-referendum-alex-salmond
2 Neal Ascherson, *Stone Voices*, Granta, 2003, p. 305
3 Alan Bold, *MacDiarmid*, Paladin, 1988
4 Hugh MacDiarmid, John Manson, Dorian Grieve and Alan Riach,
Revolutionary Art of the Future: Rediscovered Poems, Carcanet Press,
2003
5 http://theses.gla.ac.uk/1181/1/2001carrutherphd.pdf

6 https://strathprints.strath.ac.uk/31500/7/Goldie_EUP_2011_Hugh
   _MacDiarmid_the_impossible_persona.pdf
7 Alan Bold, op.cit., p. 416
8 Arthur Aughey, *The Politics of Englishness*, Manchester University
   Press, 2007
9 David Edgerton, *The Rise and Fall of the British Nation*, Allen Lane,
   2018, p.102
10 Ibid., pp. 7–8
11 Eric Kaufmann, *Whiteshift: Populism, Immigration and the Future of
   White Majorities*, Allen Lane, 2018, p. 3
12 https://www.theguardian.com/uk/1999/aug/15/theobserver.ukne
   ws1
13 https://strathprints.strath.ac.uk/47320/8/Goldie_CCBF_2015_Mo
   dern_Scottish_Fiction_Telling_Stories.pdf
14 Eleanor Yule and David Manderson, *The Glass Half Full: Moving
   Beyond Scottish Miserabilism*, Luath Press, 2014
15 Michael Shea, *State of the Nation* (1997) and *Endgame* (2002)
16 Douglas Hurd *Scotch on the Rocks* (with Andrew Osmond,1971) and
   Image in the Water (2001)
17 William McIlvaney, *Laidlaw*, Hodder and Stoughton, 1977
18 Irvine Welsh, *Trainspotting*, Secker and Warburg, 1993
19 Christopher Brookmyre, *Quite Ugly One Morning*, Abacus,
   1997
20 http://www.scottishreview.net/GerryCarruthers456a.html
21 http://www.washingtonpost.com/wp-dyn/content/article/2006/
   02/23/AR2006022301720_2.html
22 https://www.thetimes.co.uk/article/i-ll-never-be-seen-as-a-scott
   ish-writer-5pn5qr5kk

Conclusion: The Re-imagining of the Union

1 The letters are published in Stéphane Dion, *Straight Talk: Speeches
   and Writings on Canadian Unity*, McGill-Queen's University Press,
   1999
2 Text and discussion in Dion, *The Canadian Contribution to a
   Comparative Law on Secession*, Palgrave Macmillan, 2019
3 https://foreignpolicy.com/2014/09/16/the-moral-tragedy-of-scott
   ish-independence/

4 https://www.economist.com/leaders/2019/07/27/to-stop-no-deal-tory-mps-must-be-ready-to-bring-down-boris-johnson
5 Michael Ignatieff, *Isaiah Berlin: a Life*, Metropolitan Books, 1998, p. 250
6 Ibid.